D1414906

Minnesota Vikings Trivia

Minnesota Vikings Trivia

Jim Hoey

NODIN PRESS

Front cover art: Paul Roff
Design and layout: John Toren
Photographs courtesy the Minnesota Vikings.

ISBN: 978-1-935666-48-6
Library of Congress Control Number: 2013945468

Published by
Nodin Press
5114 Cedar Lake Road
Minneapolis, MN, 55416

To all of the fans who have steadfastly supported the "purple and gold" since their arrival in 1961 as we patiently wait for that elusive first Super Bowl title.

Acknowledgements

I would like to thank all of the people who have been so helpful and have supported my efforts in compiling this book, and all those who gave me suggestions and counsel. To my wonderful wife Ann and son Eddie, my appreciation is endless for accepting my passion for this and past projects and for your love and understanding in allowing me the time to complete them.

A special thanks to my publisher and friend, Norton Stillman, for his guidance and direction in publishing this book; to John Toren for his expert work with design, layout, and technical expertise; and to Paul Roff for his dynamic art work on the cover. My gratitude extends to the Minnesota Vikings organization for their permission in allowing me to use their logo and photographs from their archives.

Background and resource materials were gleaned from numerous sources, including the archives of the Minnesota State Historical Society, the St. Paul Public Library, the Minnesota Vikings, the *Saint Paul Pioneer Press*, and the *Minneapolis Star Tribune*. Most statistical information was verified through *pro-football-reference.com* and *nfl.com*, both marvelous and incredibly thorough and accurate sources. I also utilized a number of books published about the Vikings.

Finally, I am indebted to the Viking organization and the fans of the Minnesota Vikings, who have inspired my work. Their loyalty and dedication to the franchise never fails and it my sincere hope that this book will bring them great enjoyment.

Contents

Introduction: the Vikings Arrive

It was shaping up as quite a year by mid-summer of 1961. For a youngster who loved playing, reading about, and watching sports, it was a downright bonanza. Just a few months earlier, the Minnesota Twins started playing at Metropolitan Stadium in Bloomington and it became an obsession for me—devouring the sports pages of the Duluth News-Tribune and listening to the radio voices of Halsey Hall, Ray Scott, and Bob Wolff on our local station (KOZY) out of Grand Rapids.

Just as we were getting accustomed to stars like Harmon Killebrew, Bob Allison, Jim Kaat, and Zoilo Versalles, stories about pro football started to circulate. In the midst of relishing our first taste of major-league baseball, there was also excitement in the air that July as another big-time sports team started training camp in Bemidji, only 80 miles west of our home in northern Minnesota. The Minnesota Vikings had been established as a new franchise the previous year; they would be playing in the same stadium as the Twins, with the inaugural regular season to begin in mid-September.

As with the Twins, I have correlated events in my life with the rhythm of Viking seasons (albeit two months shorter). Many of the team's 790 regular season games and, of course, its 46 playoff games are indelibly etched in my mind, as are most of the 1,016 players who have competed for the club over the past 52 years. One of my dreams as a kid was to find work in the Twin Cities so I could attend major-league baseball and NFL football at the same locale. While I have attended more than a thousand Twins game at three different venues, I didn't see many Viking games at either the Met or the Metrodome. However, I don't think I've missed more than a dozen Vikings games on television or radio.

With the Vikings presence in Minnesota now secured with the passage of the stadium bill in 2012, it seemed like an appropriate time to put this trivia and information book into print. It has been my good fortune to have written two books about similar passions—*Minnesota Twins Trivia* and *Puck Heaven*, a trivia book on the Minnesota State Boys High School Hockey Tournament. My hope is that readers will be able to recall specific incidents and relish memories of former players and teams as they peruse these pages. This book was inspired by you, the fans, who have shown incredible loyalty and dedication to the "purple and gold."

I was raised on Minnesota's Mesabi Iron Range in a village aptly named Taconite (it literally means low-grade iron ore). As a nine-year-old about to attend fourth-grade, there was a lot of free time to explore in and around our little village of 350 residents, about half of whom were personal relatives. It was a wonderful time and place to grow up—almost idyllic—because a boy or girl had the freedom and opportunity to be creative and just be a kid.

We trudged along in groups, brothers and cousins and buddies of various ages. There was some sort of athletic contest every day and there were plenty of kids to partake, to be sure. Our burgeoning family at that time consisted of five boys and two girls, though in time three more boys would be added. Besides playing baseball in the spring and summer at various sites with a multitude of spheres, we played every imaginable kind of contest to test our athletic prowess and elevate ourselves on the social strata. Of course, on the hockey-mad Iron Range, we played hockey at our outdoor rink from Thanksgiving to at least Saint Patrick's Day, sometimes all day and half the night.

We usually played football at two locations: on the grass of the outdoor hockey rink in the spring, summer, and fall, and at the Taconite Elementary School lot. The school setting was perfect for pigskin play as we had a nice field that was about 80 yards long. There was touch football, to be sure, but we mostly played tackle and it was rougher than any hockey competition because we didn't wear any pads or helmets. Bloody noses, scrapes and cuts, and those nasty hip-pointers were our bodily badges of honor.

The big names we dreamed about and cited during our scrimmaging included Johnny Unitas, Jim Brown, and Ray Nitschke, three of the NFL studs at the time. It was at the elementary school grounds where Mr. Norman Hecimovich, who would become my sixth-grade teacher, taught me some of the nuances of playing the game and how to throw a good spiral. At recess in the fall of 1961, we pretended to be Tommy Mason, the fleet halfback from Tulane, who was shifty and talented. Bruce Ogle, who would go on to be a star for Greenway, did the best Fran Tarkenton impression with his spins and evasive scrambling.

In the papers, there was a lot of coverage of Dick Pesonen, who had played at UMD and was taken in the expansion draft by Green Bay, and Frank Youso, a behemoth offensive tackle out of International Falls who was a former Gopher star. My father, Ed, a fan of all sports, got me started listening to Gopher football on Saturdays and watching Green Bay games on Sundays prior to the Vikings arrival. During that hot summer of 1961, while Mickey Mantle and Roger Maris were staging their remarkable threat to the single-season home run record, Minnesota fans were getting accustomed to guys named Reichow, Hawkins, Alderman, and Marshall, who all became solid players for the Vikings in its early years. In August, kids were purchasing bubble-gum cards of all the new Vikings. Suddenly, we had a new set of heroes to admire and emulate.

As was my custom, I was studying and memorizing the players' statistics and wondering if they could duplicate or even double their output with our new Vikings. I can't remember if I ever did beg Dad to drive up to Bemidji to watch the NFL hopefuls but I was visualizing them practicing their two-a-days each day during the seven weeks they spent along the shores of Lake Bemidji.

On Sept, 17, 1961, all seemed possible when the Vikings

dumped the defending NFL champion Chicago Bears at Met Stadium with rookie Fran Tarkenton playing the role of savior in their first-ever game. The team finished with a 3-11 record but coach Norm Van Brocklin's club proved to be exciting at least. We watched our new heroes on our black and white Setchell and Carlson television set for fun, but the Packers, behind Starr and Hornung and Taylor, were the real class of the league.

Over the next several years, the Vikings were an enigma, playing a brand of ball that was enticing but fundamentally unsound. They had three losing seasons in a row but Tarkenton and Tommy Mason had a lot of flair and the team was certainly worth watching. In 1964, the Vikings went 8-5-1, finishing in second place in the Western Conference, and fellows such as Carl "Moose" Eller and Bill "Boom-Boom" Brown became my favorites. I knew the name and number of every player and the college they attended.

One day during the '64 season, we were playing football between the homes of "Pack Sack" Carpenter and Pecky Guyer in the late afternoon. The Vikings were playing the San Francisco 49ers at Kezar Stadium. We had just taken a break to check on the game on my transistor radio when the announcer reported that one of our players had recovered a fumble and was heading for the end zone unopposed. We glanced at each other with smiles before learning that, indeed, defensive end Jim Marshall had just crossed the goal-line after a 66-yard dash. He had run the wrong way and it resulted in a safety for the 49ers.

After two more losing seasons in 1965 and 1966, tempestuous Norm Van Brocklin was gone as head coach and the enigmatic Tarkenton had been traded to the Giants. With general manager Jim Finks on board and former Gopher all-around athlete Bud Grant at the coaching helm, the Vikings started an incredible run of excellence. The draft became an annual gold mine, bringing in the likes of future Hall of Famers Alan Page and Ron Yary, and many other stars. We had talented and durable players at nearly every position; the Vikings were on their way to becoming a dynasty.

A first foray into the playoffs in 1968 led to a loss to Baltimore. Then came the 1969 season. Our defense, featuring the Purple People Eaters front four, put up an astounding season, setting a league mark for least points allowed. We went 12-2 and hammered Cleveland at the Met to win the NFL title. We were set to play the AFL-NFL title game (The Super Bowl) against the Kansas City Chiefs and were considered the heavy favorite.

Jan. 11, 1970, was a tough day. Not only did we get beat by the Chiefs but we played by far our worst game of the season. Watching the game on color television (it was still a big deal at the time), it didn't take long to realize our beloved Vikes were not on their game. It was so demoralizing to see the team not play the way it had all year. Hank Stram had that big smirk on his face most of the game, mocking us for our ineptitude. I didn't read a sports page for three weeks for fear of reading something about the debacle...three weeks! Forty-three years later, the memory of it still haunts me and a few million other Viking fans.

In the summer of 1972, good buddy Joe Eckel and I ventured down to Mankato in his dad's Cadillac convertible from St. Paul for an unforgettable trip to see the Vikings in their annual intra-squad scrimmage. We stayed with our pal Kevin Keenan and we were all in our glory watching our boys close-up. Determined to have a good time on a Saturday night, we left a few plays before the end of the exhibition to head down to Mettler's, a favored downtown bar. After ordering our drafts, we turn to our left and sure enough, standing there with a beer and a handshake are rookie Ed Marinaro and my favorite player, "Boom-Boom" Brown.

Fortunately, the entire decade of the 1970's was a splendid time to be a Vikings fan as we were one of the best teams in the league. Our defense was arguably one of the best in NFL history during that period. Looking back, it's incredible to think that we didn't win a least *one* Super Bowl. Yet no one will deny that the Vikings were riding the crest of excellence during my college days at St. Mary's in Winona; and it's a good thing they were, or those annoying Chicago Bears fans from the Christian

Brothers schools in the Windy City would have been even more insufferable.

Of course, much of that credit must go to Jim Finks and Bud Grant. Both are in the Hall of Fame for a reason; they were two of the best at their craft and Minnesota was the benefactor. Finks knew talent and Grant knew how to mold a team with his common-sense approach and steely-eyed determination. With Tarkenton back in the fold, success continued to come our way, though three successive Super Bowl losses following the 1973, 1975, and 1976 seasons made the Vikings poster-boys for futility in the "big" game. Nevertheless, the nucleus of players who started in all four Super Bowls (Eller, Marshall, Yary, Krause, Tingelhoff, Cox, Page, Winston, White, and Hilgenberg) is a roll call of tireless excellence, and their contributions to the franchise will never be forgotten.

In the late 1970's, after getting a teaching job in Shakopee, I could attend some games in person but soon realized that witnessing a game at Met Stadium was a lesson in frustration. Most of the seats were 50 yards from the field. Yeah, the atmosphere was great, but the viewing was brutal, even if you sat at the 50-yard line. Let's face it, football was made for television. At home on the couch, you always have perfect sight lines plus video reviews.

My brother Peanuts (to this day, even some of my relatives wouldn't know that his given name is Donald) was a fellow die-hard in those days. He got married in Taconite in September of 1976, and after a spirited party at the Marble town hall, the newlyweds headed to Hibbing (22 miles away) for their honeymoon. It must have been great because Peanuts and Nell were back at their home by noon the next day to watch the Vikings host the Los Angeles Rams at Metropolitan Stadium with Kevin and Nancy Keenan and me. Now, that's love for you! By the way, the teams tied 10-10 that day.

On Jan. 11, 1977, I was looking for work in Seattle, Washington, when the Vikings faced the Oakland Raiders in Super Bowl XI. The Vikes did well just to get to the big game out at the

Rose Bowl. Still, the Raiders were not as powerful as the Steeler and Dolphin squads from previous losses. I had called home and found it was exactly 100 degrees colder in Taconite than it was in Pasadena that afternoon. Our star running back, Chuck Foreman, had told us the Vikings were going to play carefree and let it all hang out this time. Of course, it didn't happen. It was yet another tremendous disappointment as the Raiders prevailed easily 32-14.

Tommy Kramer, Anthony Carter, Joey Browner, and Chris Doleman were stalwarts but the Vikes were mostly an average club throughout the 1980's. Quarterback switches, the Herschel Walker trade debacle, and ownership instability created a poor atmosphere until Denny Green's ten-year run of success. With running back Robert Smith and two of the best receivers in the league in Cris Carter and Randy Moss, the Vikings were nearly unstoppable in 1998, going 15-1. The improbable overtime loss to Atlanta in the NFC title game at the Metrodome was yet another bitter pill to swallow.

Despite several unseemly off-field incidents during the era, the Vikings were still an entertaining club to watch, surprising detractors when expectations were low and disappointing backers when expectations were lofty. In 2009, of course, the Brett Favre show came to town and provided fans with as much fun as we have ever had. What looked like a magical year once again turned sour in overtime at the Super Dome in New Orleans when the Saints intercepted Favre just when it looked like we would finally make it back to the Super Bowl.

In the past six years, it has been a real treat to watch the dazzling moves and feigns of one Adrian Peterson, one of the best runners in NFL history. As the 2013 season approaches, the Vikings are assembling one of the most youthful but talented rosters in the game. In three years, Viking faithful will be filling up the new stadium on the east side of downtown Minneapolis. It has been 36 years since the team's last appearance in the Super Bowl. It would be wonderful to see them win one, but after 52 seasons supporting the team, I am just happy to enjoy the games and cheer on the team. Remember that the Vikings have won 18 division titles and have made 26 playoff appearances while Green Bay has totaled 13 and 18, respectively, in those two areas since 1961.

To this day, my wife, Ann, knows that she'd better check the fall calendar to see when the Vikings play when making Sunday plans. Sure, it's great to take a walk along Mississippi River Boulevard on a lovely day (the location of our first date, by the way) but we can do that at 3:30 p.m., after the game with Green Bay is over! She has been a trooper, no doubt, in adjusting to my passion for the Vikings. This franchise has always been entertaining on the field and consistently competitive, with the shortest stretch of consecutive losing seasons (3) in the NFL the past 52 years.

Viking fans, I hope you enjoy reading this compilation of little-known facts, sterling achievements, unforgettable individual feats, and terrible collapses, as much as I did creating it. Skol Vikings!

Minnesota Vikings Trivia

Fran Tarkenton, "The Scrambler," earning his nickname.

1 The Inaugural Season, 1961

1) What was the result of the Vikings first regular season game in the NFL played at Metropolitan Stadium on Sept. 17, 1961?

2) On April 12, 1961, the NFL assigned the newly-established Minnesota Vikings to play in the Western Conference alongside Chicago, Detroit, and Green Bay. Who were the three *other* teams who competed in the conference?

3) Who scored the first points in Minnesota Vikings history?

4) What was the Vikings record in its first year of existence?

5) What man, who had been cited as the MVP of the NFL just a month earlier, was named the Vikings first head coach?

6) On Sept. 10, 1961, the Vikings played a pre-season game at home—their first actual NFL competition. Who did they face?

7) What future Viking offensive coordinator scored the franchise's first regular season touchdown at Met Stadium on Sept. 17, 1961?

8) In which Midwestern city and state did the Vikings play their first professional game on August 5, 1961?

9) In the expansion draft following the 1960 season, how many players was the new Viking franchise allowed to pilfer from each of the other NFL rosters?

10) In early August of 1960, what former Los Angeles Rams Public Relations Director was hired to become Minnesota's first General Manager?

11) What was the roster size limit for NFL squads in 1961?

12) When the Minnesota Vikings joined the National Football League for the 1961 season, how many other teams were competing in the league?

13) In what northern Minnesota city did the Viking conduct their first training camp?

14) What International Falls native and former Gopher was a starting offensive right tackle for the Vikings in 1961?

15) What future Viking great and the team's soul for the next two decades was acquired within a week of their first game in a deal with Cleveland that also brought six other players in exchange for Minnesota's second, tenth, and eleventh-round draft choices in the 1962 draft?

16) What reserve quarterback entered the first game against the Chicago Bears late in the first quarter and ended up throwing for 250 yards (17-23) and four touchdowns and ran two yards for another in the Vikings monumental upset of the Bears on Sept. 17, 1961?

17) What four players made up the starting offensive backfield in the first regular season game against Chicago?

18) What future Hall of Famer led the 1961 Vikings with 570 rushing yards on 120 carries and was the team's first Most Valuable Player?

19) A starter at left offensive tackle from the very first game, what player ended up starting every game but one on the line for the Vikings in the 1960's and started 175 games for the team overall?

20) What man was hired as the team's first chief head scout, and along with Bert Rose, made the selections in the first Viking draft on Dec. 27, 1960?

21) How many weeks did the Viking spend at their first training camp?

22) The Vikings lost their first four exhibition games on the road that first pre-season. Who was the opponent and in what

neighboring state did they play the fourth of those games on Sept. 2, 1961?

23) What UMD graduate started at right halfback (cornerback) on defense when the Vikings took the field for their first regular season NFL game?

24) Of the 20 players the Vikings selected in their first-ever draft (Dec. 27, 1960), who is the only one who started in the first regular season game against Chicago?

25) What future Hall of Fame tight end and Super Bowl coach beat out Fran Tarkenton for NFL "Rookie-of-the-Year" in 1961?

26) In the 1961 expansion draft, what former All-Pro defensive end did the Vikings acquire from the Baltimore Colts?

27) Possessing a truly fitting name for a football player, especially for someone with a reputation as a ferocious hitter, what tight end/ linebacker did the Vikings draft in the 12th round of their first NFL draft?

28) Who led the Vikings in all three receiving categories in 1961?

29) What talented newcomer led Minnesota in both punt and kick returns in 1961?

30) What nickname was rookie Fran Tarkenton tagged with after displaying an uncanny ability to avoid pass rushers with his spins and turns?

31) In an unusual twist, what team did the Vikings play two weeks in a row in 1961?

32) What fullback gained 407 yards in the first season, leading the team with 5.1 yards per carry?

33) When the Vikings acquired 36 players in the expansion draft prior to their first season, how much did they have to pay the 12 teams total for all that talent?

34) What original Viking, their 13th pick in the first draft, actually started play as a 26 year-old because he spent more than three years in the Air Force after playing at Central Oklahoma?

35) What under-sized lineman, a teammate of head coach Norm Van Brocklin, was selected in the expansion draft and started at left guard for the first three seasons?

36) What was the yearly salary for starting running back Tommy Mason, the top overall pick in the 1961 NFL draft?

37) What original Viking and defensive tackle played in 10 games in the first season and served as the defensive captain but had to be restrained from mauling coach Norm Van Brocklin on the flight home after the final game at Chicago?

38) What establishment's workers became quite familiar with Viking hopefuls in Bemidji on summer nights in 1961?

39) Before he joined the Vikings as a defensive back in 1961, what Kent State player had his name incorrectly spelled not only in college but in his first year in the NFL with Cleveland?

40) There were 40 free agents in the first training camp in 1961. How many made the original roster?

41) What player was issued the number "70" in the inaugural season by equipment manager Stubby Eason and wore it with such distinction over 19 seasons that it is the only number that has never been worn by another player?

42) Who became the first Viking player to have 100 yards receiving in a game?

Norm Van Brocklin

43) What former Indiana star started every game at right guard in 1961 and again in 1962 after being nabbed in the expansion draft?

1) The Vikings upset the Chicago Bears, the defending NFL champions, 37-13 in perhaps the most astounding first-ever game for a new franchise in league history with a partisan crowd of 32,236 roaring their approval.

2) Baltimore Colts, Los Angeles Rams, and San Francisco 49ers.

3) Mike Mercer. A place-kicker and punter, the 26-year-old kicked a 12-yard field goal in the first quarter in the team's first-ever regular-season game, a stunning 37-13 upset of Chicago. Mercer was 9-21 in field-goal attempts and was 36 of 37 on extra points in 1961 but was 0-4 in field goal attempts in 1962 before being released.

4) 3-11. The three victories came against Chicago, Baltimore, and Los Angeles.

5) Norm Van Brocklin, who was the star quarterback for the NFL champion Philadelphia Eagles in 1960. Van Brocklin played for 12 years in the NHL and is a member of the Pro Football Hall of Fame. "Dutch" would go on to coach Minnesota for six seasons (1961-66).

6) The Los Angeles Rams beat the Vikings 21-17 in front of 27,892 onlookers at Met Stadium in Bloomington.

7) Bob Schnelker. A receiver from Bowling Green, Schnelker caught a 14-yard pass from Viking quarterback Fran Tarkenton to give the Vikings a 10-0 second-quarter lead over Chicago in the first NFL game played by the team. Schnelker played in just six games for the team, with six grabs for 70 yards. However, he was a Pro Bowl player for the New York Giants in 1958 and 1959. He served as an assistant coach for six NFL teams, including tenure as the much-reviled Vikings offensive coordinator under Jerry Burns.

8) Sioux Falls, South Dakota. The Vikings lost 38-13 to the Dallas Cowboys in their first-ever exhibition game in front of 4,954 fans at Howard Wood field. The Cowboys trained that summer at St. Olaf College in Northfield.

9) Three. Each team could protect 30 of its 38 players from their active roster. Dallas was exempt because they had just joined the

league as an expansion team the previous season. The expansion draft took place on Jan. 26, 1961; in all, the Vikings acquired 36 players from 12 other NFL teams.

10) Bert Rose, who resigned in June of 1964 after the team went 10-30-2 overall in its first three seasons.

11) 36

12) 13. The NFL had just 12 teams for several seasons until the Dallas Cowboys became the 13th in 1960 and the Vikings the 14th in 1961.

13) Bemidji (Bemidji State University), the first of six such camps for the newest NFL franchise playing in that city and at that university.

14) Frank Youso, who started in 26 of the team's first 28 games in 1961 and 1962.

15) Jim Marshall, the defensive end who would go on to become one of the most durable players in NFL history. Two others in the deal, defensive tackles Paul Dickson and Jim Prestel, also became starters for the Vikings. Linebacker Dick Grecni, cornerback Billy Gault, guard Bob Denton and running back Jamie Caleb also joined the Vikings. All seven players were on the season-opening roster.

16) Fran Tarkenton, the third-round pick from Georgia.

17) Quarterback George Shaw, left halfback Dick Haley, right halfback Hugh McElhenny, and fullback Mel Triplett.

18) Hugh McElhenny

19) Grady Alderman

20) Joe Thomas, who later became an executive with the Miami Dolphins. Thomas visited 92 colleges in his first spring scouting for talent.

21) Seven weeks. Norm Van Brocklin had his players report to Bemidji on July 7 and the regular season didn't begin until Sept. 17.

22) Chicago Bears. The game was played in Cedar Rapids, Iowa and the Bears hammered the first-year team 30-7. No one who watched that game could have imagined what would happen when

the two teams would meet two weeks later in the regular season opener!

23) Dick Pesonen, who started 11 games in 1961 with one interception and one fumble recovery. Pesonen had played for the Packers in 1960 and later played two years with the Giants.

24) Rip Hawkins, who started at middle linebacker. Hawkins, a second-round pick out of North Carolina, played five seasons for the Vikings and was a Pro Bowler in 1963. Hawkins intercepted five passes in his rookie season and later returned two interceptions for touchdowns in 1964.

25) Mike Ditka, who caught 56 passes for 1,076 yards and 12 touchdowns. Tarkenton, who started 10 of the 14 regular season games, finished with 18 touchdowns and 17 interceptions and passed for 1,997 yards (157-280). Fran rushed for 308 yards and five touchdowns.

26) Don Joyce, who started seven of the team's 14 games in 1961. Joyce was reputed to have consumed 75 beers in a 24-hour period at a Bemidji watering hole during the first camp.

27) Steve Stonebreaker, a Louisiana native who played at Detroit Mercy.

28) Jerry Reichow, who had 50 catches for 859 yards and 11 touchdowns. His scoring total for a receiver wasn't surpassed until 1995, when Cris Carter scored 17 times.

29) Tommy Mason. The first-round choice from Tulane averaged 10.4 per punt and 24.1 yards per kick return. A halfback, he didn't start any games and rushed 60 times for 226 yards.

30) "The Scrambler", who once scrambled for 18 seconds before completing a pass.

31) Green Bay. On Oct. 22, the Packers beat the Vikings 33-7 in Bloomington. A week later, on Oct. 29, the Vikings lost 28-10 in a game played at County Stadium in Milwaukee.

32) Mel Triplett, who had played several years for the Giants. The Toledo grad started eight games in that first year and finished his NFL career with Minnesota in 1962.

33) $600,000

34) Ray Hayes, who rushed for 319 yards in his only season with Minnesota.

35) Gerry Huth, who was only 5'11" and 228 pounds. He won two NFL titles as a player with the Giants and Eagles and retired prior to the 1964 season.

36) $15,000. Meanwhile, fellow rookie Fran Tarkenton made $12,500.

37) Bill Bishop. A former All-Pro with the Bears out of North Texas State, it was no surprise that his career as a Viking ended after that high-flying conflict.

38) Duchess Tavern

39) Rich Mostardi, who started nine games at left safety in the first season and had two interceptions and three fumble recoveries. His name had been spelled...Mostardo.

40) One (Gordy Smith, a tight end from Missouri).

41) Jim Marshall

42) Jerry Reichow, who had 103 yards and a touchdown on just three catches in their very first game against Chicago.

43) Mike Rabold, who played for the Bears from 1964-67. Unfortunately, Mike died at age 33 in a car accident just three years after retiring from the NFL.

Bill "Boom-Boom" Brown grinds out an extra yard against the Bears.

2 The 1960s

1) In what year did the Vikings have their first winning season in the NFL?

2) What former NFL player became the team's second general manager just two days prior to the 1964 season and was responsible for assembling many of the players who helped the Vikings win 11 division titles in a 13-year span?

3) What four men formed one of the most famous front fours in NFL history for the Vikings in the late 1960's and early 1970's?

4) In what year did the Vikings move their training camp from northern Minnesota to Mankato?

5) When the Detroit Lions faced the Vikings at Metropolitan Stadium on Oct. 11, 1964, what uniform snafu complicated matters for both players and referees?

6) What Concordia-Moorhead graduate played for the Vikings as a kicker and backup linebacker in 1962 and later became the head coach at his alma mater for 32 years?

7) With the popularity of the Vikings increasing, the demand for more seats at Metropolitan Stadium was fulfilled with the construction of a double-decked grandstand beyond the left-field baseball area. For which season was this addition ready?

8) In what year did the NFL create the Central Division, which included Minnesota, Chicago, Detroit, and Green Bay?

9) What was the nickname of bruising fullback Bill Brown, who was one of the most versatile and effective running backs in football in the 1960's?

10) What center from Nebraska came on the scene in 1962 and became entrenched as one of the best centers in the NFL for the next 17 seasons, starting 240 consecutive games from 1962-78?

11) What shifty halfback from Tulane, who had been the team's first-round draft choice in 1961, was stellar for the fledgling franchise in the early years, earning Pro Bowl status in three straight seasons (1962-64)?

12) Did the Vikings play an NFL game on Sunday, November 24, 1963, two days after the assassination of President John F. Kennedy?

13) What hard-nosed Viking running back from the late 1960's and early 1970's played on the national champion Arkansas Razorback team in 1964 and later ran for Governor of Arkansas?

14) What two prominent members of the Viking organization left after the 1966 season?

15) What rookie led the Vikings in receptions in 1963 with 51 and with 867 receiving yards and went on to become the first Minnesota player to be "Rookie-of-the-Year"?

16) He wore number 82 both seasons, but what Viking player was

a starting tight end in 1962 but a starting right linebacker the following season?

17) Who led the Vikings in both punt return and kick return yardage in 1968?

18) In 1967, the NFL draft was cut from 20 rounds per team to how many?

19) What former Wisconsin star and Rose Bowl hero signed as an undrafted free agent with the Vikings in 1963 and served as a backup to Fran Tarkenton for four seasons?

20) What Viking running back became the full package in 1964 as a regular, rushing for 866 yards and adding 703 yards receiving and totaling 16 touchdowns?

21) What Viking punter ran five times for 82 yards in 1966, including a long of 45 yards?

22) What was the rallying cry for the Vikings during their monumental 1969 season, when they went 12-2 and reached their first Super Bowl?

23) What former and future Viking quarterback was the starter for Atlanta when the host Falcons ended Minnesota's record 12-game winning streak with a 10-3 win in the regular season finale in 1969?

24) What third-year halfback rushed for only two touchdowns in 1967 after totaling nearly 1,000 yards (972) as a workhorse for Bud Grant's first Viking squad?

25) What man, a fourth-round pick from LSU in 1962, became one of the most under-rated yet valuable players to the Vikings for the next 15 years with his steady play at outside linebacker?

30) Despite a terrific season in 1963, which led to him being named to the Pro Bowl, what Viking offensive player fumbled the ball a whopping 14 times?

31) On Thanksgiving Day in 1969, what two Viking defensive players combined to complete one of the most amazing touchdowns in NFL history in a driving snowstorm at Detroit's Tiger Stadium?

32) A sixth-round draft choice in 1962, what Purdue guard started for five years at that position for the Vikings?

33) What Hopkins native and Montana player played seven games for the Vikings late in the 1963 season as a safety but died tragically prior to the 1964 season when he drowned while working on a construction project near Missoula, Montana?

34) What 6'5", 252-pound Baylor alum started on the defensive line for six-straight seasons from 1962-67 and was noted for his consistent play and leadership?

35) What University of Minnesota star from Minneapolis was drafted 20th in the 1964 draft and ended up as a durable and reliable starting offensive guard for nine seasons?

36) What positions did the following players play for the Vikings in the 1960's - Mel Triplett, Ray Hayes, and Bill Barnes?

37) In what year did the Vikings gain their first-ever victory over the Green Bay Packers and legendary coach Vince Lombardi?

38) A second-round pick out of Oklahoma, what rookie led the team in kick return average (26.2) in 1965, including a 101-yard touchdown?

39) In what year did the Vikings not only finish first in the league in team offense but first in team defense (scoring not yards)?

40) Considered one of the biggest blunders in the history of the NFL, what stalwart defensive player for the Vikings ran 66 yards the wrong way (resulting in a safety) in a game against San Francisco on Oct. 25, 1964?

41) How many times did the Vikings score at least 50 points in 1969?

42) What Viking offensive player was 10th in the league in scoring and was also fourth in punting average in 1963?

43) What huge defensive tackle out of Idaho started every game from 1961-64 and was in the same trade that brought teammate Jim Marshall to the team?

44) Nicknamed "The Seed," what Colorado State running back was a trusted backup from 1968-74?

45) Who played both tight end and wide receiver for the Vikings from 1961 to 1965, averaging an eye-popping 22.4 yards per reception?

46) What tough-as-nails strong safety provided ferocious hitting in the defensive backfield for the Vikings from 1963 to 1971 before a motorcycle accident the day before training camp in 1972 left him paralyzed?

47) What eight-year veteran of the CFL was acquired just prior to the 1967 season and became the Vikings starting quarterback for the next three seasons?

48) Despite less than stellar speed, what cornerback became one of the most reliable Vikings in the first decade of the franchise, finishing his 12-year career with 40 interceptions?

49) Acquired on waivers from Pittsburgh before the 1968 season, what former two-way stalwart from Iowa terrorized ball carriers starting at right linebacker for the Vikings from 1968-76?

50) What Utah State player started 56 games at cornerback from 1966-69, intercepting 15 passes?

51) A Madison native and star at Wisconsin who was drafted and played for his home state Packers, what rugged defensive back was notorious for his aggressive play with the Vikings from 1966-70?

52) In what year did the Vikings finally beat Green Bay twice in one season?

53) When Bud Grant was hired as coach in 1967, he employed two assistants who were with him for the next 17 years. Who were they?

54) What menacing middle linebacker, who played at both Tennessee and Tennessee Tech, played between Roy Winston and Wally Hilgenberg for several years?

55) What 1967 top pick from Michigan State spread the field and became a true deep threat for the Vikings in 1968 and 1969?

56) What kicker led the league in field goals in 1965 and 1969?

57) What player actually played both safety and running back, in addition to punt and kick returner from 1962-64?

58) What Tennessee State receiver scored six touchdowns on just 14 receptions in 1962?

59) How many times did the Vikings fumble in a 42-41 win at San Francisco on Oct. 24, 1965?

60) What moniker was given to the Central Division because of the intense rivalries and physical style of football exhibited between the teams in the 1960's?

61) Who led the Viking defense in tackles in its first four seasons?

62) On Oct. 31, 1965, the visiting Vikings stunned the defending NFL champions 27-17 on the strength of two Bill Brown touchdowns and two Fran Tarkenton touchdown passes. Who was that team and who was the star running back held to a measly 39 yards on 18 rushes?

63) The author's physical education teacher at Greenway High in Coleraine was a former Viking receiver who played in six games with his home state team in 1962. What was the name of this Keewatin native who played his college ball at UMD?

64) What reserve defensive back in 1962-63 intercepted six passes in 28 games but was forced to retire after a severe collision in training camp in 1963?

65) In the 1960s, who were the only two Vikings other than Rip Hawkins and Lonnie Warwick to lead the team in tackles?

66) Nicknamed "Moonie," what Viking starting linebacker regularly vomited prior to games?

67) What rookie defensive back, who played wide receiver at Auburn, led the 1964 Vikings with six interceptions?

68) In what year did the Minnesota Vikings first score more points in a season than they allowed?

69) What Pro-Bowl player from the 1960's and 1970's was actually cut from the team after being acquired in a trade with Cleveland prior to the 1962 season and taught school for a year before returning the following year to become a mainstay for 15 seasons?

70) What former Gopher, a defensive back for Detroit before join-

Tommy Mason (20) gets a block from Paul Flately (85) at Met Stadium.

ing the Vikings in 1964, was a trusted wide receiver for five seasons?

71) What Viking defensive lineman who played 10 seasons (from 1965 to 1974) also served as the top reserve for the "Fearsome Foursome" of the Los Angeles Rams prior to joining the Vikings?

72) When Bud Grant arrived to take over as head coach in 1967, he made it clear that he wanted his team to look respectable when standing for the national anthem. What player did he put in charge of instructing his players for the proper etiquette for the pre-game ceremony during training camp?

73) After a disappointing loss to Green Bay in 1967, what two Vikings got into a brawl outside a bar after arguing over who was more at fault for the defeat? (Both players blamed themselves and refused to accept that it was the other's fault.)

74) What rookie receiver from Texas played in just seven games in 1963 but had two 100-yard receiving games and averaged 23.6 yards per catch that season?

1) 1964. The Vikings won their final three games of the 14-game regular season to finish 8-5-1, good for a second-place tie with Green Bay behind the champion Baltimore Colts in the Western Conference.

2) Jim Finks, who had previously been the general manager for the Calgary Stampeders in the CFL. Finks would be with the Vikings until the spring of 1974 and his ability to draft and acquire top-level talent helped Minnesota become one of the elite franchises in the league. Finks played quarterback for the Steelers ahead of a guy named Johnny Unitas before departing for Calgary, where he was also a player, assistant coach, and scout.

3) Alan Page, Jim Marshall, Carl Eller, and Gary Larsen, all members of the "Purple People Eaters". The group started 84 consecutive games together from 1968-72.

4) 1966; training camp headquarters are at the Mankato State campus, which is 70 miles from their Winter Park practice facility in Eden Prairie. The primary field for scrimmages is Blakeslee Stadium. The team's longevity in Mankato is the second-longest for an NFL team in the same training camp location.

5) Both teams wore white jerseys. In that year, home teams were to wear white but Detroit brought only their white jerseys. The Vikings retrieved their purple tops from Midway Stadium in St. Paul and the players put them on during the second quarter; they finished the game in purple pants and purple jerseys. The Lions won 24-20. It wasn't until 43 years later that the Vikings again donned both purple jerseys and purple pants (Dec. 17, 2007 in a Monday night game against Chicago).

6) Jim Christopherson, who was just 11-20 on his field goal attempts but made all 28 of his conversions. He also intercepted a pass and returned it 32 yards as he played in all 14 games in the Vikings second season. Christopherson was MVP of the MIAC as a player in 1959. As a coach, he led the Cobbers to 11 MIAC titles and won two NAIA national titles (1978 and 1981) and was enshrined in the College Football Hall of Fame in 2007.

7) 1965; the new grandstand added 6,700 seats raising the capacity to 47,900 for football.

8) 1967. The Central Division of the Western Conference of the NFL lasted until the AFL/NFL merger of 1970, at which point the division became the National Football Conference (NFC) Central Division. The Vikings, Bears, Lions, and Packers re-emerged as the NFC North for the 2002 season. Tampa Bay was also a member of the NFC Central from 1977-2001 before re-alignment with the NFC South.

9) "Boom-Boom." He was given the moniker on account of his swashbuckling running style and his bruising blocking.

10) Mick Tingelhoff, who was first-team All-Pro five times in the 1960's.

11) Tommy Mason. Wearing number 20, Mason became a threat rushing, receiving, and as a punt returner. In six years at Minnesota, Mason totaled 39 touchdowns and racked up 3,252 rushing yards and averaged 11.2 yards per reception, an exceptional average for someone coming out of the backfield.

12) Yes, the Vikings played the Lions at Met Stadium and won 34-31. Commissioner Rozelle later regretted playing the NFL schedule on that Sunday, calling it the biggest mistake of his career.

13) Jim Lindsey. Wearing number 21, Lindsey was a tough runner, a good receiver, and a top-notch special teams player and one of Bud Grant's favorite guys. Lindsey ran for the 1976 Democratic nod for Governor in Arkansas but lost in the primary.

14) Head coach Norm Van Brocklin resigned on February 11, 1967, and quarterback Fran Tarkenton was traded to the New York Giants less than a month later (March 6).

15) Paul Flately, a fourth-round pick out of Northwestern. Not blessed with great speed, Flately had expert timing and great hands. He played five seasons with the club, catching 50 passes in both 1965 and 1966. He caught 202 balls for 3,222 yards and 17 touchdowns for the Vikings overall.

16) Steve Stonebreaker. He started nine games at tight end (12 catches for 227 yards and an impressive 18.9 average) but moved to the other side of the ball to start 10 games as a hard-hitting tackler the next year. Stonebreaker's son Mike later played in the NFL for the Bears and Saints.

17) Charlie West, a rookie from UTEP, averaged 10.1 yards per punt

return and 26.2 on kick returns. He started at cornerback in both 1971 and 1972.

18) 17 rounds. In 1977 it was lowered again to 12 rounds.

19) Ron VanderKelen, who led the College All-Stars to a 20-17 win over Green Bay prior to the 1963 season. It was the last time the All-Stars defeated the defending NFL champions in the annual game kick-starting the pre-season. VanderKelen led second-ranked Wisconsin to victory over top-rated USC on Jan. 1, 1963, setting some Rose Bowl marks that still stand. VanderKelen played in only 29 games (five starts) in five seasons with Minnesota and completed just 107 of 252 passes for 1,375 yards and six touchdowns.

20) Bill Brown, who was a Pro Bowler in 1964.

21) Bobby Walden, who led the league in punting with a 46.4 average in 1964.

22) "40 for 60"

23) Bob Berry. The former Oregon Ducks star had two different stints for Minnesota as a backup (1965-67 and 1973-75) and played in 24 games with just two starts. He completed 63 of 124 passes for 708 yards and seven touchdowns.

24) Dave Osborn, who averaged a career-high 4.5 yards that season.

25) Roy Winston, a durable and steady if not spectacular player who had great instincts. Winston was a starter for 13 straight seasons (1963-75).

30) Tommy Mason, who also coughed up the ball nine times in 1962, 1964, and 1965.

31) Alan Page and Jim Marshall. With the snow pelting down on a muddy field, Page tipped a Greg Landry pass and Marshall intercepted it at the Lions 45 and raced downfield. Marshall was pursued by a Lions player down the sideline and while being tackled, he lateraled the ball to his left to Page while almost horizontal to the field. Page strode into the end zone for a 15-yard lateral/interception return.

32) Larry Bowie, who started in 64 games in the mid-1960's. Bowie retired after the 1968 season and became a part-time scout for the team.

33) Terry Dillon. Just 23, Dillon was operating a cement bucket that crashed through the bridge he was helping construct. Though he survived the crash into the river, he succumbed to the raging current. The Vikings now bestow the Terry Dillon Award to recognize a team player who overcomes adversity, does not receive much recognition, and lets his actions speak for themselves.

34) Paul Dickson, who started 81 games before losing his starting job to Alan Page.

35) Milt Sunde, who wore number 64, played in the Pro Bowl in 1966.

36) Running back.

37) On Oct. 4, 1964, Minnesota beat Green Bay 24-23 at Lambeau Field.

38) Lance Rentzel, who went to become a solid receiver for the Cowboys and Rams.

39) 1969; the Vikings scored 379 points and allowed just 133.

40) Jim Marshall. Though the Vikings won the game 27-22 at Kezar Field that day, Marshall has long been remembered for the gaffe. Quarterback George Mira completed a pass to Billy Kilmer, who promptly fumbled the ball. Marshall scooped it up at the San Francisco 34-yard line facing the Viking end zone. He raced ahead despite exhortations by his teammates that he was going the wrong way. Believing he had scored a touchdown, Marshall heaved the ball into the stands as 49ers guard Bruce Bosley put his arms around him and thanked him.

41) Three

42) Fred Cox

43) Jim Prestel, who was 6'5" and 275 pounds.

44) Oscar Reed, who had 1,968 yards in seven years, including 639 in 1972, the only year he was the starter. Reed averaged four yards a carry for the Vikings.

45) Gordy Smith, who caught 57 balls for 1,277 yards and 13 touchdowns.

46) Karl Kassulke, a Drake alum who started 117 games with 16 interceptions.

47) Joe Kapp, who became a crowd favorite over the next three seasons.

48) Ed Sharockman, a fifth-round pick in 1961, started nine years in the defensive backfield. He had at least six interceptions in four seasons and had an interception for 10 straight years.

49) Wally Hilgenberg, who played 12 years for Minnesota and was a bruising tackler with his 6'3", 229-pound frame.

50) Earsell Mackbee, who had six picks alone in 1969.

51) Dale Hackbart, who started in 1966 and 1967. Interestingly enough, Hackbart was the top draft pick for Minnesota when they participated in the first AFL draft before they reneged on their loyalty to the fledgling new league. Believe it or not, at one time, Hackbart was under contract with the Green Bay Packers, the Winnipeg Blue Bombers, and the Pittsburgh Pirates.

52) 1968; winning 26-13 at Milwaukee County Stadium on Sept. 22 and 14-10 at Met Stadium on Nov. 10.

53) John Michels and Buster Mertes.

54) Lonnie Warwick, the fierce warrior wearing #59.

55) Gene Washington. At 6'3" and 208 pounds with great speed and jumping ability, Washington was a first-team All-Pro in 1969 as he caught 39 balls for 821 yards and nine touchdowns. A year earlier, he had 46 grabs for 756 yards and six touchdowns.

56) Fred Cox

57) Billy Butler, from Tennessee-Chattanooga, led the Vikings in both punt returns and kick returns all three seasons. He also had five interceptions in 1962, including the first interception return for a touchdown in Viking history with a 39-yard score against the Rams.

58) Charley Ferguson, who totaled 364 yards for an imposing 26-yard average.

59) Eight (four lost). Tommy Mason scored three touchdowns and Paul Flately had seven catches for 202 yards and two touchdowns.

60) "Black and Blue" division.

61) "Rip" Hawkins (Ross Cooper Hawkins).

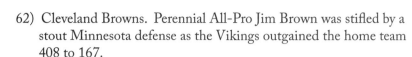

62) Cleveland Browns. Perennial All-Pro Jim Brown was stifled by a stout Minnesota defense as the Vikings outgained the home team 408 to 167.

63) Tom Adams. The 6'4", 215-pounder caught three passes in his only season. He also coached football with the Raiders and later became the athletic director.

64) Tom Franckhauser. After colliding with two teammates, he played three more plays before being helped off the field. Trainer Fred Zamberletti had to deal with a blood clot that formed on his brain, thus saving his life, and he later had emergency surgery.

65) Larry Vargo (1965) and Alan Page (1968). Hawkins led in tackles from 1961 to 1964 and Warwick in 1966, 1967, and 1969.

66) Roy Winston. Rarely out of position and an intuitive and intelligent player, Winston once intercepted three passes in a game in 1964 against San Francisco.

67) George Rose, a third-rounder. He had a single interception in each of the next two seasons before New Orleans claimed him in the 1967 expansion draft.

68) 1964 (355 points scored and 296 points allowed).

69) Fred Cox, who became not only the kicker but the punter in 1963.

70) Tom Hall. He caught 81 balls for 1,163 yards and eight touchdowns in two stints with the team (1964-66 and 1968-69).

71) Gary Larsen

72) Milt Sunde, who was a member of the National Guard.

73) Linebacker Lonnie Warwick and quarterback Joe Kapp. Warwick, a former Golden Gloves boxer, ended up with a busted nose while Kapp featured a couple of shiners.

74) Ray Poage. He caught just 15 passes for 353 yards but much of it came in a Sept. 29 tilt against San Francisco when he grabbed four balls for 137 yards and two touchdowns. Two weeks later, he had three catches for 106 yards against Green Bay.

3 The 1970s

1) The Vikings had two players chosen as MVP of the league during the decade. Who were they?

2) When Fran Tarkenton was reaquired prior to the 1972 season, anticipation was high. What was the Vikings record that year?

3) Ahmad Rashad was a star wide receiver for the Vikings in the late 1970's and early 1980's. What was his name when he was an All-American running back at the University of Oregon?

4) In what year did the Vikings start the season with a 10-0 mark?

5) In what year did the NFL expand the schedule from 14 to 16 games?

6) Years after being a stalwart and one of the best all-around backs in the NFL, what popular Viking runner became captain of the special teams in the early 1970's?

7) What player, who competed at both White Bear Lake High School and Lakewood Community College, had the difficult task of trying to fill the shoes (pun intended) of retiring kicker Fred Cox after the 1977 season?

8) During this dominant decade, how many times did the Vikings finish their regular season home schedule unbeaten?

9) What lithe receiver became one of the league's best long-ball threats in the 1970's, recording 27 touchdowns in 56 games?

10) In what year during the decade did the NFL begin playing

overtime in regular season contests?

11) Playing for a second-division team in the MIAC, what Twin Cities-area athlete from Macalester played for the Vikings in 1976 as a running back?

12) What position did the following players play for the Vikings in the 1970's: Sammy Johnson, Robert Miller and Brent McClanahan?

13) Midway through the 1974 season, what Wisconsin-Superior athlete replaced Gary Larsen in the defensive line for the Vikings?

14) A true warrior for 11 seasons (1972-82), what Viking middle linebacker was a solid run stopper and an intelligent signal caller for the defense?

15) Who threw the first overtime touchdown pass for the Vikings when they beat the Bears 22-16 on Oct. 16, 1977?

16) Jim Marshall played his final game on Dec. 16, 1979, at New England. At the time of his retirement, he held the NFL record for most recovered fumbles. How many?

17) Fran Tarkenton was traded to the New York Giants prior to the 1967 season and returned in a trade prior to the 1972 season. What receiver ended up being involved in both of those transactions?

18) What running back became the first Viking to rush for 1,000 yards?

19) A reserve linebacker in 1975, what former University of Minnesota star became the first president and CEO of the Minnesota Timberwolves?

20) What Cincinnati defender ended Fran Tarkenton's year in 1977 with a tackle that broke Sir Francis' right leg—Tarkenton's first major injury in 17 seasons?

21) A ninth-round pick in 1972, who played both offensive guard and tackle as a starter from 1973-79 and hailed from the same school as teammate Greg Coleman?

22) The largest regular-season crowd to watch a Viking game in its 52-year history took place at what road stadium on Nov. 24, 1974?

23) A first-round selection out of USC in 1974, who manned left tackle proficiently from 1974 to 1984 without much fanfare?

24) What former Gopher All-American tight end from Little Falls played three seasons for the Vikings (1971-73) and competed in two Super Bowls?

25) In 1973, many fans started to travel to places like Rochester, Winona, Moorhead, and Duluth to watch Viking home games? Why?

26) What San Diego State player became one of the best cover guys in Viking history and a two-time Pro Bowler as an outstanding cornerback from 1971-80?

27) What Tulsa stud, a third-round pick in 1976, was a solid guard, starting 92 games (1978-83) wearing #61?

28) For eight seasons (1973-80), what Arizona State grad was a part-time starter at fullback?

29) What 12-year veteran at linebacker, a first-round pick from UCLA in 1974, was a starter for eight years?

30) What Viking became the first and only player in Minnesota history to score at least 20 touchdowns in a season?

31) Almost comical in scope, what team outgained the Vikings 301 to 87 but still lost 3-0 at Met Stadium on Nov. 14, 1971?

32) One of the best players in franchise history was waived by the Vikings on October 10, 1978, and claimed by Chicago for the sum of $100. Who was he?

33) What defensive end from Colorado State was the Vikings first-round pick in the 1975 draft?

34) A long-shot to make the Vikings as a 15th round selection in 1971, what U of M defensive back endured for seven seasons with his intelligent and savvy play?

35) What Viking player came within a year of playing professional football in four decades?

36) What defensive end was acquired prior to the 1971 season from

Chuck Foreman evades a Washington tackler as Fran Tarkenton looks on.

the New York Giants and provided stellar play as a backup through 1976, though he became a household name throughout Minnesota for his off-the-field antics?

37) What future Viking return specialist returned both a punt and a kickoff for touchdowns *against* them on Dec. 17, 1977, while playing for the Lions?

38) A teammate at USC with Ron Yary, what Viking guard was a five-year starter on the line but was diagnosed with Hodgkin's disease in 1971 and retired immediately?

39) The Vikings went 12-2 in 1969. In a truly amazing twist, what two quarterbacks, one a former Viking and the other a future Viking, beat them?

40) What cornerback scored two touchdowns in a 54-13 win over Dallas in 1970?

41) As a rookie out of Grambling in 1976, who immediately became a favorite target of Fran Tarkenton?

42) What Viking punter from Tennessee earned a Pro Bowl berth in his rookie year (1975) by averaging 41.1 yards per punt?

43) What Oregon State receiver was a second-round pick in 1967 but had his best year in 1971, when he was a Pro Bowler after catching 45 passes for 691 yards and seven touchdowns?

44) Who did the Vikings defeat in their home openers in 1971 and 1974 and what was so bittersweet about those victories?

45) What popular Viking, elected MVP of the team in 1969, never even went to training camp in 1970 and finally was dealt to New England for safety John Charles and a fourth-round pick?

46) What player committed a roughing the passer penalty late in a game against Miami, keeping a Dolphin drive alive that gave the them a 16-14 win on Oct. 1, 1972? (If not for the foul, Miami's perfect season might have remained a chimera).

47) In 1971 the Vikings possessed a tremendous defense but a lack-luster offense. What three gentlemen all struggled as the starting quarterback that year?

48) What Viking running back led the team in receptions for three straight years during the 1970s?

49) With a waist about the size of a super model, what South Carolina defensive back became a starter at safety in 1969 and exhibited exceptional instincts and timing for 13 years?

50) What running back out of Cornell, the runner-up for the Heisman award, was a second-round draft pick in 1972?

51) Wearing #62, what guard from California (second pick in 1969) who came to the team as part of the trade that sent Tarkenton to the New York Giants, was a stellar blocker for the Vikings for nine seasons?

52) Born in the football-crazed Ohio town of Massillon, what third-round pick from Michigan State in 1977 became a reliable starter at strong safety for seven seasons (1978-84)?

53) In a pivotal deal just prior to the 1976 season, what classic "possession" receiver with great footwork was dealt to the Vikings from

Seattle for defensive lineman Bob Lurtsema and a fourth-round choice?

54) Who is second on the Vikings career tackles list and also leads in career blocked kicks?

55) What NFC Central star set an NFL single-game record for rushing yards with 275 against the Vikings on Nov. 20, 1977?

56) In the final game at Buffalo in 1975, what Viking player was hit in the right eye with a snowball and suffered blurry vision for several days after scoring four touchdowns?

57) Wearing #80, what receiver was a deep threat as a star in 1969 and perhaps was the only player who played up to his ability for Minnesota in Super Bowl IV?

58) Who scored four touchdowns to lead Minnesota to a 28-22 win over San Francisco in the 1979 opener at Met Stadium?

59) What team stomped the Vikings 27-0 late in the 1973 season, the first shutout under Bud Grant and the first since the 1962 season?

60) By the time the Purple People Eaters had all retired or were dealt away, how many fumbles had they recovered as a front four for the Vikings?

61) What receiver set a rookie and team record for most yards receiving in a game against Detroit on Nov. 7, 1976?

62) Though the Vikings went 99-43-2 during the 1970's, in what year did they have their lone losing season?

63) How many consecutive times did the Vikings defeat Green Bay in the decade?

64) Who holds the Vikings record for the longest rush by a receiver?

65) What three Viking stalwarts were named to the NFL's all-decade team of the 1970's?

66) Traded prior to the season by the Vikings and coached by a former Viking head coach, what quarterback led Atlanta to a 20-14 win on Monday night, Nov. 19, 1973, halting Minnesota's nine-game winning streak to start the season?

67) What productive player left as a free agent after the 1974 season for the World Football League but returned to play for the team in 1975 when the league folded after just five games?

68) In what seasons did the Viking play six pre-season games while playing a 14-game regular season schedule?

69) What Viking punter (1972-74) hailed from Upper Iowa University in tiny Fayette, Iowa?

70) Noted for their kick-blocking abilities throughout the decade, in which year did the Vikings total 16 blocked kicks?

71) In what year did the Vikings play in their first "Monday Night Football" game on ABC television?

72) What position did Fred Cox play at the University of Pittsburgh?

73) What tight end and wide receiver were teammates not only with the Vikings but also in high school and college?

74) What quarterback lost three teeth and suffered a large gash in his mouth but got stitched up and returned to lead the Vikings to a 17-7 win over Detroit on Nov. 5, 1978?

75) What player replaced the injured Bobby Bryant at cornerback in 1976 and was outstanding in 11 starts, developing a reputation for his ball-hawking style?

76) What Viking defensive lineman claims that he was bitten four times by notorious St. Louis Rams' offensive guard Conrad Dobler?

77) What Viking became the first NFL running back to play in 200 games?

78) What kick and punt returner led the NFC in kick return average (25.1) in 1979 after earning the Canadian Football League's MVP award in 1977 with Hamilton?

79) What all-around athlete from East Grand Forks, Minnesota, acquired on waivers from Houston, picked off a pass on his first play as a starter at safety on Oct. 21, 1979, a 30-27 home win over Chicago?

80) What two Vikings became the first NFL running backs on the same team to catch at least 50 passes in a season?

81) In a gut-wrenching two-year period in 1978 and 1979, no fewer than eight all-time Viking greats retired, were released, or were traded. Who were they?

82) What Viking tight end from 1967-73 convinced 10 other teammates and coaches to invest in a gold mine in Idaho that finally struck a major vein in 2004 that was worth an estimated $700 million?

1) Alan Page (1971) and Fran Tarkenton (1975).

2) 7-7 (missing the playoffs).

3) Robert Earl Moore. He changed his name in 1972, his rookie year with the St. Louis Cardinals.

4) 1975; they finally lost at Washington (31-30) on Nov. 30 when Fred Cox's 45-yard effort to win the game was blocked. Minnesota finished the year with a 12-2 log, easily winning the Central Division.

5) 1978; the Vikings finished 8-7-1.

6) Bill "Boom-Boom" Brown, the bow-legged stud with the grinder-like voice.

7) Rick Danmeier, a free agent out of Sioux Falls College. Danmeier, another straight-on kicker, was the team's kicking specialist from 1978 to 1982 and was successful on 66 % of his field-goal attempts (70 of 106). Danmeier was the second-to-last straight-on kicker, with Mark Moseley of Washington being the final holdout.

8) Four. In 1970, 1973, and 1975, the Vikings were a perfect 7-0. In 1976, they were 6-0-1. In a seven-year stretch from 1970-1976, Minnesota was 39-9 playing at Met Stadium.

9) John Gilliam, who had 165 catches for 3,297 yards from 1972-75. He was a Pro Bowler each of his four seasons with the club and averaged 20 yards per reception.

10) 1974

11) Ron Groce, a 15th-round draft pick, who played in just four games and rushed three times for 18 yards.

12) Running back.

13) Doug Sutherland. Wearing number 69, he remained in the lineup with Page, Eller, and Marshall through the 1977 season. Sutherland was a starter for seven seasons in his tenure with Minnesota (1971-80).

14) Jeff Siemon, a top choice in 1972 from Stanford. Siemon, who wore #50, was a four-time Pro-Bowler.

15) Paul Krause, the Hall of Fame safety. He was the holder for a

supposed game-winning field goal but instead of putting the ball down for Fred Cox, he tossed an 11-yard pass to Stu Voigt to win the game.

16) 30; only Rod Woodson has surpassed his mark with 32 in his career (1987-2003) with four teams.

17) Bob Grim, who was the Vikings second-round pick in '67 (one of the Giant draft picks given in return for Tarkenton). When Fran was traded back in '72, Grim was sent to New York.

18) Chuck Foreman totaled 1,070 yards in 1975.

19) Bob Stein, who became an attorney and sports agent.

20) Gary Burley. Tarkenton would return for a final season in 1978.

21) Charles Goodrum. Both Goodrum and Coleman were from Florida A & M.

22) The Los Angeles Coliseum. The Vikings lost 20-17 in 65° weather.

23) Steve Riley.

24) Doug Kingsriter, who has authored seven

Bobby Bryant.

children's books and produced several children's musicals.

25) The NFL's blackout policy, which stated that a home game could not be televised locally if not sold out at least 72 hours prior to the game's start. The radius for the blackout was 75 miles from the home team's stadium. In many cases, the NFL relaxed the rule and changed it to 48 hours if the team was a few thousand tickets short of selling out. In many cases, local TV affiliates made arrangements to buy the remaining tickets out to insure the local market was able to view the "home" team.

26) Nate Wright, who started 89 games from 1973-78 and intercepted 31 passes for Minnesota.

27) Wes Hamilton.

28) Brent McClanahan, who played alongside Chuck Foreman as a fullback in 1976 and 1977. He was also a valuable special teams player.

29) Fred McNeill. He recovered six fumbles in 1978.

30) Chuck Foreman had 22 touchdowns in 1975, 13 rushing and nine receiving.

31) Green Bay. The Vikings had just 21 yards passing on five Gary Cuozzo completions and only 66 yards rushing and five total first downs. The Packers, meanwhile, drove to the Viking 20 or better five times but didn't score as two interceptions, a lost fumble, a blocked field goal, and turning the ball over inside the Minnesota 1-yard line doomed them. The game-time temperature was 45 with a 17-mile-per-hour wind.

32) Alan Page, who played for the Bears through 1981. Page and coach Bud Grant had battled over the player's weight and other issues. Page's weight had dropped from about 270 to 230 and Grant was concerned that his lack of heft deemed him expendable.

33) Mark Mullaney, who played 13 seasons (1975-87) for Minnesota and racked up 45.5 sacks and 13 forced fumbles.

34) Jeff Wright. Only 5'11" and 190 pounds, he used his body well to position himself against receivers. He started 54 games and intercepted 12 passes.

35) Jim Marshall. He retired after the 1979 season but had he played in 1980, he would have played in the 1950's, 1960's, 1970's, and 1980's. Marshall left Ohio State after his junior season to play for the Saskatchewan Rough Riders of the Canadian Football League in 1959. After Cleveland drafted him in 1960, he played a season for the Browns. Traded just before the 1961 season, he then played 19 seasons in Minnesota.

36) Bob Lurtsema. "Benchwarmer Bob" parlayed his good humor and folksy demeanor into a public relations coup as he starred in over 150 ads for TCF Savings and Loan from 1973-84.

37) Eddie Payton

38) Jim Vellone, who died in 1977 at age 33.

39) Fran Tarkenton and Bob Berry. Tarkenton threw two fourth-quarter touchdowns to lead the New York Giants to a 24-23 win at Yankee Stadium in the first game of the season. In the final game at Atlanta, Berry threw for just 70 yards but eight (yes, eight) Viking turnovers led to a 10-3 defeat.

40) Ed Sharockman. He scored on a 34-yard interception return and a 23-yard return of a blocked punt.

41) Sammy White, a two-time Pro Bowler in 1976 and 1977. White played 10 years with Minnesota, catching 393 balls for 6,400 yards and 50 touchdowns with a sterling 16.3 yards per catch. In his rookie year, he totaled 906 yards and scored 10 touchdowns.

42) Neil Clabo

43) Bob Grim, who was involved in both trades involving Fran Tarkenton and the New York Giants.

44) The Kansas City Chiefs (1971) and the Miami Dolphins (1974). In a real twist, the victories gave them some semblance of revenge for losing to the same team in the previous year's Super Bowl.

45) Joe Kapp. Unsigned and without a contract with Minnesota, Kapp was dealt away in October and played miserably for the Patriots.

46) Bob Lurtsema. In the third game of the season, the Vikings led 16-6 entering the fourth quarter. After the Lurtsema penalty, Miami scored the game-clinching touchdown on a 3-yard pass from Bob Griese to Jim Mandich.

47) Gary Cuozzo (eight starts), Bob Lee (four), and Norm Snead (two).

48) Chuck Foreman (53 in 1974, 73 in 1975, and 55 in 1976).

49) Bobby Bryant. A seventh-round pick in 1967, Bryant was a slight 6'1", 170-pound concoction of tendon and sinew who continually came up with big plays. He had 51 career interceptions and started 121 games and made the Pro Bowl in 1975 and 1976.

50) Ed Marinaro. The curly-haired Italian from New York City rushed for 1,007 yards in four seasons but also became a fine receiver out of the backfield with 125 grabs for 1,008 yards. In 1975, he was

Ahmad Rashad (28) hauls in a pass against the Philadelphia Eagles at Met Stadium.

a starter and rushed for a career-high 358 yards and caught 54 passes for 462 yards and three touchdowns.

51) Ed White, a Pro Bowler in 1975, 1976, 1977, and 1979. Ed was also noted for his huge appetite and his arm-wrestling capabilities.

52) Tommy Hannon. From 1979-81, he had four interceptions each season.

53) Ahmad Rashad. The dynamic wide receiver became a four-time Pro Bowler (1978-81) and finished with 400 receptions for 5,489 yards and 34 touchdowns in seven memorable seasons in Minnesota. Rashad performed with the artistry of a ballet dancer and the timing of a symphony conductor.

54) Matt Blair (1,452 tackles and 20 blocked kicks).

55) Walter Payton. "Sweetness" rushed 40 times and scored Chicago's only touchdown in a 10-7 Bears win.

56) Chuck Foreman, who scored twice on rushes and twice on pass receptions. O.J. Simpson scored twice in Minnesota's 35-13 win.

57) John Henderson. The Michigan grad had 34 catches for 553 yards and five touchdowns in 1969. In Super Bowl IV, he had seven catches for 111 yards in the 23-7 loss to Kansas City.

58) Ahmad Rashad. All four scoring receptions (52, 32, 8, and 32) came in the second half from quarterback Tommy Kramer. Rashad totaled seven completions for 152 yards.

59) Cincinnati. The Vikings were 10-1 entering the game but still finished 12-2.

60) 86; Jim Marshall (29), Carl Eller (24), Alan Page (18), Gary Larsen (12), and Doug Sutherland (3). Sutherland replaced Larsen in the defensive line for the 1974 season.

61) Sammy White. The Grambling star caught seven balls for 210 yards with two touchdowns in a 31-23 win over the Lions at Met Stadium.

62) 1979 (7-9)

63) Seven. Minnesota swept the Packers from 1975-77 and won the first game in 1978 before Green Bay finally tied the Vikings 10-10 in the second game. It is the longest winning streak by either team in the rivalry.

64) Bob Grim, who ran for 54 yards against the New York Giants on Oct. 31, 1971.

65) Carl Eller (DE), Alan Page (DT), and Ron Yary (T).

66) Bob Lee, who was 11-23 for 171 yards and two touchdowns. The Falcons were coached by Norm Van Brocklin.

67) John Gilliam. The fleet receiver had 20 catches for 390 yards and two touchdowns with the Chicago Wind but the team folded and Gilliam rejoined the Vikings. He caught 50 passes for 777 yards and seven touchdowns and a sterling 15.5 average per grab.

68) 1969-1971; 1975-77.

69) Mike Eischied, who is just one of two Peacock players to make

it in the NFL. Eischeid punted for Oakland for six years prior to coming to Minnesota as they made way for Ray Guy, who many say was the best punter in league history.

70) 1976 (seven extra-points, six field goals, and three punts). Alan Page had five while Nate Allen and Matt Blair each had three.

71) 1970 (Oct. 26). It was a gorgeous night at Metropolitan Stadium, with the temperature at 51 degrees and a mild breeze as the hosts beat the Los Angeles Rams 13-3. Both teams were 4-1 entering the game and it was rated a toss-up. However, Minnesota dominated the Rams, holding them to just five first downs and only 100 total yards. Los Angeles had just 34 net yards passing as Alan Page and company harassed Roman Gabriel. The Rams had five turnovers (four fumbles). Bill Brown scored the only touchdown of the game and Fred Cox added two field goals.

Stu Voigt

72) Halfback

73) Steve Craig and Jim Lash. Craig was a third-round pick in 1974 and was mostly a reserve from 1974-78. Lash, a third-rounder in 1973, played four seasons for the team and caught 75 balls for 1,252 yards and three touchdowns. Both players competed at Garfield High in Akron, Ohio, and in the collegiate ranks at Northwestern together.

74) Fran Tarkenton, who was mauled by Lions' end Dave Pureifory.

75) Nate Allen. Just 5'11" and 175 pounds, the Texas Southern product intercepted 3 passes, forced 2 fumbles, returned a blocked punt for a touchdown, blocked 3 kicks, and made 66 tackles in one of the most impressive "substitute" jobs in team history.

76) Doug Sutherland. Dobler was universally known as the meanest and dirtiest NFL player in his 10-year career with the Rams, Saints, and Bills. What else for a guy who punched Mean Joe Greene, spat on an injured Bill Bergey, and kicked Merlin Olsen in the head, to mention a few of his transgressions.

77) Bill Brown (205 games).

78) Jimmy Edwards

79) Kurt Knoff. The former Minnesota High School Athlete of the Year started every game in 1980 and 1981 and finished his four-year career with nine interceptions in 43 games.

80) Chuck Foreman (73) and Ed Marinaro (54) in 1975.

81) Alan Page was released during the 1978 season and picked up by Chicago. Following the 1978 season, Fran Tarkenton and Mick Tingelhoff retired and Carl Eller was traded to Seattle. Chuck Foreman was traded to New England after the 1979 season and Paul Krause, Jim Marshall, and Wally Hilgenberg retired. All of them, of course, were regulars, including four future Hall of Famers and a few more that should be.

82) John Beasley. Coaches Jack Patera and Jocko Nelson and players Bob Berry, John Henderson, Joe Kapp, Bob Lurtsema, Jim Marshall, Mike Wells, Nate Wright and Godfrey Zaunbrecher all contributed $1,000 to $2,000 to purchase a controlling interest in Golden Chest Mine in Murray, Idaho. Beasley was the president.

4 The 1980s

1) In what year during the decade did the NFL utilize so-called "replacement" players to compete in regular season games during a players' strike?

2) Which defensive player became the first player in the NFL to wear a helmet shield on his facemask after suffering an eye injury in 1984?

3) What strong safety from USC was a terrific open-field tackler, especially with his vice-grip hands, for the Vikings from 1983 to 1991 and was on the NFL's all-decade team for the 1980's?

4) What defensive genius worked for Jerry Burns in the late 1980's and then for Denny Green in the early 1990's before moving on to Tampa Bay, where he became widely known and imitated for his "Tampa Cover 2" defense?

5) From 1982 to 1985, what hyperactive middle-aged man was hired to be a cheerleader for the team, always present with his hand drum?

6) What Winona athlete and Gopher star played tight end for the Vikings in 1985?

7) What position did Jarvis Redwine and Alfred Anderson play for the Vikings during the 1980's ?

8) What veteran tight end and future Hall of Famer, who played most of his career with Oakland, played a partial season with Minnesota in 1983?

9) When Chuck Foreman was traded to New England prior to the 1980 season, the Vikings received a third-round pick in 1981. They chose a tackle from Tennessee who became a reliable force on the right side of the line from 1981 to 1993. Who was he?

10) What Viking quarterback has two sons who won the Super Bowl at that same position?

11) What MIAC school supplied two players who filled backup roles superbly on the same Vikings team during the 1980s?

12) In 1984, what two running backs from Baylor did the Vikings select among their first five picks, both of whom went on to play for the team for at least seven years?

13) His father was a world-renowned surgeon and he was a star linebacker for the Gophers but played just one season (1987) for the Vikings, playing five games and starting three of them. Who was he?

14) Who became one of the team's all-time great punt and kick returners from 1980-82, playing in the same division as his more famous younger brother?

15) What player always seemed to play at 100% of his ability as a special teams ace and defensive back (1979-85) out of St. Cloud State?

16) What fourth-round pick from Oklahoma set an NFL single-season record (since broken) for kick return yardage with 1,345 in 1985?

17) What quarterback out of East Texas State who played with the Vikings from 1981 to 1991 was nicknamed "Whiskey"?

18) Who was the team's kicker in 1983, a fellow born in Paraguay who now happens to be a standup comedian and sports broadcaster?

19) What 37-year-old played quarterback for the Vikings in the three games played by "replacement" players during the 1987 players' strike?

20) What runner churned out 1,063 yards in the 1981 season and tacked on 83 receptions for another 694 yards?

21) Which two Vikings became the first teammates to gain at least 1,000 yards receiving in 1981?

22) Just 5'7" and 170 pounds, what punt returner was a great special teams player and a solid backup receiver from 1981-91 and whose father played with and was coached by Bud Grant?

23) What was the nickname of big Curtis Rouse, who played guard from 1982-86?

24) He wore #83 and he proved that Ivy League players could not only make NFL rosters but become pro standouts? Who was this superlative tight end?

Anthony Carter

25) Wearing Carl Eller's old number, what smooth-as-silk receiver from Michigan was one of the top deep threats in the league for the Vikings from 1985-93?

26) Looking like a sure bet to make the playoffs, what year did the Vikings lose their final five games to finish 7-9 and out of the post-season frolic?

27) Who proved to be an expert pass-catcher coming out of the backfield for the Vikings from 1978 to 1983 and was a backfield mate of the great Walter Payton at Jackson State?

28) In what year was there a 57-day players' strike following the second week of the season, leading to a nine-game regular-season?

29) A Pacific grad, what Viking linebacker was a force for four years from 1989-92 and won a game on Nov. 5, 1989, by blocking a punt by Los Angeles Rams punter Dale Hatcher out of the end zone in overtime?

30) What Viking quarterback became known as "Two-Minute Tommy" for orchestrating late scoring drives for the Vikings?

31) In one of the most memorable runs in NFL history, what San Francisco quarterback weaved his way through what seemed like the entire Viking defense for a game-winning 49-yard touchdown run on Oct. 30, 1988?

32) Who scored the only points for the Vikings in the final game at Met Stadium on Dec. 20, 1981, when Kansas City beat them?

33) What linebacker from Penn State intercepted Chicago's Mike Tomczak and returned the ball 94 yards for a touchdown as Minnesota edged the Bears 28-27 in the regular season finale at the Metrodome in 1988?

34) Although no front four could match the Purple People Eaters of the 1960's and 1970's, what four talented athletes made up defensive line coach Floyd Peters' pride and joy during the 1980s?

35) What Viking tight end caught six passes for 179 yards and a touchdown in a 44-38 overtime loss at Washington on Nov. 2, 1986?

36) What two quarterbacks staged a full-fledged battle to win the starting job for the Vikings from 1986 to 1989?

37) What well-conditioned athlete was a standout for the Vikings from 1978-87 as the longest-tenured punter in team history and an expert at downing punts in the "coffin corner"?

38) Besides perhaps being the most unsung of all the players who were honored as part of the "50 Greatest Vikings" in 2010, what defender was as consistent as any Viking cornerback at pass defense from 1983 to 1993?

39) A heralded All-American at Nebraska, what second-round pick in 1981 with a magnificent name was a major disappointment in a brief three-year career?

40) What Hall of Fame kicker ended his career by kicking for Minnesota in 1984 and 1985 when he was past the age of 40?

41) Who was the talented Viking cornerback from 1985 to 1989 who hailed from the same southern school as current head coach Leslie Frazier?

42) What defensive tackle was a true beast in the line for the Vikings in the late 1980's after playing in the USFL?

43) What third-round pick from LSU was the bulwark in the Vikings defensive line from 1987 to 1994?

44) A little water-bug who became one of the best all-purpose backs in the NFL in the 1980's, who was the Vikings top pick in the 1982 draft?

45) A future NFL head coach, what gentleman served as a reserve tight end from 1983-88?

46) In what year did the NFL institute limited use of "instant replay"?

47) Just 5'10" and 175 pounds, what skinny receiver was a valued backup from 1979 to 1983 and again in 1987?

48) The vaunted Chicago Bear "47" defense was a fearsome group back in 1984. What Viking quarterback was sacked a team record 11 times in a 16-7 loss at Chicago?

49) What two Viking defenders combined for 39 sacks in 1989?

50) Who set a team single-game mark with 490 yards passing in a 44-38 overtime loss at Washington on Nov. 2, 1986, to become the first NFL quarterback to pass for more than 450 yards twice in his career?

51) What player, wearing number 47, holds the Viking career record for sacks by a defensive back?

52) Originally selected by New England out of Delaware in 1987 and projected as a running back, what future Viking quarterback was acquired by the team two weeks after the draft?

53) Perhaps the most amazing play in Viking history, what Viking receiver made a miraculous touchdown catch with no time remaining to give the Vikings a 28-23 win over Cleveland to secure a playoff berth on Dec. 14, 1980 at Met Stadium?

54) As tough as his name might suggest, what fourth-round pick in 1978 from Utah State was a trusted offensive guard from 1978-86?

Chris Doleman

55) Which Viking quarterback threw four first-quarter touchdown passes and six by early in the third quarter but was pulled from the game (Sept. 28, 1986) before he could get a chance for a record-tying seven or a record eight TD passes?

56) What Hall of Fame running back set an NFL record with a 99-yard touchdown run in the last game of the 1982 regular season (Jan. 3, 1983)?

57) The Vikings started 6-2 in 1983 but went 2-6 to finish 8-8 and missed the playoffs. Whose injury in the third game of the season, which caused him to miss the rest of the campaign, put a major dent into their hopes and helped lead to Bud Grant's resignation?

58) What Viking veteran showed up for training camp in 1984 saluting the team's new head coach and wearing military fatigues?

59) Which three Vikings were named to the NFL's all-decade team for the 1980's?

60) In what two years during the decade was the Viking defense number one overall in the NFL?

61) What Florida State linebacker, a 12th round pick in 1986, was mostly a reserve in college but became a starter with the Vikings?

62) What unheralded eighth-round pick in 1987 was a tough fullback for five seasons with his bruising runs and stellar blocking?

63) What two Viking teammates in 1989 were also brothers-in-law?

64) Who is the only Viking player to leave the team and play in the United States Football League and then return to finish his career with Minnesota?

Steve Jordan

65) What vaunted Viking player from this era had three of his brothers also compete in the NFL?

66) In what season during the decade did the Viking score 336 points and allow 335 points?

67) In 1986, no fewer than five Vikings had at least 500 receiving yards. Who were they?

68) What defensive back from 1982-87 spent many years as the football coach at Minneapolis North High School?

69) Who was the Vikings top pick in the 1980 draft, a defensive tackle from Washington, who led the NFL in sacks in 1982?

70) Born in Canton, Ohio, what Ohio State center became a mainstay at that position for eight years from 1985-92 and was known as a fiery team leader?

1) 1987. The Vikings, unfortunately, lost all three games that the replacement players participated in. However, they were 8-4 with their regular players and finished 8-7 and made the playoffs as a wild-card.

2) Mark Mullaney. In 1986, Mullaney also became the first player to wear a darkened shield. Equipment manager Dennis Ryan helped Mullaney create both shields.

3) Joey Browner

4) Monte Kiffin, who is considered one of the best defensive minds in NFL history and one of the best defensive coordinators ever. He coached Tampa's defense for 13 years and in 10 of those years, his teams finished in the top ten in fewest points allowed and fewest yards gained.

5) "Krazy George" Henderson, a balding yet long-haired gentleman who graduated from San Jose State in 1968 and was a member of a judo team that won a national title. "Krazy George" worked for four other NFL teams, three major-league baseball teams, and many other sporting organizations. Henderson claims that he invented the "wave", which became popular at sporting events 30 years ago. However, the University of Washington still disputes his claim.

6) Jay Carroll, who played in 15 games but caught just one pass.

7) Running back; though Payton was also a punt and kick returner.

8) Dave Casper. The Notre Dame alum caught only 13 passes for 172 yards in 10 games before being traded to Houston late in the season.

9) Tim Irwin, who missed just three games in his 13-year run with the Vikings. He became an attorney during his tenure with Minnesota and has been a judge in juvenile court in his native Tennessee since 2005. Irwin had off-season surgery nine times during his career.

10) Archie Manning. Son Peyton won Super Bowl XLI with the Indianapolis Colts and son Eli of the New York Giants won Super Bowl XLII and Super Bowl XLVI. Archie played for the Vikings in 1993 and 1994.

11) St. Thomas University - Jim Gustafson, a wide receiver from 1985-90 and Neal Guggemos, a defensive back who played in 1986 and 1987. Gustafson was a fine special teams player and Guggemos was an excellent cover man on defense and a smart and effective player on special teams.

12) Alfred Anderson (1984-91) and Allen Rice (1984-90). Anderson was the third pick and Rice the fifth. Anderson rushed for 2,374 yards and 22 touchdowns while Rice rushed for 934 yards and 13 touchdowns.

13) Pete Najarian, the son of transplant surgeon John Najarian. He founded an on-line brokerage firm called tradeMONSTER in 2008 and is seen on "Fast Money", a CNBC financial show.

14) Eddie Payton, who led the league with 53 kick returns for 1,184 yards in 1980. The sibling was a guy named Walter, who played some ball with the Chicago Bears.

15) Keith Nord, who wore #49. Nord was captain of the special teams for several years and led the team in tackles four times with his incessant hustling.

16) Buster Rhymes, who averaged 25.4 yards per return. He had 182 yards against Chicago on Sept. 19, 1985, in addition to 89 receiving yards in a 33-24 loss to the Bears.

17) Wade Wilson, who quarterbacked the Vikings into the playoffs three times in the '80s and is currently the quarterbacks coach for Dallas.

18) Benny Ricardo, who was 25-33 on his field goal attempts. He also spent time on the pro racquetball circuit.

19) Tony Adams, who was 49-89 for 607 yards, three touchdowns, and five interceptions. Minnesota lost all three games. He had played sparingly for Kansas City from 1975-77.

20) Ted Brown

21) Sammy White (1,001) and Joe Senser (1,004).

22) Leo Lewis III, who had 1,868 yards on 201 punt returns and 182 catches for 2,924 yards and 16 touchdowns in his 11 seasons with the club. Leo Lewis II is in both the College Football Hall of Fame and the Canadian Football Hall of Fame. Lewis III is

currently the Associate Athletic Director at the University of Minnesota for Student-Athlete Development.

23) Boo Boo. Rouse, from Tennessee-Chattanooga, was the heaviest player in the league during his time with Minnesota at 350 pounds.

24) Steve Jordan, who is among the "50 Greatest Vikings" after starring from 1982-94.

25) Anthony Carter. Just 5'11" and 168 pounds, Carter caught 478 passes for 7,636 yards and 52 touchdowns. He earned three Pro Bowl nods and had three 1,000-yard receiving seasons. In 1987, he led the league with 24.3 yards per reception, grabbing 38 balls and recording seven touchdowns.

26) 1981; it was the first and only time a Bud Grant team lost five in a row.

27) Rickey Young, who led the league with 88 receptions in 1978. Young had 292 receptions in six seasons and rushed for 1,744 yards. Like Payton, he wore #34.

28) 1982. The Vikings finished 5-4 and in the convoluted playoff format, the Vikings beat Atlanta at home in a wild-card battle before losing at Washington.

29) Mike Merriweather. He became the first NFL player to win a game for his team by recording a safety as Minnesota won 23-21. The first 21 points were scored by kicker Rich Karlis, who booted seven field goals (tying a record that has since been broken by Rob Bironas, who kicked eight for Tennessee in a game in 2007).

30) Tommy Kramer

31) Steve Young, who shed six would-be tacklers who got a hand on him in a 24-21 win at Candlestick Park.

32) Rick Danmeier, who booted field goals in the first and third quarters in a 10-6 defeat that ended a 21-year run in Bloomington. Incidentally, it was 10 degrees with a 17 mile-per-hour wind that day with a -8 wind chill.

33) Walker Lee Ashley

34) Defensive ends Doug Martin and Chris Doleman and defense tackles Henry Thomas and Keith Millard.

35) Steve Jordan. Leo Lewis added 159 yards on just three catches, a 53-yard average.

36) Wade Wilson and Tommy Kramer. Wilson started 32 games during this period and Kramer 28 as the quarterback controversy was Jerry Burns' number one headache as head coach.

37) Greg Coleman. He holds team records for total punts (721), yardage (29,391), and games as a punter (138).

38) Carl Lee. A former seventh-round choice, Lee started 144 games and had 779 tackles and 31 interceptions in 11 strong years with Minnesota. He was head coach at West Virginia State for 10 seasons starting in 1996.

39) Jarvis Redwine. He started just once in 26 career games, rushing 17 times for 70 yards. Redwine was solid, however, as a kick returner, returning 50 kicks for a 22.5 average.

40) Jan Stenerud, who was 35-49 on field goal attempts those two seasons.

41) Isaac Holt. A second-rounder in 1985, Holt had eight interceptions in 1986 and returned one for a 90-yard touchdown in 1989. Both Holt and Frazier played at Alcorn State in Lorman, Mississippi.

42) Keith Millard. He was the Vikings top pick in 1984 out of Washington State but elected to play for Jacksonville of the USFL his rookie year. The Vikings agreed to take on his four-year, $1.9 million contract and he was a stud from 1985-91.

43) Henry Thomas. Nicknamed "Hardware Hank," he was a nose tackle from 1987-94 and a Pro Bowler in 1991 and 1992. Thomas lined up at a cockeyed angle so close to his opponent on the line that the NFL widened the space allowed along the line of scrimmage.

44) Darrin Nelson. After spending several years as an Associate Athletic Director at Stanford, he is now in the same role at California-Irvine.

45) Mike Mularkey, who coached for both Buffalo (2004-05) and Jacksonsville (2012).

46) 1986

47) Terry LeCount, who had a 15.5 average per catch with the Vikings.

48) Archie Manning. Richard Dent and friends totaled 101 yards in sack yardage.

49) Chris Doleman (21) and Keith Millard (18).

50) Tommy Kramer was 20-35 with four touchdowns. On Dec. 14, 1980, Kramer passed for 456 yards and four touchdowns in a home victory over Cleveland while completing 38 of 49 passes with no interceptions.

51) Joey Browner (9.5).

52) Rich Gannon. In his six seasons in Minnesota, Gannon started 35 games (19-16) and threw 40 touchdown passes and 36 interceptions while compiling a 55.9 % completion percentage.

53) Ahmad Rashad. Down 23-21 with 14 seconds left, Tommy Kramer hit tight end Joe Senser for a 10-yard gain. Senser lateraled to running back Ted Brown who sped 24 more yards and out of bounds at the Cleveland 36. With just a few seconds left, Kramer threw the ball high and far down the right sideline. Minnesota receivers Sammy White and Terry LeCount leapt for the pigskin but Browns defender Thom Darden deflected it up in the air. It fell to Rashad, who caught the ball at the three yard-line and actually backed into the end zone.

54) Jim Hough, who started 75 games at left guard and played in 111 overall.

55) Tommy Kramer, who was 16-25 for 241 yards in the Vikings 42-7 romp over Green Bay. Both Hassan Jones and Steve Jordan had two touchdown receptions. Wade Wilson replaced Kramer and was 3-5 passing as the Vikings kept the ball on the ground throughout most of the remainder of the game.

56) Tony Dorsett of the Dallas Cowboys. It was a Monday night game and the Vikings won 31-27. On the play, Dallas only had 10 men on the field!

57) Tommy Kramer, who suffered a knee injury. Steve Dils replaced him and passed for 11 touchdowns but had 16 interceptions.

58) Punter Greg Coleman.

59) Joey Browner (S), Keith Millard (DT), and Gary Zimmerman (T).

60) 1988 and 1989

61) Jesse Solomon, who started 33 games in four seasons with Minnesota. He was part of the trade with Dallas in the midst of the 1989 season for Herschel Walker.

62) Rick Fenney (1987-91). He gained 1,508 yards with a 4.2 career rushing average.

63) Kicker Rich Karlis and center Kirk Lowdermilk.

64) David Huffman, who played all five positions on the offensive line from 1979-83 and again from 1985-90.

65) Safety Joey Browner (1983-91). Jim was a defensive back with Cincinnati (1979-80), Keith was a linebacker with Tampa Bay, San Francisco, Oakland, and San Diego (1984-88), and Ross was a defensive end who played with Cincinnati and Green Bay.

Joey Browner gets a high-five from fellow defensive back Felix Wright following an interception.

66) 1987

67) Anthony Carter (686), Hassan Jones (570), Steve Jordan (859), Leo Lewis (600), and Darrin Nelson (593). A sixth, Alfred Anderson, even had 391 yards as quarterbacks Tommy Kramer and Wade Wilson had numerous options in the passing game.

68) Rufus Bess, who had nine interceptions during his tenure. He was also a kick and punt returner in 68 games with the Vikings.

69) Doug Martin. He was a Pro Bowler in 1982 when he had 11.5 sacks in just nine games. He had 50.5 sacks in 126 games during his 10-year career.

70) Kirk Lowdermilk. Kirk started six seasons and made the 1989 Pro Bowl.

5 The 1990s

1) What mercurial rookie receiver wowed Viking fans and NFL fans everywhere with his 17 touchdown receptions in 1998, a league high?

2) What Viking is the only quarterback in NFL history to complete a touchdown pass to himself?

3) On Nov. 13, 1994, what New England Patriots quarterback set an NFL record that still stands when he completed 45 passes in a 26-20 overtime win over Minnesota?

4) In what year during the decade did the Vikings not only win all eight of their regular season home games but dominate their opponents, winning by an average of 23.6 points?

5) A second-round pick in 1993, what Syracuse All-American receiver was nicknamed "The Missile," a take-off from his brother Raghib?

6) In what year did the NFL institute the two-point conversion option and in what year did the Vikings lead the league with six such conversions?

7) What diminutive kicker became the first NFL kicker (25 attempts minimum) to make all his field goal attempts during the regular season?

8) A future NFL head coach, what former USC stalwart was a standout middle linebacker from 1992 to 1995?

Cris Carter (80) is congratulated by fellow receiver Jake Reed (86) after snaring a touchdown pass.

9) What native Canadian, a huge specimen for a punter (6'4" and 220 pounds), was one of the league's top punters for his six years in Minnesota (1996-01)?

10) At the end of a superlative 11-year career as one of the NFL's best all-around backs of his era, what former Nebraska runner played his final two seasons (1992-93) here?

11) What former St. Thomas Academy and Notre Dame standout played safety for the Vikings in both 1990 and 1991?

12) What safety from Louisiana-Lafayette led the NFL with nine interceptions in his rookie year of 1995?

13) What nose tackle proved pretty much immovable on run defense for the Vikings from 1997-99?

14) A Stanford man, what special teams virtuoso was an absolute security blanket for the coaches from 1994-02 on both the return and coverage teams?

15) What kicker from Bogota, Columbia was a consistent performer from 1990-95 and was successful on 77.8 % of his field goal attempts (133-178)?

16) What two players hooked up on the first two-point conversion during the 1994 season?

17) What little punt returner/receiver caught one pass in his two-year stint with the Vikings but his 45-yard reception from Jim McMahon in the final seconds led to Fuad Reveiz' 22-yard field goal to give the Vikings a 15-13 win over visiting Green Bay on Sept. 26, 1993?

18) What player started his career by scoring two touchdowns in his very first game?

19) A top pick out of North Carolina State in 1994, what Viking cornerback was a standout as a rookie, intercepting three passes, including two for touchdowns?

20) Just days prior to the 1990 opener, who did the Vikings claim for a $100 waiver fee from the Philadelphia Eagles, a player who became one of the best possession receivers in NFL history?

21) A fifth-round choice out of Clemson in 1992, what aggressive defender played at both outside and middle linebacker with aplomb from 1992-2001?

22) What two Tampa Bay running backs each rushed for over 100 yards in leading the host Buccaneers to a 27-24 triumph on Nov. 1, giving the Vikings their only loss in the 1998 campaign?

23)What Michigan Wolverine displayed some of the hardest running ever by a Viking runner from 1996-99?

24) For what reason did more than a hundred Viking alumni attend the home contest against Jacksonville on December 20, 1998?

25) What Viking receiving duo became the first tandem to amass more than 1,000 yards each in four-straight seasons from 1994-97?

26) What Viking back once went 532 carries without a fumble?

27) What Viking defender averaged a startling 34.6 yards per runback for his seven interceptions in 1998?

28) What former Super Bowl winning quarterback with the Bears took over the starting job with the Vikings in 1993?

29) What Ohio State runner was working in a pharmacy during the 1993 season before getting a call and becoming the team's top ball carrier that season with 488 yards?

30) In what year did the Vikings lead the league in offensive plays of at least 25 yards and in plays of at least 40 yards?

31) Wearing #7, who booted 31 consecutive field goals combined between 1994 and 1995?

32) What Viking led the league with 2,051 all-purpose yards in 1990?

33) What 42-year-old was hired in January of 1992 as only the second African-American head coach in league history?

34) In a national "coming-out party" on Monday night, Oct. 5, 1998, in Green Bay's Lambeau Field, what Viking receiver had four catches of at least 40 yards, including touchdowns of 44 and 52 yards in a 37-24 Minnesota win?

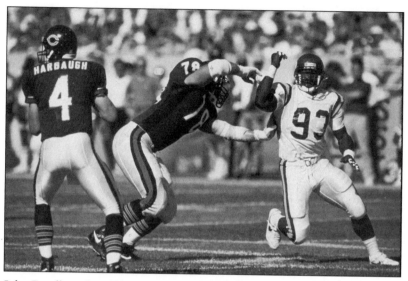

John Randle rushes Chicago QB Jim Harbaugh.

35) What Viking led the NFL in touchdown receptions three times in the 1990's?

36) With eight thefts in 1992, who led the NFL in interceptions?

37) Born in Nigeria and educated at Clemson, what Tampa Bay draftee kicked in eight games for Minnesota in 1990, converting 14 of 16 field goals?

38) What Clemson running back, who lasted until the ninth round in 1990 because of a serious knee injury, had a phenomenal 1992 season, rushing for a then team record of 1,201 yards and 13 touchdowns?

39) What current radio color analyst for the Vikings was a seventh-round pick in 1994 from Notre Dame and became a reserve line-backer and special teams player?

40) What Grambling star was the team's 3rd round choice in 1991 and was one of the top receivers in Viking history, amassing 413 receptions for 6,433 yards and 33 touchdowns?

41) The Vikings top pick in 1995, a linebacker from Alabama, who started 46 games from 1998-2000 and set an NFL record for fumble return yards in 1998 when he had 157?

42) Originally drafted by San Francisco, what Florida State star was a nifty pass receiver out of the backfield from 1994-96?

43) Never a starter in college at Florida State, what quarterback was drafted in the ninth round by the Vikings in 1992 and served the team admirably in two stints (1994-98 and 2005-06)?

44) After making San Diego State as a walk-on, what undrafted free agent played eight years with the Vikings from 1994-2001 as a first-rate strong safety?

45) What Western Carolina tight end caught 35 passes for 336 yards in his rookie year in 1994?

46) What diminutive return specialist from Alabama became one of the best returners in Viking history from 1994-2001?

47) Now a well-known football analyst, what former USC quarterback started nine regular season games for the Vikings over a three-year period (1992-94)?

48) A Gopher from Faribault, what former Viking linebacker (1989-91) is now an on-course official with the PGA?

49) Born in Honolulu and of Samoan ancestry, what Oregon State nose tackle played five years for Minnesota (1992-96), starting 28 games?

50) At the age of 35, what Viking quarterback had a monster year in 1998 by going 13-1 as the starter and throwing for 3,704 yards and 34 touchdowns?

51) On Thanksgiving Day, 1998, what Viking receiver caught just three passes against host Dallas but all three went for touchdowns of 51, 56, and 56 yards from Randall Cunningham?

52) What Viking quarterback led the NFL in completions in 1995 with 377 (606 attempts)?

53) What second-year defensive back from Louisiana-Lafayette had five interceptions in 1992, earning Pro Bowl honors?

54) While wearing a helmet that always looked extremely tight, what Arizona State offensive lineman became the second member

of the Maori tribe to play in the NFL?

55) As competitive as any Viking, what first-round pick in 1994 was a stone wall playing at left tackle from 1994-2000 wearing number 73?

56) A second-round pick in 1995, what Florida State defensive back became an immediate starter and pilfered 10 passes in his four years with Minnesota?

57) What 41-year-old was a Viking kicker for 12 games in 1997, making 12 of 17 field goal attempts after previously facing the team twice a year as a Detroit mainstay?

58) What Viking punter was second and third, respectively, in punting average in 1991 and 1992?

59) In Dennis Green's first game as Viking head coach, who rushed for 140 yards on just 12 carries and added another 53 yards on five receptions as Minnesota beat host Green Bay 23-20 in overtime?

Robert Smith races past Lion defenders.

60) What five Vikings were named to the NFL's all-decade team for the 1990's?

61) What future NFL star served as a ball-boy for the Vikings during training camps in the late 1990's?

62) What Viking became the fourth player in NFL history to record 10 or more sacks in six-straight seasons in 1997?

63) What receiving tandem combined for a startling 173 catches, 2,711 yards, and 24 touchdowns in 1999, the fourth-most productive season by two players on the same team?

64) What player, acquired off waivers from Arizona in 1993, became one of the most versatile centers in the NFL for the Vikings in a seven-year career with the local squad?

65) Signed as a Plan B free agent in 1992, what hard-hitting safety from Indiana State led the club with five interceptions in 1993 and tied for the lead in thefts in 1994 with four?

66) What two Arizona State studs were tabbed three rounds apart in the 1988 draft and ended up as the starting guards for the Vikings from 1989-91?

67) What running back ripped off a 47-yard gain in just his second carry with the team on Oct. 15, 1989 at the Metrodome despite losing one of his shoes?

68) What player took a role as the team's director of player development in 1992 after finishing his active career the previous year with the most games played at wide receiver (140)?

69) Undersized but fearless, what Clemson fifth-round draft choice in 1992 turned out to be a valuable linebacker for nine seasons with the Vikings?

70) A native of Centerville, Iowa and a graduate of Truman State in Missouri, what first-rate snapper for punts, field goals, and extra points never missed a game from 1991-99?

71) In 1994, for the first time in team history, two rookies (one offensive, one defensive) started every game. Who were they?

1) Randy Moss, the fleet wide-out from Marshall who fell to the 21st pick in the first round.

2) On Oct. 12, 1997 at the Metrodome, Brad Johnson threw a pass inside the Carolina Panthers 10-yard line toward the end zone. The pass deflected back toward Johnson, who alertly snatched the ball and scampered to pay dirt to complete a 3-yard passing play. The 4th-quarter score put the Vikings ahead 14-7 in a game they eventually won 21-14.

3) Drew Bledsoe, whose 70 pass attempts also set a league mark that still stands. The Patriots trailed 20-3 at halftime. Bledsoe threw for 426 yards and three touchdowns.

4) 1998

5) Qadry Ismail. His brother Raghib was known as the "Rocket" at Notre Dame. Qadry played four seasons for the Vikings and his best season was 1995, when he had 45 grabs for 597 yards and five touchdowns. He played 10 NFL seasons and won a Super Bowl with Baltimore.

6) Two-point conversions became optional following touchdowns in 1994 and the Vikings led the NFL with six two-point conversions (eight attempts) in 1996.

7) Gary Anderson was a perfect 35 for 35 in 1998. Mike Vanderjagt later hit all 37 of his attempts in 2003 for the Colts.

8) Jack Del Rio, who was a Pro-Bowler in 1994. Del Rio made a whopping total of 322 tackles combined in 1992 and 1993. He also intercepted 10 passes in 57 games and ended up with 440 tackles. Del Rio was the Jacksonville head coach from 2003-11.

9) Mitch Berger, who was a Pro-Bowler in 1999. Berger averaged 43.5 per boot for the Vikings and was in the top seven in punting four times. Berger also became a huge weapon as the team's kickoff man for several seasons, booming most of his kicks for touchbacks.

10) Roger Craig, who rushed for 535 yards in his final two seasons here after several great years with San Francisco.

11) Pat Eilers, who played on the 1988 national champion Irish squad.

12) Orlando Thomas, who totaled 22 interceptions in seven years and also recovered 10 fumbles. A positive force on and off the field, he died tragically at age 37 from ALS.

13) Jerry Ball, who last name was an apt description for his body build (6'1", 330 lbs.).

14) Chris Walsh, who also was a backup receiver.

15) Fuad Reveiz, who made the Pro Bowl in '94 after booting 34 field goals in 39 tries.

16) Warren Moon's pass was completed to Cris Carter in the third quarter of a 42-14 win in Chicago in the third game of the season.

17) Eric Guliford. The 5'8", 165-pounder from Arizona State was left completely uncovered down the right sideline and his reception led to the game-winning field goal. The big play was actually his first play from scrimmage in the NFL.

18) Randy Moss caught four passes for 95 yards, including scoring plays of 48 and 31 yards from Brad Johnson in a 31-7 victory over Tampa Bay at the Metrodome.

19) Dewayne Washington, who was a four-year starter. He intercepted 10 passes and returned them for an average of 25 yards in his stint in Minnesota.

20) Cris Carter. His admitted drug problems caused Eagles coach Buddy Ryan to dump him, not a lack of skill. "All he does is catch touchdowns," Ryan remarked upon his departure. Carter cleaned up his act, and yes, he continued to catch touchdowns.

21) Ed McDaniel. He started for seven seasons and totaled 607 tackles and made the Pro Bowl in 1998.

22) Mike Alstott (128) and Warrick Dunn (115). The Bucs trailed entering the final quarter but scored two touchdowns, including Alstott's six-yard scamper to take the lead. The Vikings had been undefeated at 7-0 and then finished 8-0 to complete the '98 season with a 15-1 record.

23) Leroy Hoard. Just 5'11" but 225 pounds, the hard-charging runner wearing number 44 was a dynamite backup, rushing for 1,689 yards and 26 touchdowns in 49 games.

24) To attend "Fred Zamberletti Day", in honor of the head trainer

who was completing his 38th and final season in that position Zamberletti was inducted into the team's Ring of Honor on that day, also.

25) Jake Reed and Cris Carter.

26) Robert Smith (Sept. 8, 1996-Oct. 25, 1998).

27) Jimmy Hitchcock

28) Jim McMahon. At age 34, the former Brigham Young star started 12 games (8-4) with nine touchdown passes and eight interceptions and a 60.4 % completion average.

29) Scottie Graham. The Ohio State star had been cut after a season with the New York Jets and was working in a pharmacy when he was contacted by the Vikings in September. He totaled 1,239 yards and seven touchdowns from 1993-96. Graham was an All-American in three sports in high school - football, wrestling, and lacrosse. In consecutive games in 1993, Graham rushed for 166 yards against Kansas City and 139 versus Green Bay.

30) 1998; incredibly, they had 52 plays of at least 25 yards and 22 plays of at least 40 yards.

31) Fuad Reveiz

32) Herschel Walker

33) Denny Green. Art Shell of Oakland was the first black NFL coach.

34) Randy Moss, who had five catches overall for 190 yards and had a 75-yard touchdown called back due to penalty. Randall Cunningham passed for 442 yards and four touchdowns.

35) Cris Carter (17 in 1995, 13 in 1997, and 13 in 1999).

36) Audray McMillian, who had 157 return yards and two touchdowns.

37) Donald Igwebuike, who wore number 4 in his final NFL season.

38) Terry Allen, who also added 478 receiving yards. He ran for 1,031 yards and eight touchdowns in 1994, a year after missing the entire season. Two severe knee injuries prevented him from being an all-time great but he still was a standout. He became the first NFL player to ever play after undergoing reconstructive surgery on both

knees. He rushed for 2,795 yards and 23 touchdowns in just three seasons and averaged a sterling 4.4 yards per carry.

39) Pete Bercich, who also was an assistant coach under Mike Tice.

40) Jake Reed. The 6'3" Reed played 10 years with Minnesota and was second in the NFL with 1,320 yards in 1996.

41) Dwyane Ruud

42) Amp Lee, who caught 45, 71, and 54 passes in his three seasons in Minnesota for 1,514 yards.

43) Brad Johnson. Steady and reliable, Johnson spent two years on the practice squad and didn't start a game until 1996. His best year was in 1997 when he threw for 20 touchdowns. After two years in Washington and then winning a Super Bowl with Tampa Bay, he returned to the Vikings in 2005-06 and was a part-time starter. Overall, he started 46 games and went 28-18 as a smart and effective player.

44) Robert Griffith. He intercepted 17 passes and twice was a second-team All-Pro (1998, 1999). He also served as the Executive Director of the NFL Players Association and is noted for his philanthropic activities.

45) Andrew Jordan, a sixth rounder, who played from 1994-97 and 1999-2001.

46) David Palmer, just 5'8" and 173 pounds, used his quick feet and acceleration to average 9.9 yards per punt return and 22.6 yards per kick return as one of the most dangerous returners in the league.

47) Sean Salisbury, who threw 19 touchdown passes and had 19 passes intercepted as his team went 5-4 in his starts.

48) Mark Dusbabek, who played 31 games and started in 13 of them with one interception and three recovered fumbles.

49) Esera Tuaolo, who was drafted by the Packers and once sang the national anthem prior to a game against the rival Bears while with the Pack.

50) Randall Cunningham. The rifle-armed former Eagle star completed 60.9 % of his passes and had an outstanding 106.0 quarterback rating.

51) Randy Moss, who averaged 54.3 yards per reception (163 yards) in the 46-36 win over the Cowboys.

52) Warren Moon, who completed 62.2 % of his passes and also threw 33 touchdown passes.

53) Todd Scott. With the Vikings trailing visiting Chicago 20-0 in the fourth quarter at the Metrodome, Scott intercepted Jim Harbaugh and raced 35 yards for a touchdown. They went on to score two more touchdowns in a 21-10 come-from-behind win over the Bears and their fuming coach, Mike Ditka.

54) David Dixon. The New Zealander played 11 years for the Vikings (1994-2004) at right guard and used his 6'5", 343-pound frame with a lot of leverage.

55) Todd Steussie. A beast at 6'6" and 320 pounds, the California alum started every game but one for his seven seasons in Minnesota and made the Pro Bowl in 1997 and 1998.

56) Corey Fuller

57) Eddie Murray

58) Harry Newsome, who averaged 45.5 in 1991 and 45.0 in 1992.

59) Terry Allen. Green went 11-5 and the Vikings won the NFC Central.

60) Gary Anderson (K), Chris Doleman (DE), Randall McDaniel (G), John Randle (DT), and Gary Zimmerman (T).

61) Larry Fitzgerald, Jr. The former Holy Angels and University of Pittsburgh star currently stars as a wide receiver for the Arizona Cardinals. He is the son of Larry Fitzgerald, Sr. a sportswriter in the Twin Cities who was a good friend of head coach Denny Green. Not so ironically, when the younger Fitzgerald was selected third overall in the 2004 draft, the Cardinals head coach was none other than.... Denny Green.

62) John Randle. He went on to have double-digit sacks eight years in a row.

63) Cris Carter and Randy Moss. In four seasons as teammates, the talented two-some caught 645 passes for 9,973 yards and 93 touchdowns.

64) Jeff Christy, a six-year starter from Pittsburgh University, who was considered the team's best all-around blocker on a line that included Randall McDaniel. He made the Pro Bowl in both 1998 and 1999 before bolting to Tampa Bay in free-agency.

65) Vencie Glenn. In his first season, he also picked off three passes against Green Bay, tying the team mark and earning NFC Defensive Player of the Week honors.

66) Randall McDaniel (left tackle) and Todd Kalis (right tackle). McDaniel was a first-round pick while Kalis, who was born in Stillwater, was a fourth-rounder.

67) Herschel Walker. He gained 148 yards on 18 carries in his first game, leading the Vikings to a 26-14 win over Green Bay. Walker had just been traded from Dallas in a blockbuster deal a few days before the sixth game of the year.

68) Leo Lewis, who played 11 years for the Vikings despite his diminutive size. Lewis was cited in 2000 as having the best such program in the NFL.

69) Ed McDaniel. The high-spirited McDaniel made 607 tackles in 109 games at both outside and middle linebacker. He had seven sacks in 1998, the year he made a Pro Bowl showing.

70) Mike Morris. The 6'5", 276-pounder played 144 games with the Vikings to end his career after playing for five other NFL teams previously.

71) Left tackle Todd Steussie and cornerback Dewayne Washington.

6 The 2000s

1) A huge specimen out of Central Florida, what 6'4," 265-pound quarterback had one of the best years in NFL history for a quarterback in 2004 when he threw for 39 touchdown passes with just 11 interceptions (a 69.2% completion rate), and 4,717 yards plus 406 yards rushing with two touchdowns?

2) What visiting quarterback set the league mark for most touchdown passes (surpassing Dan Marino) by throwing for his 421st scoring strike in a game at the Metrodome in 2007?

3) Entering the 2012 season, how many consecutive games had the Vikings lost to their NFC North rivals?

4) After the roof of the Metrodome caved in during a snowstorm on Dec. 12, 2010, how many home games had to be moved to other locations?

5) What two brothers played together with the Vikings for four seasons from 2008 to 2011?

6) On the same day that Adrian Peterson set the single-game rushing mark (Nov. 4, 2007), what San Diego Charger player returned a missed field goal attempt 109 yards?

7) Perhaps one of the biggest underdogs ever to make a Viking squad, what former Rochester John Marshall High and Gopher player served as a backup in the Viking secondary and a primary punt returner in both 2011 and 2012?

8) Who are the only active members of the Vikings who were

named to the squad announced as the "50 Greatest Vikings" during their 50th season celebration on December 19, 2010?

9) What crafty defensive back from Green Bay signed as a free agent prior to the 2005 season and put in four supreme years as a ball hound for Minnesota?

Culpepper and Moss.

10) Who set an NFL record with an astounding 23 fumbles in 2002?

11) Pound for pound, truly one of the toughest players in Vikings history and one of its best form tacklers, what Ohio State defensive back was a cornerstone of the defense for nine seasons (2004-12)?

12) What is the name of the new NFL overtime rule instituted for the 2012 regular season that gives both teams at least one possession unless the team with the first possession scores a touchdown?

13) What player compiled the third-highest single-season NFL rushing total by a receiver since the merger (1970) with 345 yards in 2011?

14) Tragically, what outstanding left tackle and team leader became the first player to die at an NFL training camp since 1979 when he died from complications of heat stroke on August 1, 2001?

15) What was so unusual about the results of the two NFC battles between Minnesota and Green Bay in the 2004 regular season?

16) What German-born fullback proved to be one of the best backfield blockers in Viking history in 2006 and 2007?

17) What team did Brett Favre defeat to become the first quarterback to beat all 32 teams in the NFL on Oct. 5, 2009?

18) Though he caught just eight passes the entire season, what receiver hauled in a 32-yard pass from Brett Favre with 12 seconds remaining to give the Vikings a 27-24 win on Sept, 27, 2009, at the Metrodome?

19) A top pick in 2006, who has been a mainstay at outside linebacker since 2007 after playing nine-man football at tiny Mt. Vernon, South Dakota, and at Iowa?

20) What Seattle Seahawk guard became one of Minnesota's best free-agent signings when he signed a lucrative ($49 million) deal prior to the 2006 season?

21) A former adversary with Green Bay and one of the best kickers in the league, who signed with the Vikings for the 2006 season and maintained his status as reliable in the clutch for six years?

22) A safety from 2002-05, what player became as well known for his ability to break down film and analyze college players for the NFL draft?

23) What Danish-born player who ultimately became the NFL's all-time leading scorer was the team's kicker in 2004?

24) What four players were named to the all-decade team for the 2000's?

25) What Texas Longhorn has been the Vikings long snapper since 2004 and once started 123 consecutive games?

26) What electrifying all-purpose player came to the Vikings from Florida in 2009 and wowed the fans with his speed, power, agility, and toughness for four seasons before being traded to Seattle in March of 2013 for three draft picks?

27) What defensive tackle rumbled 54 yards for a touchdown with an interception just 14 seconds into the opening game of 2007 at the Metrodome in a 24-3 win over Atlanta?

28) After Adrian Peterson left with a serious knee injury at Washington on Dec. 24, 2011, what backup running back rushed for 105 yards on just nine carries in the second half to lead Minnesota to a 33-26 win?

Adrian Peterson

29) What rookie booted four field goals in his first NFL game to open the 2012 season at the Metrodome, including a 55-yarder to tie the game on the last play of regulation, and a 38-yarder in overtime that gave the Vikings a 26-23 win over Jacksonville?

30) What Viking safety led the NFL with 276 interception return yards on nine interceptions in 2005?

31) What former Viking is the bassist for the local band "Tripping Icarus" and was the Minnesota punter from 2005 to 2012?

32) What Viking kicker made all six of his field goal attempts over 50 yards in 2008?

33) A hulk at 6'7" and 308 pounds, what Southern Cal tackle locked down a starting job after being drafted fourth overall in the 2012 draft and also has a brother playing on the offensive line in the NFL?

34) After playing eight years with Buffalo, what 6'3", 315-pound nose tackle signed as a free agent and led the Vikings to the best rushing defense in the NFL between 2006 and 2008?

35) What South Carolina jumping jack, a second-round pick in 2007, became a star receiver in 2009 with 83 catches, 1,312 yards and eight touchdowns?

36) A fourth-rounder from Tulane in 2004, what player was an expert punt returner and a fine backup running back for four seasons?

37) He had an incredibly high-pitched voice for an NFL player but what efficient tight end was an elite pass-catcher from 2004 to 2006?

38) What Nevada-Reno wide receiver had a breakout year in his second season with the Vikings in 2004 before moving on to Seattle as a free agent? (His brother Kevin once was a standout point guard for the Minnesota Gophers and a future NBA player).

39) He was the head coach at Hill-Murray High School in Maplewood in 2011 but before his coaching tenure, what Wisconsin quarterback played in seven games for the Vikings in 2006 and 2007 for a head coach who was also his offensive coordinator with the Badgers?

40) What San Diego State grad was a tremendous tackler on the kickoff and punt coverage teams from 2005-10 and was named a special team Pro Bowler in 2009?

41) A punishing runner, what former Baltimore Raven signed as a free agent with the Vikings in 2006 and produced a superlative season, totaling 1,216 yards?

42) A Cretin-Derham Hall stud, what Augustana grad played guard for four seasons and was a starter from 2000-02?

43) Talented but inconsistent, what Chicago Bears receiver signed a six-year, $42 million contract with Minnesota prior to the 2008 season?

44) What behemoth tackle, a second round choice out of Oklahoma in 2009, became an immediate starter as a rookie?

45) A versatile player at both fullback and tight end, what Carrington, North Dakota farm boy became one of the most durable and effective blockers in team history?

46) What Viking tight end and native Minnesotan was all-state in football, basketball, and tennis at Litchfield High School?

47) What free agent tight end was a godsend from 2007-11 and a vocal team leader and team spokesman?

48) What Viking safety made an interception in each of his first six games as a starter in 2003?

49) From 2010 to 2012, what Viking player scored touchdowns rushing, receiving, and by kick return each season?

50) What long-haired Texas Longhorn has been a starting defensive end opposite Jared Allen since 2011?

51) A Kentucky Wildcat drafted in the third round in 1996, what backup runner scored 11 touchdowns in 2002 and was an effective special teams player in two separate stints with the team?

52) Who set the team mark for most yards rushing as a quarterback with 609?

53) What current player has the longest tenure as a Viking player?

54) In what season in the decade did the Vikings become the first team to start 6-0 and not make the playoffs?

55) What rookie safety from Notre Dame returned two interceptions for touchdowns in 2012, providing aggressive hitting in a defensive backfield that was sorely lacking that commodity?

56) What man set records for most yards in a game and the longest run by a quarterback in a game at Detroit on Dec. 11, 2011?

57) Who has led the Vikings in tackles for the last five seasons (2008-12)?

58) When was the last time the Vikings were shut out?

59) What current Vikings were actually not only teammates but roommates in college?

60) In an incredible sequence at the end of a 24-13 home win over San Francisco on Sept. 23, 2012, what Viking running back fumbled three times (losing two) in a span of 1:33 of official game time?

61) In the first play of the 2011 season at San Diego, what player returned the opening kick by Nick Kaeding 103 yards for a touchdown?

62) In his much-heralded return to the Vikings in 2010, how did Randy Moss fare in his four games prior to his eventual release?

63) What current special teams coach is a Naval Academy graduate who flew helicopters in combat in the early 1990's?

64) Who are the only two defensive backs to ever lead the team in tackles?

65) Who rushed for 180 yards and three touchdowns to lead the Vikings to a 34-20 win on opening day at Cleveland on Sept. 13, 2009?

66) In what three-year stretch were the Vikings the top-rated team against the rush?

67) Who is the only Viking defender to score touchdowns in three different ways?

68) What defender made 22 tackles, the third-most ever in a game, versus Oakland on Nov. 20, 2011?

69) Incredibly, in what season did the Vikings have just one player with more than one interception?

70) What running back rushed for 148 yards against Chicago and then for 146 yards six days later on Dec. 14 and 20, 2003 - the only two 100-yard games of his brief career?

71) What two brothers were teammates on the 2001 club - one on offense and one on defense?

72) What Maryland linebacker was a standout for nine years (2003-11) and was a favorite of head coach Mike Tice, who liked to have guys from his alma mater?

73) On Aug. 18, 2009, head coach Brad Childress personally drove to the airport to pick up a free-agent player who had just signed a two-year, $25 million contract? What was his name?

74) In a horrendous late-game collapse by the Vikings, what Cardinal receiver caught a 28-yard touchdown pass with no time remaining in the final regular season game in 2003, knocking Minnesota out of the playoffs?

75) What 2001 top draft pick from Wisconsin rushed for 1,296 yards (5.1 average) in 2002, earning a Pro Bowl berth?

76) What tight end came to Minnesota in 2001 and caught 57 balls for 666 yards and three touchdowns and made the Pro Bowl?

77) What all-around athlete from Russell-Tyler-Ruthton and St. Cloud State star made the Vikings as a 29-year-old reserve quarterback in 2001 and proceeded to excel in five games?

78) What Viking tight end caught nine touchdown passes in 2012, tied for second in the league for tight ends and ended up as the MVP of the Pro Bowl?

79) What Viking kicker set an NFL record for most field goals by a rookie with 35?

80) Through 52 seasons, how many times have the Vikings finished in last place in their conference (Western Conference; 1961-66) or division (NFC Central, 1967-2001; NFC North (2002-12)?

81) What former Viking linebacker ran for the Illinois Congressional seat vacated by Jesse Jackson, Jr. in 2012?

82) What former Lions runner, in his only start for the Vikings, ran for 125 yards and three touchdowns in a 30-20 win over Detroit on Dec. 10, 2006?

Jim Kleinsasser

83) On Dec. 9, 2012, the Vikings started five rookies for the first time in franchise history. Who were those players (three on offense and two on defense)?

84) In 2012, Adrian Peterson led the NFL with the most runs of at least 20 yards and also with the most runs of at least 50 yards when he finished with 2,097 rushing yards, second-best in league history. How many 20-yarders and 50-yarders did he have?

85) Who did the Vikings beat 37-34 on a last-second field goal in the final game of the 2012 regular season to earn a wild-card berth in the playoffs?

1) Daunte Culpepper

2) Brett Favre. The Green Bay legend was 32-45 for 344 yards and two touchdowns in a 23-16 Packer victory.

3) 11; it ended with a 20-13 win at Detroit on Sept. 30, 2012. Their previous win over a NFC North foe had come in 2010, when they beat Detroit 24-10 on Sept. 26 at the Metrodome.

4) Two; one was rescheduled for TCF Bank Stadium on the campus of the University of Minnesota and the other at Ford Field in Detroit.

5) Erin (2008-12) and E.J. (2003-11) Henderson, both linebackers from Maryland.

6) Antonio Cromartie. It might be equaled but never surpassed as it is not possible to make a play of 110 yards (a player would be considered out of the end zone).

7) Marcus Sherels. Just 5'10" and 175 pounds, Sherels has returned 65 punts for 564 yards and one touchdown and has also played as a reserve defensive back. Sherels has averaged 8.7 yards per punt, fifth best in team history, impressive for a guy who wasn't even awarded a college scholarship out of high school.

8) Jared Allen, Antoine Winfield, Adrian Peterson, and Kevin Williams.

9) Darren Sharper, who had 18 interceptions, 250 tackles, and three touchdowns in his four seasons. He was a Pro Bowler in 2005 and 2007.

10) Duane Culpepper, who lost 17 of them.

11) Antoine Winfield. Only 5'9" and 185 pounds, Winfield was as sure a tackler as the Vikings have ever had and he totaled 21 interceptions in his nine years with the team. He was a Pro Bowler in 2008, 2009, and 2010 and is regarded as one of the best tackling cornerbacks/safeties in NFL history. Winfield signed as a free agent with Seattle in April of 2013.

12) The "fair possession" rule. In the 2012 opener, the Vikings netted a field goal on their first possession and stopped Jacksonville on

downs to win 26-23; thus, they became the first team to win under the new rule.

13) Percy Harvin, who averaged 6.6 yards per rush.

14) Korey Stringer, who was 27. Stringer became ill following a Vikings workout on the steamy morning of July 31. He was doing some post-practice conditioning when he asked trainer Chuck Barta to meet him in the air-conditioned trailer parked near the field. While inside the trailer, the 6'4", 335-pound lineman collapsed and was rushed to the hospital. The dew point was in the low 70's with the temperatures in the high 90's. His body temperature remained dangerously high and he died in the early hours of the following morning. Stringer's death brought on major changes regarding heat stroke prevention in the NFL. His jersey number, 77, was retired in 2001 and he was included in the Vikings "Ring of Honor" that same year.

15) The Packers won each game by a score of 34-31.

16) Tony Richardson, who was a Pro Bowl pick in 2007 despite rushing the ball only seven times for 13 yards. He made the team as a fullback. Richardson was a tremendous contributor off the field, too, working with the Boys and Girls Clubs and the Special Olympics. Tony also sponsored "Dictionary Project," an effort to get dictionaries to third-graders at area elementary schools.

17) Green Bay (can you believe it!). The Vikings won 30-23.

18) Greg Lewis, who snared the ball with a defender draped on him while keeping both his feet just inches from the back of the end zone. Lewis had 25 catches for 293 yards and that sole touchdown in two seasons with the team.

19) Chad Greenway, who grew up on a hog and crop farm. Greenway tore his ACL in his first pre-season game his rookie season but has been a durable and consistent performer ever since and was a Pro Bowler in 2011 and 2012.

20) Steve Hutchinson. The Michigan All-American played six solid seasons here and was a Pro Bowler four times and first-team All-Pro three times (2007-09).

21) Ryan Longwell. He made 86% of his field goal attempts (135 of 157) and scored a career-high 132 points in 2009.

22) Corey Chavous. A Vanderbilt alum, he made the Pro Bowl in 2003 after intercepting eight passes and returning them for 143 yards. He was a regular on ESPN's coverage of the NFL draft as a player and is the founder of DraftNasty.com, which specializes in coverage of major sports with an emphasis on scouting college players for the draft.

23) Morten Andersen. He booted 18 field goals and scored 99 points that season. Andersen is not only first in points scored (2,544) but games played (382) in league history.

24) Randy Moss (WR), Steve Hutchinson (G), Kevin Williams (DT), and Darren Sharper (S).

25) Cullen Loeffler. Pretty impressive for a free agent!

26) Percy Harvin, who served mainly as a wide receiver but also as a running back and a kick returner. In return, the Vikings got Seattle's first and seventh-round picks in 2013 and a third-rounder in 2014.

27) Kevin Williams

28) Toby Gerhart

29) Blair Walsh, a sixth-round selection from Georgia. Walsh earned a berth on the NFC Pro Bowl team, just the fifth Viking rookie to earn that honor.

30) Darren Sharper. He holds the NFL record for most seasons leading the league in interception returns with three, also accomplishing that feat with Green Bay (2002) and New Orleans (2009).

31) Chris Kluwe, a man noted for his avant-garde lifestyle. Kluwe was undrafted out of UCLA and was released by Seattle in the final roster cut-down in 2005 and the Vikings picked him up and he remains one of the best punters in the league.

32) Ryan Longwell

33) Matt Kalil. His brother Ryan, also an All-American with the Trojans, plays tackle for the Carolina Panthers. Kalil was an injury replacement in the Pro Bowl after starting every game in his rookie season.

34) Pat Williams, who was in the Pro Bowl each of those seasons.

35) Sidney Rice. A favorite target of Brett Favre, Rice became an expert long-ball threat but was plagued with injuries otherwise.

36) Mewelde Moore. He had a sparkling 4.9 average per carry (1,285 yards) and was also a decent receiver out of the backfield (9.4 average) and had a 10.4 average returning punts, including two touchdowns. He later won a Super Bowl in the same role with Pittsburgh.

37) Jermaine Wiggins. He caught 186 passes for 1,659 yards and six touchdowns during that three-year stretch and was remarkably agile for his 6'2", 260 pound frame.

38) Nate Burleson. He had 68 catches for 1,006 yards and nine touchdowns in 2004 and also returned a punt 94 yards for a touchdown. His father, Alvin, played in both the U.S.F.L. and the C.F.L.

39) Brooks Bollinger. A third-stringer for almost all of his tenure, he was 46-68 (67.6%) for 537 yards and started one game in his career for head coach Brad Childress.

40) Heath Farwell. The undrafted free agent was MVP of the Viking special teams in 2006.

41) Chester Taylor. At 5' 11" and 213 pounds, Taylor packed a punch. He averaged 4.3 yards a carry and totaled 2,797 yards before surrendering his status as the main ball carrier to Adrian Peterson.

42) Corbin Lacina, who was born in Mankato.

43) Bernard Berrian. The Fresno State wide-out played 51 games for Minnesota from 2008-11 and caught 138 balls for 1,925 yards and 11 touchdowns but never reached his potential.

44) Phil Loadholt, all 6'8'" and 343 pounds of him.

45) Jim Kleinsasser, a second-round pick out of North Dakota University in 1999, who played 181 games and didn't miss a game in his final seven seasons. Kleinsasser ranks second in games played for tight ends and fourth in receptions at that position. He was a big reason why the Vikings had seven of their top nine rushing seasons while he was a starter.

46) John Carlson. He won three state basketball titles playing for his father, John, Sr. and was drafted by Seattle before signing as a free agent with the Vikings prior to the 2012 season.

47) Visanthe Shiancoe. Nimble for a tight end, Shiancoe had 208 grabs for 2,424 yards in five effective seasons. He had 11 of his 24 touchdowns in 2009.

48) Brian Russell. An undrafted free agent out of San Diego State, led the league with nine picks in 2003.

49) Percy Harvin (2010 - one rushing, five receiving, one kick return; 2011 - two rushing, six receiving, and one kick return); 2012 - one rushing, three receiving, and one kick return).

50) Brian Robison. Drafted in the fourth round in 2007, Robison finally broke into the starting lineup in 2011 when he totaled eight sacks.

51) Moe Williams. In nine seasons (1996-2000 and 2002-05), Williams was a durable and smart runner, receiver, and kick returner (22.1 average). He averaged 4.1 per rush as a tough inside runner and 9.9 yards receiving out of the backfield.

52) Daunte Culpepper (2002). He also set a team mark with 10 rushing touchdowns.

53) Kevin Williams, who completed his 10th season in 2012.

54) 2003

55) Harrison Smith, the 29th pick as the team's second choice in the first round. Smith joined Dewayne Washington as the only rookies to return two thefts for a pick-six. Smith, who started all 16 games in 2012, finished with three interceptions.

56) Joe Webb rushed for 109 yards, including a 65-yarder to break standards set by Fran Tarkenton in a game at Los Angeles on November 5, 1961 (99 yards and a long of 52 yards).

57) Chad Greenway, who has played every game since 2007.

58) Nov. 11, 2007 (Green Bay beat Minnesota 34-0).

59) John Sullivan and John Carlson (Notre Dame).

60) Toby Gerhart. The reserve fullback had all eight of his carries in the final 5:59 as the Vikings attempted to run out the clock. Gerhart actually fumbled on three of four carries at one point, fumbling with 3:33 left, 2:18 left (recovered own fumble), and 2:00 remaining.

61) Percy Harvin

62) He caught four passes for 174 yards and two touchdowns.

63) Mike Priefer, whose father Chuck also was an NFL assistant for 17 years.

64) Corey Chavous had 108 (86 solo) in 2003 while Joey Browner had 139 to lead the team in 1986 and 121 to tie teammate Jesse Solomon in 1987.

65) Adrian Peterson. It was Brett Favre's first game as a Viking starter.

66) 2006, 2007, and 2008. However, they were 31st against the pass in 2006 and 32nd in 2007, somewhat muting the rushing statistics.

67) Antoine Winfield scored two touchdowns on interception returns, two on fumble recoveries, and one on a return of a blocked field goal.

68) Chad Greenway

69) Jamarca Sanford, a safety from Mississippi, had two picks in 2011 to lead the team, when they had just eight for the entire season.

70) Onterrio Smith

71) Wide receiver Jake Reed and cornerback Dale Carter.

72) E.J. Henderson, who started 105 games at both middle and outside linebacker.

73) Brett Favre, the Kiln, Mississippi resident who just happened to be the enemy quarterback for the Green Bay Packers for 16 years. At the age of 39, Favre went on to have his best statistical year of his career in 2009 with 33 touchdown passes and just seven interceptions; he was 363 for 531 for 4,202 yards and a 68.4% completion rate and a sterling quarterback rating of 107.2.

74) Nate Poole. Facing a 4th and 25 at the Viking 28, Cardinal quarterback Josh McCown threw into the right corner of the end zone. Poole caught the ball but was knocked out of bounds by Denard Walker and Brian Russell before getting both feet down. However, the officials ruled that he was forced out so the touchdown stood and Arizona won 18-17. Green Bay, thus, was handed the NFC North crown. The Vikings led 17-6 with two minutes remaining before the meltdown.

75) Michael Bennett. As a rookie starter, he had 682 yards and also had an 80-yard touchdown reception. In five seasons, the 5' 9" Bennett rushed for 3,174 yards and 12 touchdowns.

76) Byron Chamberlain

77) Todd Bouman. He went 51-89 for 795 yards with eight touchdown passes and four interceptions. In a 42-24 win over Tennessee, Bouman was sensational, throwing for 348 yards and four touchdowns. After little playing time in 2002, he later played for New Orleans, St. Louis, and Jacksonville.

78) Kyle Rudolph, a 6'6", 259-pounder who was the team's second-round pick in 2011 out of Notre Dame. Rudolph had 53 catches for 493 yards in his second season and was in the Pro Bowl following the season. He snatched five passes for 122 yards and a touchdown to lead the NFC to a 62-35 win over the AFC on Jan. 27, 2013. Not bad for a guy who became an injury replacement just two days prior to the game in Honolulu.

79) Blair Walsh. The Georgia standout also set a league mark for highest field goal percentage (92.1) for a rookie by booting 35 of 38 attempts successfully in 2012.

80) Only four times; 1961(seventh out of seven teams in Western Conference at 3-11); 1967 (fourth out of four teams in NFC Central at 3-8-3); 1984 (fifth out of five teams in NFC Central at 3-11); 2011 (fourth out of four teams in NFC North at 3-13). In 1990, Chicago finished first in the NFC Central and Green Bay, Tampa, Bay, Detroit, and Minnesota all finished tied for second with 6-10 records or you could say, tied for second through fifth. The Vikings have finished first 18 times.

81) Napoleon Harris, a linebacker who played two seasons for the Vikings (2005-06) and was the second-leading tackler for the team in 2006. Harris was an honor student at Northwestern.

82) Artose Pinner, a 5'10", 232-pounder from Kentucky. Pinner played 12 games that season. In the other 11 games, he had just 14 rushes for 65 yards.

83) Offensive tackle Matt Kalil, tight end Rhett Ellison, wide receiver Jarius Wright, safety Harrison Smith, and cornerback Josh Robinson.

84) Peterson had 27 runs of at least 20 yards and seven of at least 50.

85) Green Bay. The thrilling victory at the Metrodome on Dec. 30 allowed the sixth-seeded Vikings to play the third-seeded Packers at Lambeau Field six days later. The Packers downed the Vikings 24-10.

Antoine Winfield (26) readies to lower the boom on a San Diego Charger as Jared Allen (69) supports.

7 Kid's Stuff

1) What is the nickname of star running back Adrian Peterson?

2) How many yards long is the playing field (not counting the end zones)?

3) What is the number of Viking All-Pro defensive end Jared Allen?

4) What three positions did the versatile and exciting Percy Harvin play for the Vikings?

5) What is the uniform number of Viking quarterback Christian Ponder? (Hint: It's the same as Twins catcher Joe Mauer).

6) What term is used to describe a play when a Viking defensive player tackles an opposing player in their own end zone (earning two points for the team)?

7) What two stadiums have served as the primary home for the Minnesota Vikings since 1961?

8) How many men are on the field for the Vikings during play in an NFL contest?

9) What is the name of the Vikings theme song?

10) The Vikings are named after a horde of warriors from northern Europe because many Minnesotans hailed from this geographic area. What is this area known as?

11) What are the various ways in which the Vikings can score while on defense?

12) What type of plays are considered to be part of the so-called "special teams"?

13) How many yards behind the goal-line are the uprights?

14) Who is the present head coach of the Vikings?

15) When Jared Allen "sacks" or tackles the quarterback behind the line of scrimmage, what "act" does he perform in celebration?

16) In what city will the Vikings be playing when the new stadium is constructed?

17) Present Viking tight ends Kyle Rudolph and John Carlson both played for the same legendary college football program. What is this famous football empire located in northwestern Indiana?

18) What are the official colors of the Minnesota Vikings?

19) In what southern Minnesota city do the Vikings hold their annual training camp?

20) What term is used to describe a last-ditch attempt to score at the end of the first or second half on a long pass completion?

21) In football language, what is the "pigskin"?

22) Which other NFL team is Minnesota's biggest arch-rival?

23) What role do the "zebras" play during a Vikings game?

24) What other Minnesota professional sports franchise played its home games in the same two venues as the Vikings from 1961-2009?

25) When the Viking defense creates a turnover, the offense gets the ball back after one of two events take place. What are they?

1) A.D. (All-Day), A.P. or "Purple Jesus".

2) 100 yards

3) Sixty-nine (69)

4) Receiver, running back, and kick returner.

5) Seven (7)

6) Safety

7) Metropolitan Stadium in Bloomington (1961-1981) and the Metrodome in Minneapolis (1982-2012), also known as Hubert H. Humphrey Stadium and most recently, as Mall of America Field.

8) 11

9) "Skol Vikings"

10) Scandinavia

11) Interception return for touchdown, fumble recovery for touchdown, and safety.

12) Kickoff coverage, kickoff return, punt coverage, punt return, field goal attempts on both offense and defense, extra-point or two-point conversion plays.

13) 10 yards

14) Leslie Frazier

15) He kneels and pretends to "rope" a calf.

16) Minneapolis. The new stadium, approved by the Legislature in 2012, will be built on the same site as the Metrodome and is slated to be finished by 2016.

17) Notre Dame. Three other "Golden Domers" are also on the team - safety Harrison Smith, center John Sullivan, and safety Robert Blanton.

18) Purple, Gold, and White

19) Mankato (Minnesota State-Mankato)

20) "Hail Mary"

21) The football

22) Green Bay Packers

23) They are the black and white-clad officials.

24) Minnesota Twins. Metropolitan Stadium (1961-81); Metrodome (1982-2009).

25) An intercepted pass or a fumble recovery.

Jared Allen (69) flanked by teammates Asher Allen (21) and Madieu Williams (20).

Head Coach Bud Grant and defensive end Jim Marshall.

8 Coaches

1) Who was the first head coach of the Minnesota Vikings and what was his nickname?

2) What Viking head coach has the highest winning percentage?

3) What former Viking assistant coaches have went on to become head coaches or previously coached other teams in the NFL?

4) Which Viking head coaches never played in the National Football League?

5) What former Chicago Bear linebacker and Hall of Famer is currently the team's assistant head coach/linebackers coach?

6) Who is the only Viking head coach to serve two different stints at the helm?

7) What Viking head coaches assumed to the head job after serving as an assistant with the team?

8) For the 2012 season, how many total assistant coaches were on the Viking staff?

9) Who is the youngest man to serve as head coach of the Vikings and who has been the oldest?

10) Which Viking assistant coach was actually operating a form of the famous "West Coast" offense that was popularized by San Francisco Giant head coach Bill Walsh long before it became so widespread?

11) Did any of the Vikings head coaches ever earn first-team All-Pro as a player?

12) How many men have served as head coach of the Vikings?

13) What former Viking players eventually became head coaches in the NFL?

14) Which Viking assistant coach from 1978 and 1979 once coached a Big Ten team to the Rose Bowl in consecutive seasons?

15) Who is the only Vikings head coach to earn NFL Coach of the Year honors from the Associated Press, which is widely-regarded as the most prestigious coaching award, even by the NFL itself?

16) What Hall of Fame receiver, who held the NFL record for most career receptions upon his retirement, was an assistant for the 1984 Vikings?

17) Who is the only head coach for the team who was also a player for the Vikings?

18) What man served as an assistant for Minnesota for 27 years under four different head coaches?

19) As an assistant coach for linebackers on Viking teams for eight seasons (1994-2001), what man witnessed his son playing for the team in his final two seasons with the club?

20) What is the real first name of Viking head coach Bud Grant?

21) What Viking head coach had his brother serve as an assistant coach during his tenure?

22) How many assistant coaches were on the inaugural Viking staff in 1961?

23) What Vikings coach was an assistant coach in six Super Bowls?

24) Which Viking head coach was once a member of the Marine Corps and served as a combat infantry Lieutenant in Vietnam?

25) Which Viking coach was an assistant at Illinois when former Gopher head football coach Tim Brewster was a two-time All-Big Ten tight end in the early 1980's?

26) Which two Viking head coaches were also head coaches at Big Ten universities?

27) Which Viking head coach initiated Community Tuesdays, which had players active in the Twin Cities on their day off, a concept that spread to the entire National Football League?

28) Which two coaches have more wins in professional football (regular season only) than Bud Grant?

29) Which Viking head coach won a Super Bowl as a player for the Bears and as an assistant with the Indianapolis Colts?

30) Who is the only Viking head coach to be hired directly from the college ranks?

31) What former Gopher quarterback served as an assistant coach for the Vikings for two stints (running backs, 1985-86; quarterbacks, 1989-91) and eventually won consecutive Grey Cup titles in Canada as a head coach with the Montreal Alouettes (2009-2010)?

32) A valued assistant coach and offensive coordinator from 1992-98, what future Super Bowl-winning coach helped lead the Vikings to a league record for points with 556 in 1998?

33) What former Wisconsin Badger quarterback ended up coaching Brett Favre as the Viking quarterback coach when Favre played for Minnesota in 2009 and 2010?

34) What man served as an assistant for the team in 2000 and 2001 as the defensive coordinator, thirty years after he was a standout

defensive back for the Kansas City Chiefs in their Super Bowl win over the Vikings on Jan. 11, 1970?

35) What former Viking players later became assistant coaches for the team?

36) What Viking assistant and defensive coordinator (1992-95) played a game for Pittsburgh on Oct. 9, 1977 when he not only intercepted a pass on defense as a safety but also threw an interception after being called into duty as an emergency quarterback?

37) Who are the only Viking head coaches to become head coach of another team after being fired by the Vikings?

Dennis Green.

38) Counting time both as an assistant and head coach, what man has served the most years as a Viking coach?

39) What energetic and upbeat guy was a defensive backs coach for Minnesota from 1985-89 and is currently the head coach of the Seattle Seahawks?

40) What former William and Mary player was the Vikings defensive coordinator in 2006 and found himself the head coach of the Pittsburgh Steelers the next season?

41) Before hiring Norm Van Brocklin as their first coach on Jan. 18, 1961, what storied college coach visited team management in the Twin Cities under the condition that his visit will be kept secret from his current employer?

42) How many times did Bud Grant lead the Vikings into the post-season?

43) What Viking coach served as the team's offensive coordinator for 18 seasons?

44) Which noted Viking offensive coordinator attended both the Air Force Academy and Brigham Young University?

45) What highly-respected man was a defensive assistant under both Jerry Burns (1986-89, 1991) and Denny Green (1992-94) with the Vikings and proudly watched his own son become an NFL head coach with the Oakland Raiders?

46) A former Gopher quarterback from Jackson, Michigan, what former Viking defensive coordinator became one of the most respected head coaches in NFL history as one of the true gentleman of the game as head coach of the Buccaneers and Colts?

47) Amazingly, five assistants under Bud Grant served at least nine years for the Hall of Fame coach? Who were they?

48) What long-time NFL assistant served as the Vikings assistant head coach from 1990-93 and was Tony Dungy's offensive coordinator with the Minnesota Gophers?

49) What man was promoted from defensive coordinator to head coach when Brad Childress was fired midway through the 2010 season and went 3-3 but then faltered to 3-13 the following season?

50) What Viking head coach and Pennsylvania native was in the crowd in Hershey, Pennsylvania when Wilt Chamberlain scored 100 points on March 2, 1962 for the Philadelphia Warriors?

51) What Viking assistant coach (prior to coming to Minnesota) became the youngest assistant coach in NFL history at the age of 25 and the youngest coordinator at age 28 and later, as a head coach, became the first coach to beat all 32 NFL teams?

52) What Viking coach, as a player, led his NFL team in sacks one season and then switched to offense the next season and led them in receptions and receiving yardage?

53) What Viking head coach quit a day after a loss only to renege on the resignation 26 hours later?

54) Who is currently the senior consultant for pro personnel for

the Vikes and was a two-time Pro-Bowl defensive end (1957-67) for the Cleveland Browns and also coached his alma mater, the Stanford Cardinals?

55) What Viking head coach told the media at his introductory press conference, "There's a new sheriff in town"?

56) Which Minnesota head coach, whom some people liken in looks and demeanor to former actor Burgess Meredith, was known for his profanity-laden yet humorous rumblings?

57) Which assistants have worked under four different head coaches?

58) What assistant had a father who was a long-time NFL head coach and which former Viking assistant now watches his son coach an NFL team?

59) Who was the strength and conditioning coach in 1984 who was an assistant football coach and head track coach at Apple Valley High School for many years?

60) Who is the current Vikings offensive coordinator, a fellow who played briefly with the 49ers and Denver as a quarterback?

61) What head coach suffered seven-game losing streaks in consecutive seasons?

62) What head coach holds the team record for consecutive victories?

63) What head coach holds the team record for most division titles?

64) Who was the Vikings running backs coach for 18 consecutive years?

65) What head coach has the most consecutive division titles with six?

66) What touted special teams and linebackers coach, a Minnesota native, died 18 days after suffering a heart attack playing racquetball with fellow assistant coach Bob Holloway in November of 1978?

67) What head coach referred to the team's impact defenders and top playmakers on offense as "big knockers"?

68) What Viking head coach once played for an NBA champion?

1) Norm Van Brocklin, who was referred to as "the Dutchman." Van Brocklin was less than a month from his last game as a player when he was named coach for the 1961 season and he coached the team for six seasons, ending with a 29-51-4 overall mark (36.3%). The former Oregon University star was named to the Pro Football Hall of Fame in 1971. He also coached the Atlanta Falcons for seven seasons (1968-74). Norm was a Pro-Bowler in nine of his 12 NFL seasons.

2) Bud Grant (158-96-5) had a 62.2% win ratio, while Denny Green (97-62) is second with 61.0%.

3) Bob Hollway (St. Louis Cardinals), Neil Armstrong (Chicago), Mike Tomlin (Pittsburgh), Tony Dungy (Tampa Bay, Indianapolis), Buddy Ryan (Philadelphia, Arizona), Jack Patera (Seattle), Pete Carroll (New York Jets, Seattle), Brian Billick (Baltimore), Mike Singletary (San Francisco), Marc Trestman (Chicago), Ray Berry (New England), Scott Linehan (St. Louis Rams), Emmitt Thomas (Atlanta), Paul Wiggin (Kansas City), and Marion Campbell (Philadelphia and Atlanta).

4) Les Steckel, Jerry Burns, Denny Green, and Brad Childress.

5) Mike Singletary, who was 18-22 as head coach of the San Francisco 49ers (2008-10).

6) Bud Grant, who served his first stint from 1967-1983. He returned to coach again in 1985 before retiring for good.

7) Les Steckel, Jerry Burns, Mike Tice, and Leslie Frazier.

8) 17; four on offense, eight on defense, three on special teams, and two for strength and conditioning.

9) Norm Van Brocklin was just 34 when named the Vikings head coach in 1961 while Jerry Burns was 64 during his final year coaching the team in 1991.

10) Jerry Burns. The offense focused on the safe and short passing game.

11) Yes, Norm Van Brocklin was an All-Pro in 1960.

12) Eight (Norm Van Brocklin, Bud Grant, Les Steckel, Jerry Burns, Denny Green, Mike Tice, Brad Childress, and Leslie Frazier)

13) Mike Tice (Minnesota), Jack Del Rio (Jacksonville), and Mike Mularkey (Jacksonville and Buffalo).

14) Murray Warmath of the Minnesota Gophers, who brought his charges to Pasadena for the New Year's Day battle in both 1961 and 1962.

15) Bud Grant. However, the Maxwell Club awarded its 1998 honor to Denny Green (The Maxwell honor has been given since 1989).

16) Raymond Berry, the favorite target of Johnny Unitas with the Baltimore Colts.

17) Mike Tice. The 6'7", 253-pound tight end played for the Vikes in 1992-93 and 1995 and caught just 14 passes with two touchdowns in 22 starts.

18) John Michels, who spent 27 years with the club. The former Tennessee All-American guard was both an offensive line and running backs coach during his nearly three decades coaching the Vikings. He started in 1967 in Bud Grant's first year and finished in 1993 under Denny Green.

19) Trent Walters. His son, Troy, was an All-American wide-receiver at Stanford and the Fred Biletnikoff winner drafted in the fifth round (165th overall) in the 2000 draft. He was a receiver and a punt and kick return specialist but played sparingly. He later played for three other teams in an eight-year career. He still holds Stanford career marks for receptions and receiving yards.

20) Harry. Grant was born Harry Peter Grant, Jr. in Superior, Wisconsin on May 20, 1927. His mother, Bernice, apparently called him Buddy Boy as a child, leading to the name Bud. Later in life, he was characterized by many as The Old Trapper.

21) Mike Tice. His younger brother John served as a tight ends coach with him for four seasons (2002-05) after previously helping Denny Green from 1999-2001. Both of the Tice boys played at Maryland and then in the NFL as tight ends.

22) Four, believe it or not! (Walt Yowarsky, Darrel Brewster, Harry Gilmer, and Stan West). Yet, in his sixth and final year as head coach, Van Brocklin still had only Yaworsky and four others (Tom McCormick, Marion Campbell, Lew Carpenter, and Jim Carr) helping with the duties.

23) Jerry Burns. Burnsie was the defensive backs coach for the Packers in their first victories in 1966 and 1967 and then was the offensive coordinator for the Vikings in their four Super Bowl losses.

24) Les Steckel, who recently retired as a Colonel after 30 years in the USMC Reserves. Steckel, a former Golden Gloves Boxer, was a receivers coach for the Vikings under Bud Grant for four years prior to getting the head job. Steckel was an assistant for six teams in the NFL.

25) Brad Childress

26) Jerry Burns at Iowa (1961-65) and Denny Green at Northwestern (1981-85).

27) Denny Green, who was extremely active himself during these charity events.

Jerry Burns

28) Don Shula (328) and George Halas (318). Grant won 158 NFL games coaching the Vikings during his two stints as head coach and also won 105 games in the CFL coaching the Winnipeg Blue Bombers for a total of 263. Tom Landry had 250 wins.

29) Leslie Frazier, whose knee injury in Super Bowl XX forced him to retire after just five seasons. In 2005-06, he was Tony Dungy's defensive backs coach and helped the Colts win the Super Bowl on Feb. 4, 2007. Four days later, he was hired as Minnesota's defensive coordinator.

30) Denny Green, who had been the top guy at Stanford from 1989-91 and revived the moribund Cardinal program with a 16-18 record. Previously, he was was 10-45 at Northwestern.

31) Marc Trestman, a native of St. Louis Park. Trestman, who served as an NFL assistant for 17 years, was named head coach of the

Chicago Bears in January of 2013. He was in the Vikings training camp as a defensive back prospect in both 1978 and 1979.

32) Brian Billick, who would go on to coach the Baltimore Ravens to the Super Bowl title following the 2000 season, a 34-7 pasting of the Giants. Billick was 80-64 in nine years with the Ravens and is now an expert pro football analyst with Fox Sports. The Vikings made the playoffs in six of his seven years as coordinator.

33) Darrell Bevell, who is less than three months younger than Favre.

34) Emmitt Thomas, who also was the head coach for Atlanta for part of the 2007 season.

35) Bob Schnelker (player 1961; coach 1986-90); Mike Tice (player 1992-93, 95; coach 1996-2001); and Pete Bercich (player 1995-2000; coach 2002-05).

36) Tony Dungy, who replaced the injured Terry Bradshaw and Mike Kruczek in the game against Houston. He was 3-8 for 43 yards and was intercepted twice in that game, a 27-10 loss to the Oilers. Dungy had been a quarterback at the University of Minnesota.

37) Norm Van Brocklin (Atlanta, 1968-74) and Denny Green (Arizona, 2004-06).

38) John Michels (27 years). He came on the scene with Bud Grant in 1967 and served through 1993. Meanwhile, Jerry Burns totaled 24 years. Jerry was an assistant for 18 years (1968-85) and a head coach for six years (1986-91).

39) Pete Carroll. He also was a head coach for the New York Jets and led USC to a 34-game winning streak and one national championship.

40) Mike Tomlin, who won the Super Bowl in his second season with the Steelers.

41) Ara Parseghian of Northwestern, who went on to even greater fame at Notre Dame in the 1960's and 1970's. By the way, columnist Sid Hartman blew his cover and Parseghian was forced to issue denials.

42) 12 (1968-71, 1973-78, 1980, 1982)

43) Jerry Burns (1968-85). During that time, the team won 11 division titles and played in four Super Bowls. Following Bud

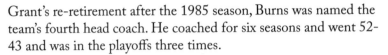

Grant's re-retirement after the 1985 season, Burns was named the team's fourth head coach. He coached for six seasons and went 52-43 and was in the playoffs three times.

44) Brian Billick, who was drafted by San Francisco in the 11th round in 1977. Billick still holds the California state high school record for interceptions with 21 as he played both cornerback and quarterback as a prep.

45) Monte Kiffin, who served 26 years as an NFL assistant but never became a head coach, despite many opportunities. Monte's son, Lane, who played at Bloomington Jefferson when Monte was working for the Vikings, became a head coach at age 31 and ran the Raiders for two seasons (2007-08), the youngest coach in modern NFL history. Monte then assisted Lane at Tennessee and also at USC.

46) Tony Dungy, who was a four-year starter at the "U" (1973-76). The mild-mannered and modest Dungy is presently doing football commentary for NBC and is also involved with motivational speaking. He is the first coach to gain the playoffs in 10-straight years and was a head coach for 13 seasons in the NFL with Tampa Bay (1996-2001) and Indianapolis (2002-08).

Assistant coach John Michels instructs center Kirk Lowdermilk (63).

47) John Michels (1967-83, 85), Buster Mertes (1967-83), Bob Hollway (1967-70, 78-83, 85), Neil Armstrong (1969-77), Jerry Burns (1968-83, 85). In addition, Jocko Nelson served eight years (1971-78) and Jack Patera seven (1969-75). Now, that's continuity!

48) Tom Moore, who has been an assistant for an amazing 36 years. Moore was Dungy's offensive coordinator when Indianapolis won the Super Bowl in 2007.

49) Leslie Frazier, whose coaching career started at tiny Trinity College in suburban Chicago.

50) Denny Green. Nearing his 13th birthday, Green witnessed Wilt score in triple figures against the New York Knicks in the "chocolate" city.

51) Tony Dungy, who also became only the third man to win the Super Bowl as a player (Pittsburgh - 1978) and as a head coach (Indianapolis - 2007) and the first African-American head coach to win the big prize.

52) Bud Grant of the Philadelphia Eagles in 1951 and 1952. Grant was drafted 12th overall in 1950 by the Eagles.

53) Norm Van Brocklin. On Nov. 15, 1965, a day after Baltimore downed the Vikings 41-21, Van Brocklin announced that he was quitting. However, the next day, he said he had reconsidered. The Vikings finished 7-7 in 1965.

54) Paul Wiggin, who won an NFL title with the Browns in 1964.

55) Denny Green, on January 10, 1992. Green would compile a 101-70 record (all games) in his 10 seasons in Minnesota.

56) Jerry Burns. A press conference defending his offensive coordinator, Bob Schnelker, was particularly entertaining and humorous.

57) John Michels and Tom Batta (each under Grant, Steckel, Burns, and Green).

58) Chuck Knox, Jr., who was an assistant from 2001-05, watched his father, Chuck Knox, Sr. be the top honcho for the LA Rams (twice), Buffalo, and Seattle in a 22-year career. Buddy Ryan, an assistant for Grant in 1976-77, has witnessed his son, Rex, be the top guy with the New York Jets since 2009. Buddy Ryan was the head coach of Philadelphia (1986-90) and Arizona (1994-95).

59) Bud Bjornaraa, who worked one season for Les Steckel in 1984.

60) Bill Musgrave, who is with his seventh NFL team as an assistant coach. Musgrave compiled a quarterback handbook entitled, "100 Ways for a QB to Lead His Team" in 2001.

61) Norm Van Brocklin (1961, 1962).

62) Bud Grant (13 in a row 1974-75). He also won 12 in a row in 1969.

63) Bud Grant (11) 1968-71; 1973-78; 1980)

64) Buster Mertes (1967-84).

65) Bud Grant (1973-78)

66) Jack "Jocko" Nelson. A star at Hibbing High School, Nelson went on to letter in five sports at Gustavus Adolphus and later became the head football coach at his alma mater for five seasons (winning two MIAC titles). In 1971, Bud Grant hired him and he was a major factor in the Vikings outstanding special teams play during the 1970's. Nelson actually died while the Vikings were playing San Diego on Nov 19, 1978. The team wore black armbands to honor Nelson the remainder of the season.

67) Jerry Burns

68) Bud Grant. A former all-around star at the University of Minnesota, Grant played in 35 games as a 6'3" forward for the Minneapolis Lakers team that copped the league title in 1949-50. Grant earned four letters in football, three in basketball, and two in baseball at the "U" from 1946-49.

Mall of America Field at the Metrodome in downtown Minneapolis in 2012.

9 Stadiums and Attendance

1) Other than its two primary home venues throughout their first 52 seasons (Metropolitan Stadium and the Metrodome), what three other stadiums have served as the team's home field for a regular season NFL game?

2) Both the Twins and the Vikings began play at Metropolitan Stadium in 1961 but what other professional sports franchise also used the Bloomington facility as their home field from 1976-81?

3) The smallest regular season crowd for a home game in Viking history occurred on Oct. 4, 1987, a 23-16 loss? Who was the opponent and what was the reason for the dearth of witnesses?

4) What was the average attendance at Metropolitan Stadium in the Vikings inaugural season of 1961?

5) The smallest crowd to witness a Viking road game came on Sept. 24, 1961, when just 12,992 fans saw Minnesota battle what opponent?

6) What Viking running back scored the first regular season touchdown in the Metrodome on Sept. 12, 1982?

7) In 21 seasons playing at Metropolitan Stadium, what was the Vikings overall record?

8) In what year did the Vikings start playing games in downtown Minneapolis at the Metrodome?

9) The Metrodome was named for former Minneapolis mayor, U.S. Senator, and Vice-President Hubert H. Humphrey. What was Hubert's middle name?

10) During their tenure playing at Met Stadium, what was the Vikings record when the temperature was below freezing?

11) In which stadium have the Vikings had a better home record (regular season only) - Met Stadium or the Metrodome?

12) What were the ticket prices when the Vikings moved into the spanking-new Metrodome in 1982?

13) Why was the home game with the New York Giants slated originally for Dec. 12, 2010, moved out of state?

14) What were the warmest and coldest game-time temperatures at Met Stadium?

15) The Vikings 10-year quest to build a publicly-owned and operated stadium culminated with the passage of stadium legislation in May of 2012. What is the expected cost to construct the stadium and what percentage of the total project will the Vikings be paying for?

16) When both the Vikings and Twins began playing at the Metrodome, what other team joined them as a major tenant?

17) What metro newspaper columnist and radio personality wrote a book on the history of Metropolitan Stadium in 1981 entitled "Once There Was a Ballpark"?

18) Groundbreaking for the new Viking stadium will tentatively start in the fall of 2013 with the stadium expected to be ready for what NFL season?

19) Where have the Vikings had a better post-season winning percentage - Met Stadium or the Metrodome?

20) How many seasons did the Vikings play without air-conditioning at the Metrodome?

21) What were the approximate construction costs for Met Stadium and the Metrodome and what are the expected costs for the new Viking stadium approved by the Minnesota legislature in 2012 (due to be completed in 2016)?

22) With the new Viking stadium being built mostly on the same site as the Metrodome, the team is expecting to continue to play at the Metrodome in 2013. Where do they intend to play in both 2014 and 2015, when the Metrodome itself will have to be torn down to make way for the new facility?

23) On Jan. 26, 1992, the Metrodome played host to Super Bowl XXVI with 63,130 fans on hand. Who were the combatants and what was the result?

24) From 1968 (the first season they reached the playoffs) though 1981, what was the Vikings home record at Metropolitan Stadium, counting the post-season?

25) What streets or roads bounded Met Stadium on four sides during its tenure as the home venue of the Vikings from 1961-81?

26) What fabric did the original Metrodome roof (1982-2010) consist of?

27) For the 1965 season, a large double-decked grandstand was installed beyond what was left field in the baseball layout, adding nearly 7,000 seats. Which tenant paid for it, the Vikings or the Twins?

28) In what year was ground broken for construction of Metropolitan Stadium in Bloomington?

29) Who was the opponent on the day the Vikings played their last home game at Metropolitan Stadium and what was the result?

30) The Metrodome includes 7,600 retractable seats, the largest such section of any stadium in the world. How long did it take to

Metropolitan Stadium on game day (Met Center in background) on the Bloomington prairie circa 1969.

convert from a baseball configuration to football and vice versa?

31) In what year was Metropolitan Stadium demolished?

32) In what fashion was the playing field for Vikings games aligned to the baseball field configuration for the baseball Twins?

33) What were the four different field substances or turfs that have been installed in the Metrodome?

34) The Metrodome is the only facility in the world to have served as a venue for all of what four major sporting events?

35) In the 1960's, the Vikings sometimes practiced at two locations less than a mile apart in St. Paul. What were those two sites?

36) From 1961 to 1994, the Vikings played the Packers at either of what two Wisconsin fields or stadiums?

37) When the Vikings "50 Greatest Vikings" team was announced to the home crowd on Dec. 20, 2010, what was so ironic about the occasion?

38) What dedicated fan sounded the Gjallarhorn prior to the start of the 2012 home opener against Jacksonville at the Metrodome, representing all the fans and supporters who backed legislation for the new downtown stadium passed that May?

39) What is the Vikings record for consecutive regular season home sellouts?

40) In what year did the Viking start garnering consistent sell-out crowds at Met Stadium?

41) What was the largest crowd to ever witness a home Viking game?

42) What opposing coach referred to the Metrodome as a "Roller-dome" prior to a Dec. 6, 1987 game in Minneapolis?

43) What was the largest crowd to watch a post-season home game?

44) What is the Vikings all-time record at the Metrodome/Mall of America Field?

45) What is the total attendance for Viking home games from 1961-2012?

46) What architectural firm was hired by the Minnesota Sports Facilities Authority in September of 2012 to design the new $975 million stadium in downtown Minneapolis?

47) What is the current capacity of the Metrodome/Mall of America Field?

48) How many acres will the new stadium footprint cover in the eastern portion of downtown Minneapolis, scheduled for completion in 2016?

49) Where have the Vikings played more playoff games - Met Stadium or the Metrodome?

50) In what year did the Vikings set the team record for single-season attendance?

1) Memorial Stadium (University of Minnesota), Oct. 5, 1969. Reason: The Twins were preparing Metropolitan Stadium for the first American League championship series in Bloomington for a game the next day. The Vikings beat rival Green Bay 19-7 on the strength of four Fred Cox field goals.

   Ford Field (Detroit, Michigan), Dec. 13, 2010. Reason: After a 17-inch snowfall, the Metrodome roof collapsed and forced the team to find another indoor facility. The Vikings lost 21-3 on a Monday night to the New York Giants.

   TCF Bank Stadium (University of Minnesota), Dec. 20, 2010. Reason: (See above) After two weeks to get the field and facilities ready, the one-year old stadium on the "U" campus played host to its first NFL game. In Brett Favre's last NFL game, the Bears walloped the Vikings 40-14 on a cold, snowy Monday night.

2) The Minnesota Kicks of the North American Soccer League. The tailgating in the parking lot became a cultural phenomenon for area youth as the Twins, Vikings, and Kicks shared the Met in its final six seasons of use. The Kicks folded after the 1981 season.

3) Green Bay! The NFL was in the midst of a players' strike and the league had decided to use so-called "replacement" players in lieu of the regular players. The fans were not enamored by the talent on the Metrodome floor, to be sure. Otherwise, the smallest attendance at a home game took place on Nov. 25, 1962 when only 26,728 fans attended a 24-24 tie with the Los Angeles Rams.

4) 34,586 (capacity was 41,200 for the first four seasons). Season ticket sales for the first season were approximately 26,000.

5) Dallas Cowboys

6) Rickey Young, on a 3-yard run in the second quarter of the Viking's 17-10 win over Tampa Bay.

7) 98-59-4 (regular season and post-season combined)

8) 1982

9) Horatio

10) 28-8 (77.7%)

11) Metrodome. The Vikings are 158-85 (65%) in 32 seasons under the teflon. At Met Stadium, the Vikings were 91-56-4 (61.9%) in 21 seasons.

12) When the team moved into the Metrodome in 1982, all seats sold for $15.

13) The Metrodome roof collapsed at 5:00 a.m. after three panels ripped and spewed ice and snow onto the stadium turf. After 17 inches of snow fell on Dec. 10 and 11, strong winds prevented workers from removing snow from the roof. Concern over the roof had already caused officials to move the game to Monday, Dec. 13. Fox Sports cameras captured the roof tearing and dumping the snow and ice into the stadium. No one was hurt and the roof sagged and came to rest on cable stays. Only a few seats and a light fixture were damaged. On Dec. 15, another panel tore, sending more ice and snow onto the field. The NFL decided to move the Vikings home game to Ford Field in Detroit and the Giants beat the Vikings 21-3 on Dec. 13.

14) Six games started with temps of at least 70 degrees but the warmest was on Sept. 11, 1978 when it was a balmy 79 with high humidity as the Vikings beat Denver 12-9 on the strength of four Rick Danmeier field goals. The coldest temperature day occurred on Dec. 2, 1972 when it was -2 below with a wind chill of -19 as visiting Green Bay won 23-7. Only six games in Met Stadium history had games where the temperature was 10 degrees or below.

15) $975 million with the Vikings guaranteeing to privately cover $477 million or 49% of the upfront capital costs, as well as $13 million annually for operating expenses/capital improvement funding during the 30-year lease. Groundbreaking is slated for October 2013.

16) The Minnesota Gopher football team.

17) Joe Soucheray, the host of "Garage Logic" on 1500 ESPN (KSTP) and a general columnist for the St. Paul Pioneer Press.

18) 2016

19) Met Stadium (7-3). At the Metrodome, they were 6-4. Thus, overall they have a 13-7 record in home post-season contests.

20) One (1982). Air conditioning was installed in June of 1983 during

the Twins' second season in the stadium. Pre-season games in August, 1982 were steamy!

21) $8.5 million for Met Stadium (1956), $68 million for the Metrodome, and $975 for the new (yet to be named) Viking stadium.

22) TCF Bank Stadium on the University of Minnesota campus.

23) The NFC Washington Redskins beat the AFC Buffalo Bills 37-24.

24) 82-29-1 (73.9%)

25) Cedar Avenue on the west, 24th Avenue South on the south, East 83rd Street on the east, and 83rd Street on the north.

26) Two layers of teflon-coated fiberglass. The roof, 195 feet from the playing surface and 16 stories high at its highest point, weighed 580,000 pounds.

27) The Vikings, who received reduced rent as part of the deal. Capacity rose to 47,900 from 1965-70. It was 49,784 from 1971-74, back to 47,900 from 1974-76, and then finally 48,446 the final five seasons from 1977-81.

28) 1955. Construction began on June 25 and concluded less than a year later at a cost of $4.5 million, financed by revenue bonds. The 160 acres of land were purchased at a cost of $2,980 per acre. Met Stadium was ready for the main tenant, the Minneapolis Millers of

An artist's rendering of the new stadium.

the American Association, on April 24, 1956.

29) On Dec. 20, 1981, the Vikings lost to the Kansas City Chiefs 10-6. The attendance was only 41,110, about 6,000 less than capacity. Maybe it was just as well because many of the people in attendance wouldn't have had room for all of the tools they used to dismantle portions of the stadium when the game ended.

30) Four hours

31) 1985; it started in January and took about four months to complete the demolition. The author has four well-preserved seats in his basement; they were located in the lower deck near the end zone that was adjacent to the third-base dugout for the Twins. On one Saturday morning, 100 fans were allowed to enter the stadium and haul away up to 10 seats for $10 each.

32) Often considered a substandard venue for football, the gridiron for NFL games ran from around third-base to right field, with barely enough room to fit the end zones. In fact, receivers had just a few feet behind the end of the end zone to stop themselves before running into the stands.

33) Super-Turf, also called SporTurf, was the original surface from 1982-86. In 1987, AstroTurf replaced it; a more cushioned turf of the same brand was installed in 1995. In 2004, another surface, called FieldTurf, was laid down. In 2010, a surface called UBU - Speed Series was laid by Sportexe. However, it necessitated replacement because of water damage (mold and fungus) caused by the roof collapse in December of that year. After a new roof was placed on the facility by Birdair (the original manufacturers), Sportexe contracted to put down UBU S5-M Sports Turf for the 2011 season.

34) World Series (1987 and 1991), NCAA Mens' Basketball Final Four (1992), Super Bowl (1992), and the Major-League's All-Star game (1985).

35) Midway Stadium and the Hippodrome (Coliseum) on the State Fair Grounds.

36) Lambeau Field in Green Bay and County Stadium in Milwaukee. The Packers played two or three games each season in Milwaukee from 1953-94 and the Vikings were their most common foe (15 times). The Pack discontinued playing in Milwaukee after the

1994 season because renovations at Lambeau made playing all their games there more lucrative. The Packers played 126 games over 42 years at County Stadium, with a .617 winning percentage.

37) It was exactly 21 years from the last time the Vikings had played an outdoor game (at Met Stadium) and nine of the players being honored played in that game on Dec. 20, 1981.

38) Larry Spooner

39) 144 games, which extended from the first game of 1998 to the final game of 2011.

40) 1969

41) 64,482 saw Green Bay beat Minnesota 30-27 on Nov. 2, 2003.

42) Chicago Bears coach Mike Ditka. The Vikings cheerleaders proceeded to promote their team with roller skates on as the Bears beat the hosts 30-24.

43) 64,060 witnessed Atlanta beat Minnesota 30-27 on Jan. 17, 1999.

44) 158-85 all-time record at the Metrodome thru 2012 (regular season only). In the playoffs, they are 6-4 for an overall mark of 164-89 (62.5%).

45) 21,367,333 for 396 regular season home games through 2012.

46) HKS, Inc, a Dallas-based firm that also built Lucas Oil Stadium in Indianapolis and Cowboys Stadium in Arlington, Texas. The new facility will seat approximately 65,000. The M.A. Mortenson Company, based in the Twin Cities, was selected as the general contractor in building the facility in February of 2013. Mortenson was also the contractor for Target Field, Target Center, Xcel Energy Center, and TCF Bank Stadium.

47) 64,126

48) 33 (7,000 construction workers are expected to work on the project for three years).

49) Met Stadium. In 11 games from 1969-77, the Vikings were 8-3 in Bloomington. They have played 10 games at the Metrodome, going 6-4 in those post-season contests.

50) In 2003, a record 513,437 fans attended eight regular season games in the Metrodome.

10 Non-playing Personnel

1) Minnesota was granted an NFL franchise at the league's owners meetings in Miami, Florida, on Jan. 28, 1960, and would begin play in the league in 1961. What five men made up the first ownership group for the Vikings?

2) Who is the all-time leader in tackles for the Vikings who has served in the team's player personnel department for the past 21 years?

3) Which one of the original owners of the Vikings once owned a piece of another Minnesota entry in the NFL?

4) Which Viking employee has worked for the team since its inception and attended the first 1,049 of the franchise's games, including pre-season, regular season, and post-season games?

5) What longtime Twins public-address announcer also worked in that role for the Vikings for a short period in the early 1960's and in a 1963 contest at the Met stated, "The Giants have been penalized 15 yards for having an illegitimate man on the field."?

6) What Memphis businessman did team president Max Winter hire to be the team's general manager on July 15, 1975, despite having absolutely no football experience?

7) What Viking general manager played seven seasons as an NFL quarterback?

8) What fellow worked for several years to secure a new Viking stadium as vice-president of public affairs/stadium development and finally succeeded when the Minnesota Legislature finally approved a stadium in May of 2012?

9) Who currently serves as the Vikings' director of ticket sales and hospitality and once worked for 12 years with the Minnesota Twins?

Dick Jonckowski, the head field usher, is shown on the Met Stadium turf in the early 1970s.

10) What role do the following men play in the operation of the Minnesota Vikings, as of 2012: Scott Kuhn, Ryan Monnens, Jeff Robinson, Steven Price, Paul Roell, Frank Acevedo, Terrance Gray, Kevin McCabe, Mike Sholiton, and Reed Burckhardt?

11) What Edina native, who originally covered the team for the *Minneapolis Tribune*, served as the Vikings director of public relations from 1974 to 1993?

12) What man was not only instrumental in bringing the Twins and North Stars to the Twin Cities but also served as part owner and president of the Vikings?

13) What beloved man served as the team's equipment manager for its first 20 years?

14) What St. Louis Park native and Vikings general manager was the NFL Executive of the Year in 1999?

15) What gentleman, who did yeoman service in scouting and player personnel for the Vikings for 32 years, once played for Bud Grant in the CFL and was an assistant under Jerry Burns at his alma mater?

16) What St. Paul Highland Park grad has worked for the Vikings since 1976, starting as an assistant equipment manager before moving up to head equipment manager in 1981?

17) What former Viking still serves as a player personnel consultant with the team more than 50 years after his playing career started

with the team in 1961?

18) What reputable former NFL referee was hired by the Vikings for the 2012 season to be a game consultant assisting with coaching decisions regarding replays?

19) Who became the president and CEO of the Vikings on Jan. 1, 1991, and remained in that position until 1998, as one of ten owners of the club?

20) What Wayzata High graduate started with the Vikings as an intern in 1991 and has served as the director of public relations since 1998?

21) What successful auto salesman from San Antonio, Texas, purchased the Vikings from the 10-person ownership group in August of 1998 for $206 million in cash and the assumption of $40 million in debt?

22) Who is the current head athletic trainer for the Vikings?

23) Which two prominent Twin Cities businessmen did Max Winter sell his 48% share of the team to in April of 1984?

24) Who has spent the past 12 years as the Vikings vice-president of sales and marketing and chief marketing officer, and will be in charge of naming rights, building partnerships, and brand integration opportunities in the new football stadium?

25) Who has been a Viking team physician for the past 28 years and is also the medical director for the Wolves, Lynx, and Wild?

26) Who are the current owners of the Minnesota Vikings?

27) Who is the vice-president of football operations for the team presently, in charge of the salary cap, the lead negotiator on high-profile contracts, and the Vikings representative at league meetings?

28) Whose resignation led to head coach Bud Grant assuming the power to make trades, determine the roster, and oversee draft selections in 1974?

29) What gentleman is the current writer/editor for the team's website—Viking.com?

30) In October of 1997, under pressure from the NFL to reorganize so that one person owned at least 30% of the team, the Vikings board of directors announced that the team was for sale. What noted author agreed to buy the club for $200 million early in 1998 but couldn't come up with the money?

31) What former player spent two years as the Vikings' director of planning and development and was responsible for overseeing the construction of the Winter Park office headquarters and training complex?

32) What current minority owner of the team had made a tentative deal with the Viking board of directors to buy the club in February of 2005 from Red McCombs for $625 million?

33) What man served as the team's ticket manager from 1974 to 1995?

34) From 1964-1983, what group from a suburban high school performed on the sidelines as the unofficial team cheerleading squad?

35) What man became the official mascot of the team for 20 years starting in 1970?

36) Who has been the Vikings executive director of community relations for 14 years, making it one of the NFL's strongest?

1) Max Winter, E. William Boyer, H.P. Skoglund, Ole Haugsrud, and Bernard Ridder, Jr.

2) Scott Studwell. The Illinois "stud" played 14 years (1977-90) at middle linebacker for Minnesota and had a total of 1,981 tackles. Studwell, who wore number 55, has been the team's Director of College Scouting since 2002. He also broke Hall of Famer Dick Butkus' collegiate record for tackles at Illinois.

3) Ole Haugsrud. The Superior, Wisconsin native and resident owned the Duluth Eskimos in the 1920's after purchasing ownership for $1 with a partner. When he sold the team back to the NFL later that decade, he was given the rights to gain part ownership in the next NFL franchise to be awarded to Minnesota. He was given 10% of the team in Jan. 1960 when the NFL owners voted to allow Minneapolis-St. Paul to join the league. He remained one of the owners until his death in 1976.

4) Fred Zamberletti. After serving as the team's trainer from 1961-98, Zamberletti became the coordinator for medical services for three years before becoming a senior consultant. Zamberletti was honored into the team's Ring of Honor in 1998.

5) Bob Casey. The lovable "Case" was noted for his malapropos but overall did an outstanding job. He is in the Twins Hall of Fame.

Fred Zamberletti

6) Mike Lynn, who had befriended Winter in his desire to acquire a team for his city. Lynn remained with the team through 1990. He was one of the driving forces for bringing the club from Met Stadium to the Metrodome, launching the Vikings Children's Fund, and spearheading the Twin Cities hosting Super Bowl XXVI.

7) Jim Finks, who was just 37 when he became the Viking general manager in 1964. Finks played for Pittsburgh from 1949-55 and led the NFL with 20 touchdowns passes in 1952.

8) Lester Bagley

9) Phil Huebner, who has worked for the local NFL franchise since 1998.

10) Each of the afore-mentioned gentlemen is a Viking scout.

11) Merrill Swanson. He took over for Bill McGrane, another former writer from the *Minneapolis Tribune*, who went to work in the same role for Jim Finks after the general manager took the same job with Chicago. McGrane wrote a book on the Vikings called, *Bud: The Other Side of the Glacier*, in 1986, and was the team's public relations director from 1966 to 1972.

12) Wheelock Whitney, who replaced Max Winter as team president in September of 1987 and served through 1990.

13) Jim "Stubby" Eason, who died of lung cancer in 1981. Eason lost a leg in combat while fighting on the beaches of Italy during WWII. With his artificial leg, he was seen retrieving the kicking tee after Viking kickoffs. He and his wife Dottie were known for annually inviting over the team's bachelors and others who were from out of town to Thanksgiving dinner at their home.

14) Jeff Diamond, who later was President of the Tennessee Titans for five years. Diamond joined the team as an intern, incidentally, and one of his first jobs was to write a book on the team called *The First Fifteen Years*. Diamond spent 23 years with the team.

15) Frank Gilliam. A former star end at Iowa, Gilliam was an assistant under head coach Jerry Burns with the Hawkeyes and he also played three years for coach Bud Grant at Winnipeg (1957-59). Gilliam worked for the Vikings from 1971 to 2002.

16) Dennis Ryan. He became the youngest head equipment manager

in the league when he took over the top duties and just finished his 37th year with the team. He won the Whitney Zimmerman award recognizing the NFL's best equipment manager in 1995.

17) Jerry Reichow, who was a wide receiver from Iowa and played for Minnesota from 1961-64. Starting in 1965, he became a scout and then moved to director of player personnel to director of football operations to assistant general manager. The last few years, he has been a senior consultant and is one of the longest-serving employees in the NFL.

18) Bernie Kukar, a Gilbert native who played football at St. John's. He was an NFL official for 22 seasons and twice was the head referee in the Super Bowl.

19) Roger Headrick

20) Bob Hagan, whose main responsibilities are coordinating print and electronic coverage of the team and producing the team's media guide and game programs.

21) Red McCombs, who owned the team for almost seven years and ended up selling the team for $600 million in 2005, a tidy little profit of about $400 million. McCombs also once owned the San Antonio Spurs and the Denver Nuggets.

22) Eric Sugarman has been in his post since 2006.

23) Carl Pohlad and Irwin Jacobs.

24) Steve LaCroix. He will also be busy overseeing new offerings related to season tickets, premier seating, club seats, and suites in the new facility, proposed to be completed by 2016.

25) Dr. Sheldon Burns

26) Zygi Wilf (owner, chairman), Mark Wilf (owner, president), Leonard Wilf (owner, vice-chairman), Jeffrey Wilf, David Mandelbaum, Alan Landis, and Reggie Fowler.

27) Rob Brzezinski, who is in his 14th year with the Vikings and his 20th in the NFL.

28) General Manager Jim Finks, who primarily left because of philosophical differences with owner Max Winter. More precisely, Finks was upset because Winter refused to allow Finks to gain ownership of company stock.

29) Mike Wobschall

30) Tom Clancy, who wasn't able to come up with the $60 million necessary to close the deal. Three months later, the Vikings were sold to Texas auto dealer Red McCombs.

31) Grady Alderman, who became a certified public accountant during his playing days.

32) Reggie Fowler, an Arizona businessman. Fowler couldn't finance the deal and eventually joined on with the Wilf family, who finally purchased the team from McCombs.

33) Harry Randolph

34) The Parkettes, from St. Louis Park High School. From 1961-63, a group called the Vi-Queens performed those duties. It was organized by Bob Patrin and included 10 members split between the St. Louis Park-based Parkettes and the University of Minnesota's Pomperettes. Since 1984, the team has sponsored the official cheerleading ensemble, which currently has 35 members.

35) Everett "Hub" Meeds. A St. Paul native, he and his brother traveled to New Orleans for the Super Bowl game between the Vikings and Chiefs. "Hub" dressed up in traditional "Norseman" clothing and walked into Tulane Stadium as the guards figured he was with the team. He cheered from the sidelines that day and at all home games (and many road games) through 1989 when the team asked him to be a part of their entourage.

36) Brad Madson, who is in his 21st year with the team.

11 The Media

1) What veteran scribe has not only covered the Vikings since their inception but also served as the presenter for Bud Grant when he was inducted into the Pro Football Hall of Fame in Canton, Ohio, in 1994?

2) What gentleman, who has served as the play-by-play man for the team since 2002, has the same name as the owner of the Seattle Seahawks (co-founder of Microsoft)?

3) Who was the first beat reporter covering the Vikings for the *Minneapolis Star*?

4) What KSTP-TV sports reporter hosted a half-hour show with Bud Grant on local television in the 1970's on Monday evenings?

5) What former NFL defensive back, who was one of the regulars on the CBS pre-game show *The NFL Today* from 1975 to 1989, works with Jim Rich at Fox station KMSP on a post-game show during the NFL season?

6) What former Viking defender and 12-year NFL veteran was the publisher of *Viking Update* for many years?

7) What veteran Twin Cities sports columnist wrote a book on the team in 2008 entitled, *Minnesota Vikings: The Complete Illustrated History*?

8) What longtime pro football scribe wrote a book on the Vikings in 2007 called, *The Good, The Bad, and The Ugly: Heart-Pounding, Jaw-Dropping, and Gut-Wrenching Moments in Minnesota Vikings History*?

9) What WCCO-TV sportscaster has covered the Vikings thoroughly for the local CBS station for over 40 years, specifically highlighting them on his Sunday night half-hour sports specials at 10:30 p.m.?

10) What former Viking tight end spent nine years as the color analyst on Viking radio from 1981 to 1989?

11) What former Viking receiver later worked for WCCO radio for 15 years as the color analyst on broadcasts of Gopher football?

12) What *St. Paul Pioneer Press* columnist used to poke fun at the Green Bay Packers and their fans by referring to the Wisconsin team and its supporters as "Green Bush"?

13) Tagged the Superstar, what former Vikings long-snapper analyzed his former team as a host of the *Power Trip* morning show at KFAN radio from 6-9 a.m. for 10 years?

14) What gentleman published *Tough Enough to Be Vikings* in 1999, a 382-page masterpiece which reviewed every player in Viking history to that point?

15) What Benilde-St. Margaret's graduate is currently covering the Vikings on his weekly morning talk show on 1500 ESPN (KSTP) and in posts on 1500ESPN.com?

16) What journalist, formerly an expert *Star Tribune* beat writer for the Vikings from 2000 to 2008, now covers Minnesota as part of his job for ESPN.com covering the NFC North?

17) Possessor of one of the great voices in broadcast history, what gentleman covered the Viking for 18 years for WCCO-TV?

18) What long-time *St. Paul Pioneer Press* and *Dispatch* writer started covering the Vikings in 1967?

19) What award-winning journalist, now a senior editor at 1500ESPN.com, formerly covered the Green Bay Packers as assistant editor for the *Green Bay Press-Gazette* prior to covering the Vikings?

20) How many Viking players, coaches, or executives have earned the wrath of veteran newspaper scribe Patrick Reusse by being

chosen as Turkey of the Year, a negative honor he has bestowed on a local or national sports personality during the week of Thanksgiving since 1978?

21) What former Viking tight end has served two stints on the Minnesota Viking radio network as a color commentator?

22) What lady won three local Emmy's for her work producing and hosting *Vikings Weekly* on Fox Sports North?

Star Tribune **columnist Sid Hartman (right) and Bud Grant at Grant's Hall of Fame induction in Canton, Ohio, in 1994. Hartman was Grant's presenter.**

23) What Hall of Fame baseball broadcaster worked as a play-by-play announcer for CBS for the first four seasons of the Vikings?

24) One of the biggest names in Minnesota sports history, what former Gopher All-American football and baseball player worked color commentary of Viking radio broadcasts from 1962 to 1969 for WCCO?

25) Firmly established as one of the top football play-by-play announcers for either college or pro football, what St. Charles, Minnesota, native was the main announcer on Viking radio broadcasts in 1988 and 1989?

26) What excitable announcer broadcast the Vikings on radio in two separate stints (1971-76 and 1985-87) with the team?

27) What former Notre Dame All-American and Viking offensive lineman did yeoman work with his easy-going style as a color commentator on the Viking Radio Network?

28) What former player and assistant coach is currently the color commentator for Vikings radio broadcasts?

29) Pre-season games are generally not shown on national networks. What local station has produced Viking pre-season games

for the past few decades?

30) What Viking play-by-play announcer lasted just one preseason game into the 2001 season?

31) What noted Minnesota reporter, columnist and author has written no less than seven books on the Vikings?

32) What consummate professional was the play-by-play announcer for radio broadcasts from 1991 to 2000?

33) What local radio station has had control of Viking broadcasts for four different stints?

34) What player wrote a 1977 book with Jim Klobuchar entitled, *Will the Vikings Ever Win the Super Bowl?*

35) What former Viking star currently writes weekly articles analyzing the team for TwinCities.com and the *St. Paul Pioneer Press*?

36) What Heisman Trophy winner and member of the Pro Football Hall of Fame was a colorful radio analyst from 1970 to 1974?

37) What former Gopher kicker, who was cut twice by coach Bud Grant in the 1960's, wrote a book in 2012 about the top players in Viking history titled, *Vikings 50*?

38) In 1990, what suburban mayor and former professional athlete was hired to be a color analyst on the Viking radio broadcasts?

39) What award-winning photographer has covered the Vikings for the past 31 years?

40) A ten-year Viking veteran, what former specialist has been a longtime sideline reporter and a pre-game and post-game interviewer for Viking radio broadcasts?

41) Since 2001, the Twin Cities chapter of the Pro Football Writers of America has awarded the Korey Stringer Good Guy Award (most cooperative and best attitude with the media) in honor of the late Vikings lineman. What three players have won it twice?

42) What two radio stations serve as the flagship stations for the Minnesota Vikings Radio network, which includes outlets in six states?

43) Despite growing up a Packer fan in Wisconsin, what television reporter has covered the Vikings extensively for 30 years, especially with his Sunday night half-hour program called *Sports Wrap*?

44) What daily sports radio talk show host for KFAN 100.3 FM has been fostering opinions on the Vikings as a part of his afternoon gig since 1992?

45) What offensive tackle once did color commentary for the Vikings on radio and later became general manager of the Denver Broncos?

Viking play-by-play radio announcer Paul Allen of KFAN broadcasts from Mall of America field in 2012.

46) What local AM station had broadcast rights to the Vikings from 1970 to 1975 and from 1985 to 1987?

47) What Hall of Fame broadcaster, who became famous broadcasting Packer games for CBS, did Vikings play-by-play for WCCO radio from 1978 to 1980?

48) What *Star Tribune* writer has covered the NFL for 22 years and has been a beat writer for the Vikings since 2003?

49) What Minnesota broadcasting legend, a longtime fixture at WCCO Radio who was the primary Gopher football announcer for 50 years and the Gopher basketball play-by-play man for 45 years, did play-by-play on Viking radio from 1966 to 1969?

50) In 2012, a new half-hour television show premiered focusing on rare inside access to the team. What is it called?

1) Sid Hartman. "Sidney," the Minnesota journalistic legend, has covered the Vikings for all of their 52 seasons and was still a first-rate reporter in 2012 at the age of 92.

2) Paul Allen, who broadcasts for KFAN, the team's broadcast partner. Allen, who also announces races at Canterbury Park, has done Vikings play-by-play since 2002.

3) Jim Klobuchar, the father of current U.S. Senator Amy Klobuchar, who has covered the Vikings in one form or another for 52 seasons. Roger Rosenblum was the beat writer for the *St. Paul Pioneer Press and Dispatch* in 1961.

4) Bob Bruce

5) Irv Cross, who became the first African-American to work full-time as a football analyst on national television in 1971 for CBS. Cross played 10 years in the NFL and made two Pro Bowls with the Eagles in the 1960's.

6) Bob Lurtsema. The tabloid started as a newspaper in the 1970s and is now a monthly feature magazine with a website.

7) Patrick Reusse, who has written several hundred columns on the team in his tenure with both the *St. Paul Pioneer Press* (1979-1988) and the *Star Tribune* since 1988. He has also thoroughly entertained listeners with his Viking views on AM 1500 ESPN (KSTP) radio for 30 years.

8) Steve Silverman

9) Mark Rosen, who started covering the Vikings in 1970. In his book, *Best Seat in the House*, Rosen writes generously about his experiences covering the team. His show, *Rosen Sports Sunday*, which airs weekly during the fall and early winter, often focuses its attention on the Vikings.

10) Stu "Chainsaw" Voigt, who is currently chairman of First Commercial Bank in Bloomington.

11) Paul Flately, who was on the air from 1983 to 1997. He also did pre-game and post-game shows for the station from 1971 to 1990.

12) Don Riley, whose daily column, "The Eye Opener", was a must-read for Vikings fans for over 30 years. Purposefully controversial

and always entertaining, it certainly must have sold a lot of newspapers in western Wisconsin.

13) Mike Morris, who played 144 games for Minnesota from 1991 to 1999. Morris also co-hosted post-game shows after Vikings broadcasts on the station.

14) Bill Ballew

15) Judd Zulgad, who spent 22 years writing about the Vikings for the *Star Tribune*. He can be heard weekdays from 9 a.m. to 1 p.m.

16) Kevin Seifert

17) Hal Scott, who was a mainstay on Channel 4 in the 1960's and 1970's. Scott, the brother of Hall of Fame broadcaster Ray Scott, was also assigned to be the CBS play-by-play announcer for the Vikings for three seasons (1965-67).

18) Ralph Reeve, who many times wrote two articles on the team; one in the morning for the *Pioneer Press* and one in the afternoon for the *Dispatch*.

19) Tom Pelissero, who also is a contributor to *Pro Football Weekly* and co-hosts *Sunday Morning Sports Talk* with Jim Souhan each week on 1500 ESPN (KSTP).

20) Nine (or more than 25% of the 35 awardees). They include owner Zygi Wilf (2011), quarterback Brett Favre (2010), owner Red McCombs (2004), players Cris Carter and Randy Moss (2001), coach Dennis Green (1997), quarterback Warren Moon (1995), defensive end Chris Doleman (1991), general manager Mike Lynn (1989) and coach Les Steckel (1984).

21) Joe Senser (1993-94 and 2001-06), who also owns Joe Senser's Restaurant and Sports Theater in both Roseville and Bloomington.

22) Ann Carroll. The show aired for six years and she won the Emmy's in 2008, 2009, and 2010.

23) Herb Carneal. The legendary Twins broadcaster actually worked for the Vikings in 1961 before joining Twins broadcasts in 1962. He worked with former Gopher football and NFL great Clayton Tonnemaker on Vikings broadcasts from 1961 to 1964 as CBS assigned commentating crews (play-by-play and color analysts) to specific teams for the entire season from 1956 to 1967.

24) Paul Giel. The two-time Big Ten MVP in football (1952-53) was also the athletic director at his alma mater from 1971 to 1989.

25) Brad Nessler

26) Joe McConnell. The Purdue alum also did Twins broadcasts in 1978 and 1979 in a career that saw him broadcast for five NFL teams and two NBA teams, in addition to college football and basketball.

27) David Huffman

28) Pete Bercich, who started with KFAN in 2007. His father, Bob, played safety for Dallas in 1960 and 1961.

29) KARE-TV (Channel 11) with Ari Wolfe and Mike Mayock.

30) Lee "Hacksaw" Hamilton resigned after local journalist Larry Fitzgerald, Sr. (father of Arizona star receiver Larry Fitzgerald, Jr.) brought about concerns over alleged racist and sexist comments Hamilton made on his talk show.

31) Jim Klobuchar. The books include *Purple Hearts and Golden Memories, Always on Sundays, Tarkenton, True Hearts and Purple Heads, Will The Vikings Ever Win the Super Bowl, Knights and Knaves,* and *Love at Halftime.*

32) Dan Rowe, who worked with both KFAN and WCCO.

33) WCCO-AM (1961-69, 1976-84, 1988-90, and 1996-2000).

34) Jeff Siemon, who had played in the last three Super Bowl losses. As for the answer to the title's question, I hope I am alive to answer in the affirmative.

35) Fran Tarkenton, the former Viking quarterback and Hall of Famer. A walking conglomerate, Tarkenton also is an advocate for small business and the founder of OneMoreCustomer.com.

36) Paul Hornung. The former Notre Dame and Green Bay Packer great was a great complement to play-by-play announcer Joe McConnell with his Kentucky drawl and common sense approach.

37) Jim Bruton. The ex-Gopher has written six books relating to the local sports scene, including *A Tradition of Purple: An Inside Look at the Minnesota Vikings* published in 2007 and *Every Day is Game Day* published in 2009 with Fran Tarkenton and Roger Staubach. Bruton was in training camp in both 1967 and 1971.

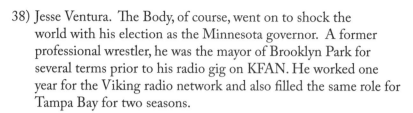

38) Jesse Ventura. The Body, of course, went on to shock the world with his election as the Minnesota governor. A former professional wrestler, he was the mayor of Brooklyn Park for several terms prior to his radio gig on KFAN. He worked one year for the Viking radio network and also filled the same role for Tampa Bay for two seasons.

39) Brian Peterson of the *Star Tribune*, who has worked for the paper since 1987. Peterson also photographed the team for the *St. Paul Pioneer Press* from 1982 to 1986.

40) Greg Coleman, who is also an ordained minister and prior to each game presents a sideline homily moments before kickoff called Pre-Game Preach.

41) Daunte Culpepper and Ben Leber.

42) KFAN (100.3 FM) and KTCN (1130 AM). There are 42 stations in outstate Minnesota.

43) Joe Schmit, who first joined KSTP in 1985.

44) Dan Barreiro, who worked for 17 years as a columnist for the *Star Tribune*.

45) Grady Alderman, who worked the airwaves from 1976-80, just prior to his short stint as a Broncos executive.

46) KSTP-AM

47) Ray Scott, whose minimalist style of broadcasting was notable throughout the NFL. He also was the primary play-by-play announcer for the Twins from 1961-66 and also worked part-time from 1973-75 covering the local major-league team.

48) Mark Craig, who is one of the 44 selectors for the Pro Football Hall of Fame.

49) Ray Christensen. "Gentleman Ray" also did broadcasts of Twins baseball and Lakers basketball during his classy career.

50) "Beyond the Gridiron," a documentary-style format that had its debut just prior to training camp.

Daunte Culpepper (11) audibles at New England in 2000. Culpepper was the Vikings top draft pick (11th overall) in 1999 out of Central Florida and along with Tommy Kramer and Christian Ponder, is one of only three quarterbacks ever taken by the team in the first round.

12 Draft, Trades, Free Agency

1) Who was the first player to be drafted by the Vikings, the top overall selection in the draft for the 1961 season?

2) What Minnesota Gopher all-around athlete was drafted in the 17th round by the Vikings in 1973?

3) For its first six seasons (1961-66), the Vikings participated in an NFL draft that included how many rounds?

4) What position has been picked most often by the Vikings in the first round?

5) Who was the only Minnesota Gopher football player to be drafted in the first round by the Vikes?

6) How many players have the Vikings picked in their 53-year history (1961-2013) of selecting players in the NFL draft?

7) On only three occasions have the Vikings nabbed a quarterback in the first round of the NFL draft. Who were those quarterbacks?

8) In a monumental trade which was a key factor in building the Vikings into a true power in the NFL, what original Viking was traded on March 7, 1967, to the New York Giants but returned to greater glory with the team five years later?

9) How many times have the Vikings gone without making a selection in the first round of the NFL draft?

10) What Gopher gridiron great became the first "U" player to be drafted by the Vikings?

11) The Ivy League is noted more for its academic prowess, of

course, than for developing football talent. Who are the only five Ivy players to be drafted by Minnesota?

12) The trade for this Dallas running back on Oct. 12, 1989, is considered one of the two or three worst trades in NFL history; it led to the loss of first-round draft picks in 1990, 1991, and 1992 and helped the Cowboys catapult themselves to three Super Bowl wins within a four-year period. Who was he?

13) What player went undrafted but then signed a free-agent contract with the Vikings and ultimately was inducted into the Pro Football Hall of Fame after an 11-year career in Minnesota (1990-2000)?

14) Following the 2004 season, disgruntled wide receiver Randy Moss was traded for linebacker Napoleon Harris and two draft-choices: a first-round pick (7th overall) and a 7th-rounder. What team took on Moss?

15) What running back out of Ohio State became one of the worst draft busts in Vikings history as the first-round selection in 1971?

16) Throughout its history, how many Minnesota Gophers have been drafted by the Minnesota Vikings?

17) Though not speedy or even quick, what 13th-round draft pick out of North Dakota in 1965 became one of the Vikings most popular players as a hard-nosed running back?

18) How many players drafted by the Vikings have been inducted into the Hall of Fame?

19) Except for their initial season, when is the only other year when the Vikings had the top overall selection in the NFL draft and who did that player turn out to be?

20) In what year did the Vikings fail to sign either their first- or second-round draft pick?

21) What Minnesota Gopher quarterback, whose three sons would later be hockey stars for the Gophers, was drafted in the eighth round by the Vikings in 1965?

22) Since 1994, the NFL draft has been limited to how many rounds?

Carl Eller pursues Detroit QB Greg Landry.

23) In the 1963 draft, the Vikings drafted two standouts from the MIAC in the 17th and 18th rounds. Who were they?

24) What three individuals form the current three-man hierarchy in charge of the annual NFL draft for the Vikings?

25) From the rosters of what university have the Vikings made the most first round draft selections?

26) What All-Pro guard from the Seattle Seahawks signed a free-agent deal with the Vikings prior to the 2006 season?

27) Was current star defensive end Jared Allen a draft choice, a trade acquisition, or a free-agent signing?

28) In 2005, the Vikings received Oakland's first-round pick in exchange for the disgruntled Randy Moss. Who was this wide receiver out of South Carolina?

29) What Georgia kicker was a 6th round pick in the 2012 draft, the highest-ever for a kicker by Minnesota?

30) Who was the Vikings #1 pick in the 1965 draft, a swift receiver out of Notre Dame, who never played for the team?

31) What outstanding all-around athlete from UMD was the Vikings' sixth-round selection in the 1976 draft?

32) What Oklahoma running back was Minnesota's top choice in the 2007 draft and the seventh selection overall?

33) In 1976, the first two picks for the Vikings had the same last name. What was it?

34) Players from what Big Ten schools have been drafted in the first round by the Vikings?

35) A native of tiny Mount Vernon, South Dakota, what Iowa linebacker became the Vikings top choice in the 2006 draft?

36) In the 1993 draft, what dynamic running back did the Vikings pick from Ohio State University?

37) A third-round choice from Minnesota in 1972, what offensive tackle from Mounds View High School competed in football, hockey, and track with the Gophers?

38) What Miami runner brought an immediate spark to the Vikings running and passing game when he was Minnesota's top pick in 1973?

39) What Marshall wide receiver finished fourth in the Heisman voting in 1997 but fell to the 21st overall pick in the first round in 1998?

40) One of the better late-round Viking picks, what Cretin-Derham Hall product became an outstanding center for his home state team after being nabbed in the 6th round in 1998?

41) What three players from Oklahoma State have been top draft picks of the Vikings?

42) Jeff Siemon (1972) and Darrin Nelson (1982), who were both number one Viking picks, both played at what Pac 10 school?

43) In one of the most exciting days in Viking history (August 18, 2009), what retired NFL legend signed a free-agent contract with

the club and went on to have the best statistical season of his illustrious career?

44) Who is the only Heisman Trophy winner to be drafted by Minnesota?

45) What Stanford wide receiver and punt and kick returner was a fifth-round selection in 2000, thus joining a team where his father, Trent, was already employed as an assistant coach?

46) A future giant in coaching circles, what offensive and defensive tackle from Nebraska was a 15th-round draft pick for Minnesota in 1965?

47) He never played for the Vikings but what Tulsa wide receiver was a 14th-round pick in 1966 after setting several NCAA receiving marks as a collegian?

48) What tight end from California was the Vikings eighth-round selection in 1967 and a vital member of the offense for seven seasons? (He later was working a college football broadcast that featured perhaps the most bizarre play in gridiron history.)

49) The Vikings first choice in the 1966 draft and the seventh overall, what Purdue defensive tackle turned out to be a major disappointment, playing in only 15 games for the Vikings?

50) In 2000, the Vikings were able to select the winner of the Jim Thorpe Trophy, which is given to the best defensive back in the nation. Who was this Gopher great?

51) Who was the most recent player to be drafted from the Minnesota Gophers?

52) Their first-rounder in 2004, what defensive end from Southern California had a promising future cut short when he was diagnosed with acute lymphoblastic leukemia prior to the 2008 season?

53) In what year's NFL draft did the Vikings actually have to move down two positions in the draft because they didn't make their selection in the time allotted?

54) In 1982, the Vikings drafted a linebacker from Minnesota out of St. Cloud. He never made the team but later played seven years

for the San Francisco 49ers and competed in three Super Bowls. Who was this player, who played with his older brother Keith with the 49ers, an offensive tackle who also starred for the Gophers?

55) Drafted in the top two rounds in 1974, what linebackers from UCLA and Iowa State started on defense for the Vikings together for eight years and were roommates at training camp and road trips for 12 seasons?

56) In what magical year did the Vikings have the foresight and the privilege to select the following individuals to compete for Minnesota: Clinton Jones, Gene Washington, Alan Page, Bob Grim, Bobby Bryant, and John Beasley?

57) Of the 20 players they picked in their first NFL draft before the 1961 season, how many actually played a game for the Vikings?

58) Perhaps one of the best late-round draft picks for the Vikings, what quarterback was taken in the eighth round from East Texas State and played 11 years for Minnesota?

59) Who was the Vikings sixth-round choice in 1979, a football and basketball star out of West Chester State who became one of their best tight ends?

60) In 1967, the Vikings had two of the top eight picks in the draft as part of the trade of Fran Tarkenton to the New York Giants. Which two Michigan State teammates did they select?

61) The Vikings top choice (19th overall) in the 1983 draft turned out to be probably the most athletic defensive back in their history. Who was he?

62) What North Carolina State runner was Minnesota's top pick in the 1979 draft and established himself as a fine all-around player for the next eight years?

63) What North Dakota farm boy, a second-round selection in 1999, proved his mettle on every play of his 13-year career with the Vikings?

64) What Owatonna star athlete, who lettered in football, hockey, and baseball at the U of M, was a 12th-round pick in 1969 and played 14 games as a linebacker in 1971?

65) Perhaps the most versatile and athletic offensive guard in NFL history, what Arizona State stud was nabbed in the first round by Minnesota in 1988?

66) What future Hall of Fame quarterback joined the Vikings in a trade with the Houston Oilers on April 14, 1994?

67) A 6'5", 335-pound offensive tackle with great quickness, what Ohio State Buckeye was the team's first-round pick in the 1995 draft and started 100 games from 1995-2000?

68) In a franchise-changing move on draft day in 1967, the Vikings traded halfback Tommy Mason and tight end Hal Bedsole for tight end Marlin McKeever and the rights to the 15th overall pick in the first round. Who did the Vikings select with that choice?

69) A huge man (6'8", 335 pounds) playing at Miami of Florida, who was the team's first pick in 2002 as a left tackle?

70) On Jan. 28, 1972, the Vikings re-acquired quarterback Fran Tarkenton from the New York Giants in exchange for what players?

71) How many times has a punter been drafted by the Vikings?

72) What quarterback from Alabama State, a second-rounder in 2006, was a surprising pick by the Vikings and became a part-time starter over the next four seasons?

73) What draft year ranks as the worst in Vikings history as none of the picks were with the team just five years later?

74) A defensive tackle from Oklahoma State, who was the first-rounder in 2003 who became a five-time first-team All-Pro and is still a dominant force on the defensive line?

75) A Brett Favre-baiter, what defensive tackle from Boston College was the Minnesota first-rounder in 2000 and was noted for his face-painting and intensity?

76) Tight end Marlin McKeever and a seventh-round pick in the 1969 draft were sent to Washington in a trade prior to the 1968 season that brought the Vikings what future Hall of Fame defender?

77) In a big trade following the 1972 season, quarterback Bob Lee and linebacker Lonnie Warwick were traded to Atlanta for quarterback Bob Berry and a first-round pick in the 1974 draft. Who did the Vikings pick?

78) In what two years did the Vikings have three picks in the first round?

79) Who are the only four defensive backs to be drafted by the Vikings in the first round?

80) Of the 10 players drafted in 2012, how many were on the active roster in their rookie year?

81) In what three seasons did only two of the drafted players earn a roster spot?

82) What were the real first and middle names of 1987 first-round draft choice (14th overall) D. J. Dozier?

83) What Green Bay Packer receiver was signed to a five-year, $47.5 million free agent contract on March 15, 2013?

84) After Percy Harvin was traded to Seattle in March of 2013 for three draft picks, who did the Vikings draft with the 25th overall pick in the first round?

85) In which consecutive draft years did the Vikings select three pairs of college teammates?

1) Tommy Mason, a shifty halfback from Tulane University in New Orleans. The 1961 draft class was actually selected on Dec. 20, 1960.

2) Dave Winfield. The St. Paul Central product was a star in both baseball and basketball at the "U" but never played football for the Gophers. However, out of tribute to his skills, the home town team tabbed him as a possible tight end, though everybody knew he was headed for a big-league baseball career. A star for San Diego, he eventually was enshrined into the Baseball Hall of Fame. He remains the only athlete to be drafted by four professional sports teams - San Diego Padres (MLB), Atlanta Hawks (NBA), Utah Stars (ABA), and Minnesota Vikings (NFL).

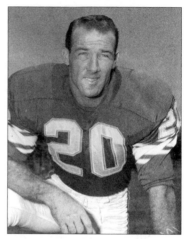

Tommy Mason.

3) 20

4) Running back (10 times). Linebacker and defensive ends have both been chosen first on eight occasions and defensive tackle and wide receiver six times each.

5) Carl Eller, a future Hall of Famer who was the sixth overall pick in 1964. The defensive end played 15 seasons and in 209 games for the Vikings.

6) 608

7) Tommy Kramer (Rice, 27th round, 1977); Daunte Culpepper (Central Florida, 11th round, 1999), and Christian Ponder (Florida State, 12th overall, 2011).

8) Fran Tarkenton. General Manager Jim Finks traded the disgruntled quarterback in exchange for four draft choices (first-round in 1967 and 1968 and second-round in 1967 and 1969).

Those picks turned out to be Clinton Jones and Bob Grim in 1967, Ron Yary in 1968, and Ed White in 1969.

9) Nine (1962, 1969, 1981, 1989, 1990, 1991, 1992, 2008, 2010)

10) Bobby Bell, an All-American linebacker, who was the team's second-round pick (16th overall) in the 1962 draft. Bell never played for the Vikings, instead signing with the AFL Kansas City Chiefs. He was outstanding for the Chiefs as one of its best-ever players and is enshrined in the Pro Football Hall of Fame.

11) Matt Birk (Harvard, offensive tackle, sixth round, 1998); Steve Jordan (Brown, tight end, seventh round, 1982); Ed Marinaro (Cornell, running back, second round, 1972); Brian Dowling (Yale, quarterback, 11th round, 1969); and Cosmo Iacavazzi (Princeton, running back, 20th round, 1965).

12) Herschel Walker. The former Georgia great and Heisman Trophy winner was acquired for defensive back Isaac Holt, linebacker David Howard, running back Darrin Nelson, and linebacker Alex Stewart. Also, included were the following draft choices: a 1st-round choice in 1992, conditional first-round choices in 1990 and 1991, conditional 2nd-round choices in 1990, 1991, and 1992, and a conditional 3rd-round choice in 1992. Meanwhile, the Vikings got Walker, a 3rd-rounder (Mike Jones), a 5th-round choice (Reggie Thornton) and a 10th-round choice (Pat Newman) in 1990 and a 3rd-round choice (Jake Reed). The final results for Dallas netted a 1st, 2nd, and 6th round choice in 1990, a 1st and 2nd-round choice in 1991 and a 1st, 2nd, and 3rd-round choice in 1992.

13) John Randle (Texas A and M - Kingsville). The 6'1", 287-pound defensive end had a tryout with Tampa Bay before being acquired by the Vikings during training camp in 1990. Randle became a seven-time Pro Bowler and recorded 137.5 sacks and was Brett Favre's main tormentor.

14) Oakland. Moss, with questionable effort, struggled somewhat with the Raiders. He caught 102 passes for 1,558 yards and 11 touchdowns in his two seasons with Oakland while battling injuries and still exhibiting the petulant behavior that has led to several unhappy endings.

15) Leo Hayden, the 24th overall choice, who was on the roster in 1971 but never carried the ball for the team.

16) 19, including two each in both 1963 and 1964.

17) Dave Osborn. "Ozzie", from Cando, North Dakota, played 11 seasons with the Vikings and rushed for 4,320 yards (sixth all-time) and 29 touchdowns.

18) Seven; six primarily played for the Vikings: Fran Tarkenton (3rd pick, 1961); Carl Eller (1st pick, 1964); Alan Page (3rd pick in first round, 1967); Ron Yary (1st pick, 1968), Chris Doleman (1st round, 1985); Randall McDaniel (1st pick, 1988). Plus, Bobby Bell, the second pick in the 1963 draft, never signed with the Vikings but had a Hall of Fame career with the Kansas City Chiefs.

19) In 1968, the Vikings selected USC tackle Ron Yary with the top pick. Yary didn't disappoint, playing 14 years (1968-81) for the team, earning Hall of Fame status in 2001.

20) 1963. Jim Dunaway, a defensive tackle from Mississippi State and their top pick, signed with the Buffalo Bills. Bobby Bell, the Outland Trophy winner from the Gophers who had played defensive tackle but was projected as a linebacker, was their choice in the second round but he signed with the Kansas City Chiefs. The NFL and the upstart AFL were at war over signing players in that era.

21) John Hankinson

22) Seven. In 1993, the draft was eight rounds after being a 12-round draft from 1977-1992.

23) Tom Munsey, a running back from Concordia and Tom McIntyre, an offensive tackle from St. John's. Neither made the roster, however.

24) Rick Spielman is the General Manager, George Paton is the Assistant General Manager, and Scott Studwell is the Director of College Scouting.

25) University of Southern California (1968, 1983, 2004, 2012).

26) Steve Hutchinson. The two-time All-American at Michigan played six years for the Vikings, earning Pro Bowl status each of his first four years. The contract was for seven years for $49 million, the largest ever for an offensive lineman.

27) Trade. Allen was traded from Kansas City prior to the 2008 draft for Minnesota's first-rounder and two third-round choices.

28) Troy Williamson, whose tenure with Minnesota was disappointing as he had trouble catching the ball, sort of a prerequisite for being a receiver. Williamson played three years with the Vikings, started 22 games, caught 79 balls for 1,067 yards and scored three touchdowns before being traded for a 6th-round pick to Jacksonville.

29) Blair Walsh. The Vikings have only drafted six kickers in 52 years. Walsh was the first kicker drafted since Mike Wood in the eighth round in 1978.

30) Jack Snow, who didn't want to play in the snow. A California native, he had no desire to play on the northern tundra and made it clear he wouldn't play in Minnesota. He was traded to Los Angeles and was a standout for 11 years with the Rams. His son, J.T. later played major-league baseball.

31) Terry Egerdahl, a wide-receiver and defensive back. Egerdahl was a three-sport star at Proctor High before attending nearby UMD, where he was all-conference in both baseball and football. In his career playing for the legendary Jim Malosky, Egerdahl played quarterback, running back, wide receiver, kicker, punter, and punt returner and was Little All-American first-team in 1975. He died of a heart attack at age 27 in Duluth.

32) Adrian Peterson

33) White. James White, a defensive tackle from Oklahoma State, in the first round and Sammy White, a wide receiver from Grambling, in the second round.

34) Michigan State (2), Ohio State (2), Wisconsin (2), Minnesota (1), Purdue (1), Iowa (1).

35) Chad Greenway, who has been the team's top tackler since 2008.

36) Robert Smith, who became the team's leading career rusher with 6,818 yards (since broken by Adrian Peterson early in 2012).

37) Bart Buetow, whose twin brother Brad also competed in all three sports for the Gophers. Bart played two games for the Vikings in 1976 after playing part-time for the Giants in 1973. Brad later became coach of the Gopher hockey team.

38) Chuck Foreman, who became a five-time Pro Bowler, and is still entrenched as the most versatile running back in Viking history.

39) Randy Moss, who was bypassed for the standard "character" issues.

40) Matt Birk, who was a standout at Harvard. Birk played 11 years with the Vikings and was a Pro-Bowler six times at center.

41) John Ward (offensive tackle, 1970); James White (defensive tackle, 1976), and Kevin Williams (defensive tackle, 2003).

42) Stanford

43) Brett Favre, who threw for 4,202 yards, 33 touchdowns and just seven interceptions with a 107.2 quarterback rating. Favre led his former arch-rivals to a 12-4 regular-season mark and nearly led them to the Super Bowl.

44) Gino Torretta, the seventh-round pick in 1993. Torretta won the Heisman in 1992 after quarterbacking the Miami Hurricanes. Torretta was on the roster for one game in 1993 but never threw a pass for the Vikings. His only NFL action came in 1996, when he played in one game for Seattle (5-16 for 41 yards, one touchdown, and one interception).

45) Troy Walters, whose father coached linebackers from 1994-2001.

46) Monte Kiffin, who would later be an assistant coach and defensive coordinator with the Vikings and would go on to establish himself as one of the top defensive gurus in NFL history and the impetus behind the so-called "Cover 2" defense.

47) Howard Twilley, who was the Heisman runner-up to Steve Spurrier. Twilley was a 12th round pick of the AFL Miami Dolphins, played nine years for the Dolphins and competed in three Super Bowls.

48) John Beasley, who as a color commentator on the USA broadcast, was involved in The Play, the amazing ending to the California-Stanford game in 1982. That was the play, of course, when several laterals turned a kickoff return into a 25-20 "Cal" win over John Elway's club. Barry Tompkins did the play-by-play.

49) Jerry Shay, who started two games in 1966 and one in 1967.

50) Tyrone Carter. The Florida native played two years for the Vikings and later won a Super Bowl with Pittsburgh.

51) Nate Triplett, a linebacker, in the fifth round in 2010.

52) Kenechi Udeze, whose last season was 2007.

53) 2003. The Vikings were set to draft seventh but confusion reigned in their draft room as they attempted to trade down. Jacksonville and Carolina selected ahead of them, taking Byron Leftwich (quarterback from Marshall) and Jordan Gross (offensive tackle from Utah) with Viking fans alarmed over the stupendous oversight. While Minnesota was becoming the laughing stock of the league, they managed to get the last laugh (eventually) as their eventual selection of Oklahoma State defensive tackle Kevin Williams turned out to be one of the league's best defensive linemen over the next decade. In 2002, the Vikings were also castigated for not being ready when it came time for the sixth overall pick. Kansas City swooped in and took Ryan Sims, a highly-touted defensive tackle from North Carolina. Minnesota then nabbed Miami offensive tackle Bryant McKinnie with the seventh choice. Again, they lucked out as McKinnie was a key starter in their line for years while Sims underperformed.

54) Jim Fahnhorst. He was a fourth-round pick in 1982 but was cut from the Vikings and signed with the 49ers and played 82 games. Brother Keith, six years older, started for 10 years in a 14-year career with San Francisco and was a first-team All-Pro in 1984. The Fahnhorst boys played four years together on the West coast.

55) Fred McNeill (UCLA, first round) and Matt Blair (Iowa State, second round) started at linebacker together from 1977-1984.

56) 1967

57) 10, including their top five picks—Tommy Mason, Rip Hawkins, Fran Tarkenton, Chuck Lamson, and Ed Sharockman. Of course, many of the roster spots were filled with players selected in the expansion draft.

58) Wade Wilson, who ended up playing 17 years in the NFL. Wilson started 48 times for the Vikings and had a 27-21 record. He threw 66 touchdown passes in his 76-game career here.

59) Joe Senser, whose promising career was cut short by a knee injury after an outstanding season in 1981, when he caught 79 balls and made the Pro Bowl.

60) Running back Clinton Jones (second overall) and wide receiver Gene Washington (eighth overall).

61) Joey Browner, a four-time All-American from USC, who became a six-time Pro-Bowler.

62) Ted Brown, who rushed for 4,546 yards and had 339 receptions and 53 touchdowns as a durable and dependable back.

63) Jim Kleinsasser, one of the most powerful and effective blockers in team history.

64) Noel Jenke, who reached AAA in baseball. Jenke later played for Atlanta and Green Bay.

65) Randall McDaniel, the quiet and unassuming leader of the Viking line from 1988-99.

66) Warren Moon, who was the Vikings starter from 1994-96. Houston received two draft picks (4th-rounder in 1994 and 3rd-rounder in 1995) in return.

67) Korey Stringer, who earned a Pro Bowl nod in 2000.

68) Alan Page, who only turned out to be one of the most devastating defensive linemen in NFL history.

69) Bryant McKinnie, who was eighth in the Heisman voting as an offensive lineman and the winner of the Outland Trophy, emblematic of the top lineman in the nation.

70) Quarterback Norm Snead, quarterback Vinnie Clements, and receiver Bob Grim. The Vikings also gave the Giants their first-round draft picks in 1972 and 1973.

71) Six times. The highest draft pick used on a punter came in the 2013 draft when the Vikings tabbed Jeff Locke of UCLA in the fifth round.

72) Tarvaris Jackson, who was 10-10 as a starter with 24 touchdown passes.

73) 2005; Troy Williamson (2005-07), Erasmus James (2005-07), Marcus Johnson (2005-08), Ciatrick Fason (2005-06), C.J. Mosley (2005). Dustin Fox and Adrian Ward never made the team.

74) Kevin Williams, who was one of five active Vikings to make the "50 Greatest Vikings" list in 2010.

75) Chris Hovan, who started 70 games from 2000-2004.

76) Paul Krause, who went on to pick off 53 passes as the ultimate "centerfielder" in Bud Grant's defense from 1968-79.

77) Fred McNeill

78) 1967 and 2013. In 1967, the Vikings drafted running back Clinton Jones from Michigan State second, receiver Gene Washington from Michigan State eighth, and defensive tackle Alan Page from Notre Dame 15th. In 2013, Florida defensive tackle Sharrif Floyd was the 23rd pick, cornerback Xavier Rhodes of Florida State was 25th, and receiver Cordarrelle Patterson of Tennessee was 29th overall.

79) Joey Browner (1983), Dewayne Washington (1994), Harrison Smith (2012) and Xavier Rhodes (2013).

80) Nine (Matt Kalil, Harrison Smith, Josh Robinson, Jarius Wright, Rhett Ellison, Robert Blanton, Blair Walsh, Audie Cole, Trevor Guyton). Only wide receiver Greg Childs wasn't on the active roster, having torn patellar tendons in both knees making a catch in a training camp scrimmage.

81) 1969 (Ed White - 2nd and Noel Jenke - 12th); 1971 (Leo Hayden - 1st and Jeff Wright - 15th), and 1989 (David Braxton - 2nd and Darryl Ingram - 4th).

82) William Henry. The Penn State running back played four underwhelming years for the Vikings and rushed for 643 yards and seven touchdowns as a reserve.

83) Greg Jennings. The former Western Illinois star had 425 catches for 6,537 yards and 53 touchdowns with the Pack from 2006-12.

84) Xavier Rhodes, a cornerback from Florida State.

85) 2012 and 2013. In 2012, the Vikes took teammates from USC (Matt Kalil and Rhett Ellison), Notre Dame (Harrison Smith and Robert Blanton), and Arkansas (Jarius Wright and Greg Childs. In 2013, Minnesota tabbed Jeff Locke and Jeff Baca from USC, Xavier Rhodes and Everett Dawkins from Florida State, and Gerald Hughes and Michael Mauti from Penn State.

13 Uniform Numbers

The following list includes most of the greatest players in Vikings history. Most of the numbers have been worn by several players, though only one player has worn #70 and only two have worn #10. Some numbers have been worn by a string of obscure bench-warmers, while others have been worn by six or seven stars, in which case I have selected the best of the lot to include. Please mark the uniform number worn by each player through all or most of his career with the team. Mark the numbers/names that are now retired by the Vikings with an asterisk.

___ Fran Tarkenton	___ Alan Page	___ Bill Brown
___ Carl Eller	___ Jim Marshall	___ Paul Krause
___ Mick Tingelhoff	___ Tommy Mason	___ Grady Alderman
___ Dave Osborn	___ Fred Cox	___ Wally Hilgenberg
___ Gary Larsen	___ Roy Winston	___ Matt Blair
___ Bobby Bryant	___ Ed Sharockman	___ John Gilliam
___ Gene Washington	___ Clint Jones	___ Karl Kassulke
___ Ed White	___ Nate Wright	___ Rip Hawkins
___ Milt Sunde	___ Doug Sutherland	___ Chuck Foreman
___ Jeff Wright	___ Stu Voigt	___ Ron Yary
___ Sammy White	___ Joe Senser	___ Jeff Siemon
___ Tommy Kramer	___ Rickey Young	___ Ahmad Rashad
___ Anthony Carter	___ Joey Browner	___ Carl Lee

___ Steve Jordan	___ Mike Merriweather	___ Joe Kapp
___ Wade Wilson	___ Fred McNeill	___ Chris Doleman
___ Bob Grim	___ John Beasley	___ Ted Brown
___ Keith Millard	___ Scott Studwell	___ Henry Thomas
___ Doug Martin	___ Terry Allen	___ Greg Coleman
___ Darrin Nelson	___ Herschel Walker	___ Randall McDaniel
___ Cris Carter	___ Gary Zimmerman	___ Tim Irwin
___ Brad Johnson	___ Dwayne Rudd	___ Paul Flately
___ David Palmer	___ Mitch Berger	___ Jake Reed
___ Robert Griffith	___ Korey Stringer	___ Michael Bennett
___ Matt Birk	___ Todd Steussie	___ Jack Del Rio
___ Randall Cunningham	___ Jeff Christy	___ Todd Scott
___ Warren Moon	___ Fuad Reveiz	___ John Randle
___ Randy Moss	___ Robert Smith	___ Gary Anderson
___ Duante Culpepper	___ Pat Williams	___ Percy Harvin
___ Adrian Peterson	___ Steve Hutchinson	___ Antoine Winfield
___ Brett Favre	___ Darren Sharper	___ Bryant McKinnie
___ Jared Allen	___ Kevin Williams	___ Ryan Longwell
___ Chris Kluwe	___ Chad Greenway	___ Orlando Thomas
___ Hassan Jones	___ Jim Kleinsasser	___ Alfred Anderson
___ Oscar Reed	___ David Dixon	___ Steve Riley
___ Ed McDaniel	___ Rich Gannon	___ Dale Hackbart
___ Bob Lurtsema	___ Mark Mullaney	___ Ben Leber
___ Chester Taylor	___ Moe Williams	___ Leo Lewis
___ Harry Newsome	___ James White	___ Brent Boyd
___ Gary Cuozzo	___ Jerry Ball	___ Earsell Mackbee
___ Ray Edwards	___ Charles Goodrum	___ Jim Vellone
___ Jan Stenerud	___ Bob Lee	___ Nate Allen
___ Reggie Rutland	___ Al Noga	___ Dennis Swilley

___ Kirk Lowderwilk	___ Keith Nord	___ Willie Teal
___ Lonnie Warwick	___ Paul Dickson	___ Derrick Alexander
___ Larry Bowie	___ Qadry Ismail	___ Scottie Graham
___ Leroy Hoard	___ Wes Hamilton	___ Sidney Rice
___ Mike Morris	___ Dennis Johnson	___ Brent McClanahan
___ Jim Prestel	___ Jerry Reichow	___ Brian Robison
___ Darren Bennett	___ Bucky Scribner	___ Mewelde Moore
___ Tony Galbreath	___ Terry Tausch	___ Robert Miller
___ Allen Rice	___ Phil Loadholt	___ Hugh McElhenny
___ Ed Marinaro	___ Duane Clemons	___ Esera Tuaolo
___ Tim Newton	___ Darrion Scott	___ Chris Hovan
___ E. J. Henderson	___ Rick Fenney	___ Bubby Brister
___ Jim Hough	___ Jesse Solomon	___ John Henderson
___ Jim Lash	___ John Turner	___ Isaac Holt
___ Lance Rentzel	___ Terry Brown	___ Jimmy Hitchcock
___ Roger Craig	___ Vencie Glenn	___ Bob Berry
___ John Ward	___ Bob Tucker	___ Charlie West
___ Fernando Smith	___ Gerald Robinson	___ Derrick L. Alexander
___ Tommy Hannon	___ Sammy Johnson	___ Andrew Jordan
___ Buster Rhymes	___ John Kirby	___ Adam Schreiber
___ Teddy Garcia	___ Blair Walsh	___ Erin Henderson
___ Kyle Rudolph	___ Archie Manning	___ Donovan McNabb
___ Neil Clabo	___ Mike Mularkey	___ Jim McMahon
___ Norm Snead	___ Neal Guggemos	___ Everson Griffen
___ Tony Williams	___ Phil King	___ Jim Gallery
___ Artie Ulmer	___ Brian Habib	___ Greg Manusky
___ Tim Baylor	___ Ken Byers	___ John Sullivan
___ Marcus Sherels	___ Steve Bono	___ Fred Evans

Many players wore more than one number during their tenure with the Vikings but the list below cites the player wearing the number he wore for most of his career. The asterisk appears in front of those players whose number was retired due to his outstanding play while wearing it.

1 - Gary Anderson, Warren Moon
2 - Darren Bennett, Teddy Garcia
3 - Jan Stenerud, Blair Walsh
4 - Brett Favre, Archie Manning
5 - Chris Kluwe, Donovan McNabb
6 - Bubby Brister, Jim Gallery
7 - Randall Cunningham, Fuad Reveiz
8 - Greg Coleman, Ryan Longwell
9 - Tommy Kramer, Jim McMahon
10 - *Fran Tarkenton, Phil King
11 - Wade Wilson, Duante Culpepper, Joe Kapp
12 - Percy Harvin, Neil Clabo
13 - Bucky Scribner, Steve Bono
14 - Fred Cox, Brad Johnson
15 - Gary Cuozzo, Ron VanderKelen
16 - Rich Gannon, Norm Snead
17 - Mitch Berger, Bob Berry
18 - Harry Newsome, Sidney Rice
19 - Bob Lee, Lance Rentzel
20 - Bobby Bryant, Tommy Mason, Darrin Nelson
21 - Terry Allen, Moe Williams
22 - Paul Krause, David Palmer
23 - Michael Bennett, Ted Brown, Jeff Wright
24 - Robert Griffith, Terry Brown
25 - Nate Allen, Vencie Glenn
26 - Robert Smith, Antoine Winfield, Clinton Jones
27 - Bob Grim, John Turner
28 - Adrian Peterson, Ahmad Rashad

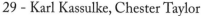

29 - Karl Kassulke, Chester Taylor

30 - Bill Brown, Mewelde Moore, Isaac Holt

31 - Rick Fenney, Scottie Graham

32 - Oscar Reed, Tony Galbreath

33 - Brent McClanahan, Roger Craig

34 - Herschel Walker, Rickey Young

35 - Robert Miller, Marcus Sherels

36 - Allen Rice, John Kirby

37 - Willie Teal, Jimmy Hitchcock

38 - Todd Scott, Bob Tucker

39 - Carl Lee, Hugh McElhenny

40 - Jim Kleinsasser, Charlie West

41 - Dave Osborn, Neal Guggemos

42 - John Gilliam, Darren Sharper

43 - Nate Wright, Orlando Thomas

44 - Chuck Foreman, Leroy Hoard

45 - Ed Sharockman, Tommy Hannon

46 - Alfred Anderson, Earsell Mackbee

47 - Joey Browner, Tim Baylor

48 - Reggie Rutland, Sammy Johnson

49 - Dale Hackbart, Keith Nord, Ed Marinaro

50 - Jeff Siemon, Erin Henderson

51 - Ben Leber, Jim Hough

52 - Chad Greenway, Dennis Johnson

53 - *Mick Tingelhoff, Artie Ulmer

54 - Fred McNeill, Jesse Solomon

55 - Scott Studwell, Jack Del Rio

56 - Chris Doleman, E.J. Henderson

57 - Dwayne Ruud, Mike Merriweather

58 - Wally Hilgenberg, Ed McDaniel, Rip Hawkins

59 - Matt Blair, Lonnie Warwick

60 - Roy Winston, Adam Schreiber

61 - Larry Bowie, Wes Hamilton

62 - Ed White, Brent Boyd, Jeff Christy

63 - Jim Vellone, Kirk Lowderwilk

64 - Randall McDaniel, Milt Sunde

65 - Gary Zimmerman, John Sullivan

66 - Terry Tausch, Ken Byers

67 - Grady Alderman, Dennis Swilley

68 - Charles Goodrum, Mike Morris

69 - Doug Sutherland, Jared Allen

70 - *Jim Marshall (only player to wear)

71 - David Dixon, Phil Loadholt

72 - James White, John Ward

73 - Ron Yary, Todd Steussie

74 - Bryant McKinnie, Brian Habib

75 - Bob Lurtsema, Keith Millard

76 - Tim Irwin, Steve Hutchinson, Paul Dickson

77 - *Korey Stringer, Mark Mullaney, Gary Larsen

78 - Matt Birk, Steve Riley

79 - Doug Martin, Jim Prestel

80 - *Cris Carter, John Henderson

81 - Carl Eller, Anthony Carter, Joe Senser

82 - Qadry Ismail, Jim Lash, Kyle Rudolph

83 - Steve Jordan, Stu Voigt

84 - Randy Moss, Gene Washington, Hassan Jones

85 - Sammy White, Paul Flately

86 - Jake Reed, Mike Mularkey

87 - John Beasley, Leo Lewis

88 - *Alan Page, Buster Rhymes

89 - Jerry Reichow, Andrew Jordan

90 - Derrick L. Alexander, Fred Evans

91 - Ray Edwards, Greg Manusky

92 - Duane Clemons, Ray Barker

93 - John Randle, Kevin Williams

94 - Pat Williams, Tony Williams

95 - Fernando Smith, Gerald Robinson

96 - Jerry Ball, Tim Newton, Brian Robison

97 - Henry Thomas, Everson Griffen

98 - Darrion Scott, Esera Tuaolo

99 - Al Noga, Chris Hovan

Note: Orlando Thomas wore both 42 (1997-98) and 43 (1995-96).

14 Infamous Happenings, Unusual Incidents

1) No doubt one of the most dynamic athletes in Viking history, what controversial player became infamous for the following line: "I play when I want to play."?

2) In one of the strangest off-the-field incidents in team history, what running back was arrested at the Minneapolis-St. Paul airport on April 21, 2004 in possession of a fake penis referred to as "The Original Whizzinator"?

3) What immensely talented defensive lineman once got into trouble at a Bloomington hotel and when detained by police, stated "Go ahead and shoot because my arms are more powerful than your guns"?

4) What is the name of the leadership training facility in New Mexico where Vikings general manager Mike Lynn sent the Vikings for a mini-camp in May of 1990?

5) What Viking employee was embarrassed and later fined by the NFL for selling his Super Bowl tickets for profit?

6) What term was coined to describe the scurrilous antics of some Vikings players on board two party boats on Lake Minnetonka on October 6, 2005?

7) What Viking kick returner/wide receiver was arrested for DWI after the 2006 pre-season opener at the Metrodome and never played again for the team, despite being a Pro Bowler the previous season?

8) In one of the most notorious non-plays in Viking history, quarterback Randall Cunningham faced a third-and-three situation at the Viking 27 with 30 seconds remaining in the NFC championship game at the Metrodome on Jan. 17, 1999. Instead of attempting to get a first down, Cunningham knelt down and let the clock run out. What name have fans given to this event?

9) What Viking defensive back was suspended for most of the 2011 season when he was charged with domestic assault?

10) What was the name of the backfield official (field judge) who was struck in the back of the head with a whiskey bottle hurled on the field following Drew Pearson's 50-yard game-winning catch in the 1975 NFC divisional playoff game at Met Stadium?

11) What Viking head coach wrote a book titled *No Room for Crybabies*, in which he threatened to sue members of the ten-member ownership group for trying to replace him with Lou Holtz?

12) What Viking executive provided some chuckles when he showed up at a training camp in the 1990's wearing coaching shorts and bearing a whistle?

13) What 29th overall draft choice (second in the first round after Daunte Culpepper) left training camp after the first morning practice in 1999 and never played for the Vikings?

14) What Viking wide receiver received some bad publicity after his boorish comments regarding the food prepared by Tinucci's Restaurant and Catering of Newport at the team's training facilities in Eden Prairie in 2010?

15) Between 1986 and 1990, how many Viking players were arrested for DWI or chemical abuse?

16) What man, one of the key organizers of the American Football League in 1959, had secured a franchise in the fledgling new league for the 1960 season for the Twin Cities but later dumped the AFL when the NFL offered the area a franchise in January of 1960?

17) What Viking player, an established NFL icon, was accused of sexual impropriety in 2010 when it was revealed he had texted photos of his genitalia to New York Jets on-air personality Jenn Sterger

when he played for the team in 2008?

18) What Viking defensive back faced some negative publicity when he was caught having sex with a woman in the stairwell outside Minneapolis nightclub in August of 2006?

19) In the last game of the 2004 regular season, at Washington, what player walked off the field with time still remaining on the clock, angering teammates, Viking officials, and Minnesota fans?

20) What four Viking players were charged with crimes associated with the Love Boat incident on Lake Minnetonka in 2005?

21) What player pulled off what a Fox announcer called a "disgusting" act when he fake-mooned the partisan Green Bay crowd at Lambeau Field in a playoff upset of the Packers on Jan. 9, 2005?

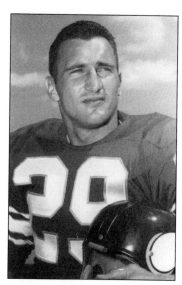

Karl Kassulke

22) What former Green Bay cornerback and Texas All-American did Mike Lynn sign in the midst of the 1988 season before a public outcry over his criminal past led to his release before he ever played for Minnesota?

23) What Viking quarterback dealt with some serious chemical dependency issues while playing for the team in the 1980's?

24) Prior to the 2002 season, what name was used to describe head coach Mike Tice's announced plan to throw at least 40 percent of the team's passes to #84?

25) In February of 2003, what charitable fundraising affair at Lake Mille Lacs became an embarrassment for the Vikings when allegations of sexual assault were levied against some current and former Viking players and officials?

26) On Dec. 6, 1964, at Yankee Stadium in New York, what Viking

offensive guard started a bonfire behind the team's bench that eventually ignited him?

27) What Viking rookie was embarrassed when he lost the ball short of the goal line after catching what appeared to be a sure touchdown pass from Fran Tarkenton in a game against Detroit at the Met in 1976?

28) By the late 1970's, what Viking official was calling Metropolitan Stadium "a piece of crap"?

29) What starting Viking defender in the 1980's once had his helmet start on fire as it was being warmed on the sideline at Cleveland's Municipal Stadium?

30) On Sept. 26, 1976, the late-arriving Vikings caused a 40-minute start delay to a nationally televised game against what NFL team?

31) What chief field usher at Met Stadium (the current public-address announcer for Gopher basketball and baseball games), gave a swift kick to Dallas receiver Drew Pearson during the infamous "Hail Mary" playoff game that ended the 1975 season?

32) At the first training camp, what three Viking players had to undergo a 90-minute "special" practice on the final morning of camp at the behest of coach Norm Van Brocklin after missing curfew the night before?

1) Randy Moss. The Marshall flash uttered this unfortunate quote moments after leading Minnesota to a 28-16 win over the New York Giants at the Metrodome on Nov. 19, 2001. He had just caught 10 passes for 171 yards and three touchdowns on a night when Korey Stringer's jersey was retired.

2) Onterrio Smith. The Oregon product, a fourth-round pick in 2003, was in possession of this product apparently because he was trying to beat urine tests administered by the NFL. Smith was trying to sneak it through security in a "carry-on" bag. Smith was suspended for the entire 2005 season because his arrest with the device was treated as a positive drug test.

3) Keith Millard

4) Pecos River Learning Center, located near Santa Fe, New Mexico. The event, billed as a team-bonding retreat, was supposed to build communication, teamwork and trust. Unfortunately, the team went 14-18 the next two seasons and missed the playoffs after averaging 10 wins the previous three seasons.

5) Head coach Mike Tice. As an assistant coach, he had purchased tickets from the players and sold them, splitting the profits with the players. After becoming the head coach, he used assistant coach Dean Dalton as a middle man but was caught by the league. At first, he denied selling the tickets but soon recanted and admitted his mistake. He was fined $100,000, a hefty figure for a guy making just $800,000 at the time.

6) Love Boat. The boats, rented from Al and Alma's Supper Club, left the docks and sailed into NFL football and maritime infamy.

7) Koren Robinson, who was a Pro Bowler in 2005 after averaging 26 yards a return. Robinson was clocked at 104 miles per hour in St. Peter and led the authorities on a 15-mile chase that ended at training headquarters at Mankato State. He had signed a three-year deal that stated that if he got into legal trouble, his contract would be null and void. The Vikings cut him and he later served 20 days in jail in 2007.

8) The Kneel-down or the Denn-Knee. Coach Denny Green took a lot of heat for that decision after the Vikings lost to Atlanta in overtime, preventing Minnesota's fifth Super Bowl appearance.

9) Chris Cook, who was later acquitted of the charge of striking and choking his partner.

10) Armen Terzian, who was struck at about the Vikings 10-yard line. While he went down and was momentarily unconscious, Terzian was bandaged and left the field for the final two plays (11 seconds). He later received 11 stitches. Following the Pearson touchdown, rage filled the field, both with the fans and Viking players. Alan Page was flagged for a 15-yard unsportsmanlike conduct penalty prior to the kickoff and shortly thereafter, Fran Tarkenton was sacked near the end zone. Terzian was reaching down to pick up a bottle when he was struck. With fools losing their heads in the disappointment, Chuck Foreman maintained some class and ran to the grandstands to urge the fans to stop their desultory actions.

11) Denny Green. In the book, which was published mid-season in 1997, he also included a copy of the lawsuit he might file.

12) Roger Headrick, the team's President and CEO.

13) Dimitrius Underwood. A defensive end from Michigan State, he hitchhiked back to the Twin Cities and flew east. The next day, he told the Vikings he wanted to return but the team wasn't interested. He was found six days later in a Philadelphia hotel. After being released by Minnesota, he later played briefly with Miami and Dallas after being diagnosed with a bipolar disorder.

14) Randy Moss, who told owner Gus Tinucci, "I wouldn't feed this food to my dog." Actually, the real account was a bit more vulgar. The food served, incidentally, was a buffet of beef, chicken, and ribs provided for the team's locker room.

15) 10

16) Max Winter. The AFL owners never forgot this slight and were overjoyed when Kansas City upset Winter's team in Super Bowl IV.

17) Brett Favre

18) Dwight Smith, a safety in 2006 and 2007 out of Akron.

19) Randy Moss. Matt Birk confronted Moss in the locker room to let him know about his displeasure with his actions at the end of the 21-18 loss to the Redskins.

20) Daunte Culpepper, Fred Smoot, Bryant McKinnie, and Moe

Herschel Walker (34) and Randall McDaniel (64).

Williams. Each faced misdemeanor charges for indecent conduct, disorderly conduct, and lewd and lascivious conduct. Smoot and McKinnie were found guilty and fined $2,000 and 48 hours of community service; Williams was dealt a $300 fine and 30 hours of community service. Culpepper's charges were dropped.

21) Randy Moss. After catching a 34-yard touchdown pass late in the fourth quarter to put the game away, Moss faked pulling his pants down against the goal-post as Minnesota beat Green Bay 31-17.

22) Mossy Cade, who had spent 15 months in jail after being found guilty of two second-degree sexual assaults in 1987.

23) Tommy Kramer, who kept the bartenders along the 494 strip busy with his liquid requests.

24) The Randy Ratio, in reference to wide-out Randy Moss. With Cris Carter gone from the team, Tice wanted to appease Moss and motivate him, and new offensive coordinator Scott Linehan tried to oblige. Tice later admitted that it was a bad idea because it tipped off opposing defenses. Moss caught 106 passes for 1,347 yards but his yardage per catch dipped to a career-low 12.7 yards and he had just seven touchdowns, the only time in his first seven-year stint with the team he didn't catch double-digit touchdowns.

25) The Arctic Blast, a snowmobile event.

26) Palmer Pyle. The Michigan State alumnus, attempting to ward off frostbite, built a tent out of warm-up coats before becoming a part of the flames in a 30-21 win by Minnesota.

27) Sammy White. The Grambling speedster raced down the field well ahead of the Lion defenders but when he reached the 10-yard line, he hoisted the ball well over his head in celebration. Suddenly, Lem Barney dove and tripped him up. White fumbled and Levi Johnson recovered for a touchback. White sauntered back to the sideline for a quick one-sided conversation with Bud Grant, who told him there was a difference between showbiz and showboating. Later in the game, White caught the clinching 36-yard touchdown to wrap up a truly spectacular day. He snatched seven passes in all for 210 yards in the 31-23 win over Detroit; the yardage total remains a Viking record.

28) General Manager Mike Lynn.

29) Doug Martin. The defensive tackle from Washington liked his size 8.5 helmet kept warm so he set it atop a big burner designed to keep the players warm behind the bench. Suddenly, flames emanated from the helmet. The fire was put out quickly and the equipment people struggled mightily to get it back into condition for play, as Martin had the largest helmet on the team and no other helmet would fit.

30) Detroit. The game, played at suburban Pontiac's Silverdome, was won by the Vikings 10-9. A massive traffic jam caused the delay.

Coach Bud Grant, who usually wanted his team to show up just an hour and 15 minutes before kickoff, wasn't alarmed but network and NFL officials were frantic and not pleased with the visitors.

31) Dick Jonckowski, who has a virtual sports memorabilia museum in his basement. Facing 4th and 16 from his own 25, Dallas quarterback Roger Staubach hit Pearson at the sideline but he landed out of bounds at the 50 after being hit by Viking cornerback Nate Wright. However, the officials ruled that he was forced out and the catch stood. Jonckowski, frustrated and disgusted, was just a few steps away and kicked toward Pearson and hit his shoe. Two plays later, Pearson made his controversial "Hail Mary" catch to give Dallas a stunning 17-14 win. Jonckowski, "The Polish Eagle", was noted for his behind-the-back passes to officials after returning field goal attempts and errant passes as he worked for Sims Security Services.

32) Bill Bishop (tackle), Charley Sumner (defensive back), and Ray Hayes (fullback). All three players missed the Saturday night curfew (11 p.m.) but were on the field at 8:00 a.m. the following morning. For two hours, Van Brocklin had the players roll down the entire field and back in full gear in the hot and humid August air.

Ed White in the trenches vs. Green Bay.

15 Top Vikings by Position

Quarterback
1) Fran Tarkenton
2) Tommy Kramer
3) Daunte Culpepper
4) Warren Moon

Running Back
1) Adrian Peterson
2) Chuck Foreman
3) Bill Brown
4) Robert Smith

Wide Receiver
1) Cris Carter
2) Randy Moss
3) Anthony Carter
4) Sammy White

Tight End
1) Steve Jordan
2) Stu Voigt
3) Visanthe Shiancoe
4) Joe Senser

Offensive Tackle
1) Ron Yary
2) Gary Zimmerman
3) Grady Alderman
4) Tim Irwin

Offensive Guard
1) Randall McDaniel
2) Ed White
3) Steve Hutchinson
4) Korey Stringer

Center
1) Mick Tingelhoff
2) Matt Birk
3) Kirk Lowderwilk
4) Jeff Christy

Kicker
1) Fred Cox
2) Ryan Longwell
3) Fuad Reveiz
4) Gary Anderson

Punter
1) Kris Kluwe
2) Mitch Berger
3) Greg Coleman
4) Neil Clabo

Kick Returner
1) Percy Harvin
2) Eddie Payton
3) David Palmer
4) Darrin Nelson

Punt Returner
1) David Palmer
2) Leo Lewis
3) Tommy Mason
4) Mewelde Moore

Defensive Tackle
1) Alan Page
2) John Randle
3) Keith Millard
4) Kevin Williams

Defensive End
1) Carl Eller
2) Chris Doleman
3) Jim Marshall
4) Jared Allen

Middle Linebacker
1) Scott Studwell
2) Jeff Siemon
3) Ed McDaniel
4) Jack Del Rio

Outside Linebacker
1) Matt Blair
2) Wally Hilgenberg
3) Roy Winston
4) Fred McNeill

Safety
1) Paul Krause
2) Joey Browner
3) Karl Kassulke
4) Darren Sharper

Cornerback
1) Carl Lee
2) Bobby Bryant
3) Antoine Winfield
4) Ed Sharockman

16 Awards and Honors

1) What Viking stalwart became the first defensive player to win the league MVP award and later became an associate justice of the Minnesota State Supreme Court?

2) What undrafted Vikings player became a seven-time Pro Bowler and eventually earned entrance into the Pro Football Hall of Fame?

3) What Viking player became the first from the franchise to earn first-team All-Pro status?

4) On August 2, 1986, who became the first player to be inducted into the Pro Football Hall of Fame who had played the majority of his career with the Vikings?

5) What man became the first non-player or coach associated with the team to earn Hall of Fame recognition in 1995?

6) What number-one overall draft pick from 1968 definitely lived up to his billing and was inducted into the Hall of Fame in 2001 after fifteen outstanding seasons at right tackle?

7) Who is the only Viking to win the NFC Defensive Rookie of the Year award?

8) What Royalton, Minnesota, native and South Dakota State player finished his career with the Vikings in 1980 and 1981 after playing most of his career with Miami?

9) What Viking won two NFL Defensive Player of the Year Awards in a three-year span?

Alan Page and (88) and Jim Marshall (70) walk off the gridiron after a game.

10) What active Viking player has been a Pro Bowler in five of his six NFL seasons?

11) In what two seasons did an astounding ten Viking players compete in the Pro Bowl?

12) Who became the first Viking player to be named NFL Rookie of the Year?

13) Who was the first Viking to be inducted into the Pro Football Hall of Fame?

14) What free-agent center made six consecutive Pro Bowl teams and was first-team All-Pro five times between 1964 and 1969?

15) Who were the first two Vikings to play in the Pro Bowl, representing the Western Conference All-Stars?

16) The only Hall of Famer from the state of Arizona, what Viking

guard went to eleven straight Pro Bowls and was a seven-time first-team All-Pro between 1989 and 1999?

17) Who won the NFL Most Valuable Player award in 1975?

18) Who is the only Viking to be cited as the NFL Comeback Player of the Year?

19) The first person to be enshrined in the Pro Football Hall of Fame who grew up in Canton, Ohio (where the hall is located) played for the Vikings. Who was he?

20) Who are the only Viking players to have their number retired by the club?

21) Although he was drafted as a linebacker out of Pittsburgh, what Viking defensive end became one of the most feared pass rushers during his era and was ultimately honored with his Hall of Fame induction in 2012?

22) What tackle from USC was a first-team All-Pro six straight years between 1971 and 1976?

23) Though he spent his best years with Kansas City, what Danish-born kicker played for the Vikings in 1984 and 1985?

24) What seven Viking players played in the Pro Bowl following the 2012 season?

25) What five Viking players have been the MVP of the Pro Bowl?

26) What all-time NFL interception leader and twelve-year Viking safety was honored with enshrinement in the NFL Hall of Fame in 1998?

27) Who is the only Viking to garner the NFL Man of the Year award, given to the player who best serves his team, community, and country in the spirit of Byron "Whizzer" White, a former NFL rushing champion, Supreme Court justice, and humanitarian?

28) What five Vikings have won the NFC Offensive Rookie of the Year award?

29) Who is the only former Viking to be given the NFL Alumni Career Achievement Award?

30) What kick-blocking linebacker from Iowa State was in the Pro Bowl every year between 1977 and 1982?

31) Perhaps the most underrated player in team history, what original Viking earned six Pro Bowl nods in the 1960's?

32) Who were the first six people to be inducted into the team's Ring of Honor?

33) Who is the only Vikings special-teams player to ever win the Player of the Month award more than once?

34) What defensive end was enshrined in the Hall of Fame in 2004 after fifteen illustrious years with the Vikings (1964-78), including six Pro Bowl appearances and five first-team All-Pro recognitions?

35) What Viking player holds the team record for most consecutive Pro Bowl honors with 11?

36) He had three solid seasons (1994-96) as the Minnesota quarterback and joined Bud Grant as persons who are in both the CFL and NFL Hall of Fames. Who is he?

37) Who is the only Minnesota native to earn Pro Bowl status for the Vikings besides Milt Sunde (1966)?

38) The all-time Viking leader in receptions (498) for tight ends, what Brown University graduate made the Pro Bowl every year from 1986 to 1991?

39) Unquestionably one of the top running backs of the 1970's, what spinning dervish was a Pro-Bowler from 1973 to 1977?

40) What Viking strong safety, who played more like a linebacker, was a a six-time Pro Bowler, first-team All-Pro in 1987, 1989, and 1990, and a member of the 1980s all-decade team?

41) Who were the only three Vikings selected to play in the Pro Bowl in their first three pro seasons?

42) What current Viking has made the Pro Bowl six times (2004, 2006-08, 2009-10)?

43) Who are the offensive players who are inducted into the team's Ring of Honor?

44) What Viking standout was named the NFL Defensive Player of the Year in 1989?

45) Who are the defensive players included in the Vikings Ring of Honor?

46) Who is the only Viking to earn Pro-Bowl status in two different stints with the club?

47) What free-agent guard, acquired in 2006, paid immediate dividends and made the Pro Bowl his first four years with the team?

48) Who is the only Viking to win a Player of the Week award in his first game in the NFL?

49) Amazingly, the powerful 1998 Viking contingent was awarded the NFC Player of the Week award ten times. What three players won the award in back-to-back weeks?

50) What 17 players have been named to all three of the noteworthy anniversary teams named by the Vikings (25th, 40th, and 50 Greatest Vikings)?

51) What five Vikings have been named Playoff Players of the Week?

52) In what years did the Vikings have six starters in the Pro Bowl?

53) Who is the only Viking player to be named Rookie of the Month twice?

54) In what year was the entire Viking front four named to the Pro Bowl?

55) What Viking has the most Player of the Month awards with five?

56) What player has been named Player of the Week the most times?

57) Who became the 20th member of the Vikings Ring of Honor on Oct. 25, 2012?

58) In 1966, the Vikings had three offensive linemen start for the Western Conference in the Pro Bowl. Who were they?

59) Which Viking rookies have made the Pro Bowl?

60) What Viking became the third player in franchise history to be the MVP of the entire NFL with his extraordinary 2012 season?

61) How many individuals associated with the Vikings (players, coaches, or executives) have been enshrined in the Pro Football Hall of Fame?

62) Who are the only Viking rookies ever to be chosen first-team All-Pro by the Associated Press?

John Randle in Tampa Bay's backfield.

1) Alan Page. The defensive tackle won the NFL's top honor for his outstanding 1971 season when he amassed 18 sacks and was relentless as one of the famed Purple People Eaters along with Carl Eller, Jim Marshall, and Gary Larsen. He earned nine Pro Bowl nods and was enshrined in the Hall of Fame in 1988.

2) John Randle. The defensive tackle, who played collegiately at Texas A & M - Kingsville, played 11 years (1990-2000) for the Vikings and had double-digit sacks in eight seasons with the club. He totaled 137.5 sacks for Minnesota and was named to the all-decade NFL team for the 1990's. Randle was noted for his fierce rivalry with Packer quarterback Brett Favre and for his eccentric face-painting and trash-talking. He was enshrined in the Hall of Fame in 2010.

3) Tommy Mason. The first overall draft pick in the draft for the 1961 season, the Tulane product played in the Pro Bowl in 1962 after rushing for 740 yards (4.6 per carry) and totaling 603 in receiving yards. Mason also made the Pro Bowl in 1963 and 1964.

4) Fran Tarkenton, who owned four major career passing marks at the time of his induction (touchdown passes – 342; completions – 3,686; yards passing – 47,003; pass attempts – 6,467). He also had the most career rushing yards as a quarterback (3,674) and most games as a quarterback (246).

5) Jim Finks, who was the Minnesota General Manager from 1964-74. Finks later was in the same position with the Chicago Bears and New Orleans Saints and was hugely successful with all three of his NFL teams. Finks died in 1994 at age 66, a year before his enshrinement.

6) Ron Yary, who wore #73.

7) Dewayne Washington (1994).

8) Jim Langer, a center, who was enshrined in the Hall of Fame in 1987.

9) Alan Page (1971 and 1973).

10) Adrian Peterson (2007-10, 2012). He was first-team All-Pro in 2008, 2009, and 2012.

11) 1998 and 2009

12) Paul Flatley, a wide receiver out of Northwestern, in 1963.

13) Hugh McElhenny. The former 49er great played for the Vikings in his final two seasons (1961-62) and was inducted into the Hall of Fame in 1970.

14) Mick Tingelhoff

15) Running back Hugh McElhenny and wide receiver Jerry Reichow participated in the Jan. 14, 1962 contest at the Los Angeles Coliseum. The West won 31-30.

16) Randall McDaniel, who could arguably be the most effective player to ever play for the Vikings. He was justifiably inducted into the Hall of Fame in 2009.

17) Fran Tarkenton, who guided the team to a 12-2 record as he completed 64.2% of his passes for 2,994 yards and 25 touchdowns.

18) Tommy Kramer (1986)

19) Alan Page. Ironically, Page had worked on the building during the construction of the Hall of Fame. Dan Dierdorf, an offensive tackle and longtime Monday Night Football analyst, became the second Canton native to be honored.

20) Fran Tarkenton (#10), Mick Tingelhoff (#53), Jim Marshall (#70), Korey Stringer (#77), Cris Carter (#80), and Alan Page (#88).

21) Chris Doleman, who played 10 years for Minnesota (1985-93, 99) and totaled 96.5 sacks in 142 starts. He recovered 16 fumbles and had 737 tackles.

22) Ron Yary

23) Jan Stenerud, who made the Pro Bowl after kicking 20 of 23 field goals that year. He was inducted into the Hall of Fame in 1991.

24) Adrian Peterson (RB), Jared Allen (DE), Jerome Felton (FB), and Blair Walsh (K) were all selected to the team and Chad Greenway (LB), Matt Kalil (T), and Kyle Rudolph (TE) were injury replacements for the NFC.

25) Fran Tarkenton (1964), Ahmad Rashad (1978), Randy Moss (1999), Adrian Peterson (2007) and Kyle Rudolph (2012). The year denotes the season, not the year the game was played.

26) Paul Krause, who was a six-time Pro Bowler.

27) Cris Carter (1998)

28) Chuck Foreman (1975), Sammy White (1976), Randy Moss (1998), Adrian Peterson (2007), and Percy Harvin (2009). Paul Flately won the NFL award in 1963 prior to the formation of the NFC.

29) Alan Page (1995).

30) Matt Blair, a first-team All-Pro in 1980.

31) Grady Alderman

32) Bud Grant, Jim Finks, Paul Krause, Alan Page, Fran Tarkenton, and Fred Zamberletti.

33) Punter Mitch Berger, who won once each in 1998, 1999, and 2000.

34) Carl Eller

35) Randall McDaniel (1989-99). Alan Page (1968-1976) reached nine in a row and Cris Carter (1993-2000) eight in a row.

36) Warren Moon

37) Matt Birk, a St. Paul native and Cretin-Derham Hall graduate who was a standout center for his home-state team. Birk was a Pro Bowler six times.

38) Steve Jordan, who is third all-time in receptions behind Cris Carter and Randy Moss. He also holds the club record for touchdowns for tight ends with 28.

39) Chuck Foreman

40) Joey Browner

Randall McDaniel

41) Chuck Foreman (1973-75), Randy Moss (1998-2000) and Adrian Peterson (2007-09). Foreman made it his first six seasons.

42) Defensive tackle Kevin Williams.

43) Fran Tarkenton, Ron Yary, Korey Stringer, Mick Tingelhoff, Cris Carter, Bill Brown, Chuck Foreman, and Randall McDaniel.

44) Keith Millard, who had 18 sacks in his best year as a pro.

45) Alan Page, Paul Krause, Jim Marshall, Carl Eller, John Randle, Chris Doleman, and Scott Studwell.

46) Fran Tarkenton (1964-65 and 1974-76).

47) Steve Hutchinson

48) Blair Walsh. After converting all four field goal attempts, including the game-tying effort on the last play of regulation and the winning points in overtime, he was cited as the Special Teams Player of the Week after the Vikings 23-20 win over Jacksonville on Sept. 9, 2012.

49) Randall Cunningham, Mitch Berger, and Randy Moss.

50) Fran Tarkenton (QB), Bill Brown (RB), Chuck Foreman (RB), Sammy White (WR), Ahmad Rashad (WR), Ed White (G), Ron Yary (OT), Mick Tingelhoff (C), Fred Cox (K), Jim Marshall (DE), Alan Page (DT), Carl Eller (DE), Matt Blair (LB), Scott Studwell (LB), Jeff Siemon (LB), Bobby Bryant (CB), and Paul Krause (S).

51) Eddie Murray, Robert Griffith, Robert Smith, Daunte Culpepper, and Antoine Winfield.

52) 1969 and 2007.

53) Adrian Peterson (September and October, 2007)

54) 1969 (Carl Eller, Jim Marshall, Alan Page, and Gary Larsen). All but Larsen started in the game. Paul Krause, Gene Washington, and Mick Tingelhoff also started.

55) John Randle (defense). Mitch Berger (special teams) was honored three times with Chris Doleman (defense) and Daunte Culpepper (offense) both honored twice.

56) Daunte Culpepper (eight times).

57) Matt Blair, the 12-year linebacker (1974-85).

58) Tackle Grady Alderman, guard Milt Sunde, and center Mick Tingelhoff.

59) Running back Chuck Foreman (1973), wide-receiver Sammy White (1976), wide-receiver Randy Moss (1998), running back Adrian Peterson (2007), kick returner Percy Harvin (2009) and kicker Blair Walsh (2012). Also, tackle Matt Kalil was an injury replacement in 2012.

60) Adrian Peterson, who also won the "Offensive Player of the Year" award. He ran for 2,097 yards, just eight yards short of the single-season mark held by Eric Dickerson (2,105 in 1984). Peterson averaged 6.0 yards per carry and scored 13 touchdowns.

61) Seventeen. (head coach Bud Grant, general manager Jim Finks, and players Cris Carter, Dave Casper, Chris Doleman, Carl Eller, Paul Krause, Jim Langer, Randall McDaniel, Hugh McElhenny, Warren Moon, Alan Page, John Randle, Jan Stenerud, Fran Tarkenton, Ron Yary, and Gary Zimmerman. Norm Van Brocklin, the team's first head coach, is also in the Hall of Fame as a player with the Rams and Eagles.

62) Receiver Randy Moss (1998) and kicker Blair Walsh (2012).

17 The Post-Season

1) What is the Vikings all-time post-season record?

2) In what season did the Vikings actually win an outright NFL title?

3) After what season did the Vikings play a consolation-round game after being eliminated from advancing in the playoffs?

4) Since the AFL-NFL merger in 1970, how do the Vikings rank among franchises in regard to the number of playoff appearances?

5) What is the Vikings record in NFC conference championship games?

6) How many division titles have the Vikings won?

7) On how many occasions have the Vikings lost a post-season game at home?

8) What is the Vikings record in playoff overtime games?

9) In perhaps the most pathetic performance in Viking playoff history, what was the score in the NFC Conference Championship played against the New York Giant at Giants Stadium in East Rutherford, New Jersey on Jan. 15, 2001?

10) Following their inception in 1961, how many years did it take for the Vikings to make their first playoff appearance?

11) What was the Vikings record at Met Stadium while playing playoff games during December or January?

12) What foe did the Vikings beat to claim their first-ever playoff win?

13) What was the largest point-differential in Viking post-season history between the point-spread established before the game and the actual game result?

14) The 1987 Vikings became the team with the worst regular season record to win two playoff games. What was their regular season mark that year?

15) On how many occasions have the Vikings played a division rival in the playoffs?

16) Who did the Vikings face when they hosted the largest crowd in post-season play at Metropolitan Stadium on Christmas Day, 1971?

17) What year did the Vikings go 15-1 in the regular season and yet not reach the Super Bowl?

18) Not counting their first six seasons, when they were an expansion team, what is the longest number of years the Vikings have gone between playoff appearances?

19) What overtime rule was changed for the playoffs after the Vikings 31-28 loss to New Orleans on Jan. 24, 2010, in the NFC conference championship?

20) How many different men have started at quarterback for Minnesota in a playoff game?

21) Deeply disappointed with the Vikings 17-14 loss to Dallas on Dec. 28, 1975, in a divisional playoff game at Met Stadium, what tragic news did quarterback Fran Tarkenton receive shortly after the game?

22) What is the franchise record for post-season games at home, on the road, and at neutral sites?

23) What is the Vikings longest losing streak in the playoffs?

24) Which Viking head coaches do *not* have a losing record in the playoffs?

25) Have the Minnesota Vikings ever won three straight games in the post-season?

26) How many times has Minnesota earned a wild-card berth in the playoffs?

27) Who has been the most frequent playoff opponent for the Vikings?

28) Why were so many people appalled when the NFL announced the date for the Vikings divisional playoff game against Dallas following the 1971 regular season?

29) In the NFL championship game at the Met on Jan. 4, 1970, what Viking player kicked Cleveland linebacker Jim Houston in the head attempting to leap over him and knocked him out cold?

Wally Hilgenberg (58) battles Pittsburgh in Super Bowl IX; Paul Krause (22) is in the background.

30) What was so unusual about the Vikings playoff loss to the Bears following the 1994 regular season and the Vikings playoff win over the Packers following the 2004 regular season?

31) In a playoff loss at Philadelphia on Jan. 3, 1981, the Vikings led 14-0 but eventually lost 31-16. What problem led to their defeat?

32) In the first-ever playoff game hosted by the New Orleans Saints on Jan. 3, 1988, what Viking ruined Al Hirt's party by returning six punts for 143 yards and catching six passes for 79 yards in a 44-10 Minnesota victory?

33) The largest post-season crowd ever to witness a home playoff game occurred on Jan. 17, 1999 when the Vikings lost a heartbreaker to what team?

34) What receiver hauled in three TD passes from Brett Favre in a 34-3 win over Dallas in a divisional game on Jan. 17, 2010?

35) In the NFC title game at Washington on Jan. 17, 1988, facing fourth and four from the Redskin's six-yard line, who dropped Wade Wilson's pass in the flat to give the host team a 17-10 win and deny the Vikings a chance to win in overtime and get to their fifth Super Bowl?

36) What Cretin-Derham Hall alum quarterbacked the Chicago Bears to a 35-18 upset win over the Vikings at the Metrodome in a wild-card playoff game on Jan. 1, 1995?

37) What Vikings player has played the most seasons in the playoffs with 11?

38) Under Denny Green, the Vikings had seven different starting quarterbacks in eight post-seasons. Who were they?

39) What Viking defender intercepted Los Angeles Rams quarterback Jim Everett on their first two possessions in a 28-18 Minnesota wild-card win on Dec. 26, 1988?

40) Who holds the playoff mark for most field goals made in a game?

41) Who has the highest rushing total in a playoff game?

42) What is the largest deficit overcome to win a playoff game?

43) What reserve running back had 159 yards receiving in a 35-18 wild-card loss to Chicago on Jan. 1, 1995?

44) What is the largest margin of victory in a playoff game?

45) In a truly remarkable effort, what Viking wowed a Candlestick Park crowd with 227 yards receiving in a 36-24 win over San Francisco on Jan. 9, 1988?

46) What player attacked a chalkboard in the Viking locker room at halftime of a divisional playoff game against Washington on Dec. 22, 1973 at Met Stadium and was credited with inspiring his teammates to a come-from-behind victory over the Redskins?

47) Who is the career leader in post-season touchdowns?

48) Of the five Viking quarterbacks who have started at least four playoff games, who has the best and worst quarterback rating?

49) What Dallas passer and receiver hooked up on a controversial "Hail Mary" 50-yard touchdown play with under a minute to play to beat the Vikings 17-14 in a divisional playoff game at Met Stadium on Dec. 28, 1975?

50) On a very cold day on Jan. 12, 1975, the Vikings beat the Los Angeles Rams 14-10 on their way to their second Super Bowl. What Viking helped preserve the victory with a late-game interception in the end zone after the Rams had driven 98 yards?

51) What player had good timing to compile his first and only 100-yard rushing game in his Viking career by rushing for 101 yards in a 35-20 win over Washington on Dec. 18, 1976?

52) Who scored the first touchdown in Viking playoff history?

53) Who became the first Viking to score three touchdowns in a playoff game in a 41-21 win over Arizona on Jan. 9, 1999?

54) On a day when the Vikings played a playoff game at Met Stadium, why did the New York Times feature a story and photo about another event at the Metropolitan Sports Center?

55) What three quarterbacks all engineered scoring drives in Minnesota's 44-10 upset over host New Orleans in a wild-card playoff game on Jan. 3, 1988?

56) What Viking defender returned a blocked field goal 90 yards on the game's first possession to propel the Vikings to a 24-13 win over Los Angeles in the NFC title game on Dec. 26, 1976?

57) How many years have the Vikings played in the post-season?

58) Who became the only quarterback in NFL history to start a playoff game without throwing a pass during the regular season?

1) 19 wins and 27 losses

2) 1969. The Vikings, who went 12-2 in the regular season, defeated the Los Angeles Rams 23-20 in the NFL Western Conference finals at Met Stadium on Dec. 27, 1969, and then downed the Cleveland Browns 27-7 at Met Stadium on January 4 to win the NFL title. In the final year before the AFL-NFL merger, the AFL champion Kansas City Chiefs then beat the favored Vikings 23-7 at Tulane Stadium on Jan. 11 to win Super Bowl IV.

3) The 1968 season. On Jan. 5, 1969, the Vikings faced the Dallas Cowboys in Miami, Florida and lost the so-called Playoff Bowl game by a score of 17-13 in front of just 22,961. Two weeks earlier, as the NFL Central champions, they had lost to Baltimore 24-14 in the Western Conference title game. The Cowboys had been defeated by Cleveland in the Eastern Conference finals. The so-called Playoff Bowl games that were played from 1960 to 1969 were so inconsequential that the NFL doesn't even consider the team or individual statistics from those games as valid. However, the games actually did take place!

4) Second (25). Only Dallas (26) has more while Pittsburgh is third with 24 appearances and San Francisco fourth with 23.

5) 4-5; however, they are 0-5 in their last five appearances!

6) 18 (17 outright)

7) 7 times; 1970 - lost to San Francisco 17-14 in divisional playoff; 1971 - lost to Dallas 20-12 in divisional playoff; 1975 - lost to Dallas 17-14 in divisional playoff; 1992 - lost to Washington 24-7 in wild-card game; 1994 - lost to Chicago 35-18 in wild-card game; 1998 - lost to Atlanta 30-27 (OT) in NFC Championship; and 2008 - lost to Philadelphia 26-14 in wild-card game. The Vikings are 14-7 overall in home playoff games.

8) 0-2; they lost to Atlanta 30-27 in the NFC Conference Championship game on Jan. 17, 1999 and lost to New Orleans 31-28 on Jan. 24, 2010 in the NFC Conference Championship.

9) 41-0 Giants. At halftime, New York led 34-0 and held a 386-45 yardage advantage. Kerry Collins tossed five touchdown passes while Daunte Culpepper was just 13-28 for only 78 yards and three interceptions.

10) Eight years. In 1968, the Vikings won the NFL's Central Division title with an 8-6 record but lost to the Baltimore Colts 24-14 at Memorial Stadium in the Western Conference championship. They would make the playoffs 11 times in a 13-year span to become one of the top franchises in the NFL.

11) 8-3, including 3-0 versus the Los Angeles Rams.

12) Los Angeles Rams (23-20) on Dec. 27, 1969 at Met Stadium. The next week, Jan. 4, 1970, the Vikings won the NFL title with a 27-7 thrashing of the Cleveland Browns on the same field. On Jan. 11, 1970, they faced the Kansas City Chiefs, the winner of the AFL title, in the Super Bowl. It was the final year before the two leagues merged and formed the NFC and the AFC within the umbrella of the National Football League.

13) 43 points. In the 2000 NFC championship (Jan.14, 2001), the Vikings were favored to beat the host New York Giants by two points. Gulp! They lost 41-0.

14) 8-7 (they beat New Orleans and then San Francisco).

15) Three times. On Jan. 1, 1995, the Bears beat the host Vikings 35-16. On Jan. 9, 2005, Minnesota downed Green Bay 31-17 at Lambeau Field. On Jan. 5, 2013, the Vikings lost 24-10 at Green Bay.

16) Dallas Cowboys. The Vikings were upset 20-12 in front of 49,100 onlookers.

17) 1998. The Vikings were upset by Atlanta 30-27 in the NFC conference championship on Jan. 17, 1999. Green Bay also went 15-1 in 2011 and never reached the Super Bowl.

18) Four years (1983-86).

19) Instead of allowing a team to win by a field goal on the first possession, the other team has a chance to get the ball and tie the game or win it with a touchdown. If the first team scores a touchdown, the game is over. If both teams each record a field goal on their possession, whichever teams scores next wins.

20) 16; Fran Tarkenton (6-5) and Tommy Kramer (3-2) are the only ones who have a winning record.

21) His 63-year-old father, Reverend Dallas Tarkenton, had died of a

Matt Birk (78) blocks for Robert Smith (26) at Tampa Bay.

heart attack while watching the game with two of Fran's brothers at home in Savannah, Georgia.

22) Home - (14-7); Road - (5-16); Neutral Site: (0-4)

23) Six (Jan. 1, 1989-Dec. 28, 1996)

24) Jerry Burns (3-3) and Mike Tice (1-1). Bud Grant was 10-12, Dennis Green 4-8, Brad Childress 1-2, and Leslie Frazier 0-1.

25) No. They have won two in a row on five occasions.

26) 12 times; (6-6 record).

27) Dallas (8). The Cowboys hold a 6-2 record over the Vikings in the playoffs.

28) It was slated for Christmas Day at Met Stadium; the first NFL game ever played on that religious holiday.

29) Joe Kapp. The Vikings went on to win their only NFL title 27-7 but lost the last of the four AFL-NFL Super Bowl battles to Kansas City the next week.

30) In both of those seasons, the home team lost in the playoffs after winning both of the regular season meetings.

31) Eight turnovers, all in the second half! (Yup, eight, one more than seven, including five interceptions by Tommy Kramer).

32) Anthony Carter. He had an 84-yard punt return in the first quarter and later added a 10-yard touchdown reception.

33) Atlanta (30-27 loss in overtime in the NFC title game).

34) Sidney Rice, who had six grabs for 141 yards.

35) Darrin Nelson. Even if he hadn't let the ball go through his fingers, it appeared that standout Redskin defender Darrell Green was prepared to make the tackle short of the first down at the two-yard line.

36) Steve Walsh. The former Miami Hurricane was 15-23 for 221 yards and two touchdowns.

37) Ron Yary (1968-71; 1973-78, 1980). Carl Eller, Wally Hilgenberg, Paul Krause, Jim Marshall, and Mick Tingelhoff all played in 10 post-seasons. Yary has also played in the most playoff games with 20.

38) Sean Salisbury (1992), Jim McMahon (1993), Warren Moon (1994), Brad Johnson (1996), Randall Cunningham (1997, 1998), Jeff George (1999), and Daunte Culpepper (2000).

39) Joey Browner. Alfred Anderson rushed for two touchdowns. The following week, Jerry Rice scored three touchdowns in a 34-9 romp in San Francisco.

40) Chuck Nelson, who kicked five in a 36-24 upset win over San Francisco on Jan. 9, 1988.

41) Robert Smith gained 140 yards in a 27-10 wild-card win over Dallas on Jan. 9, 2000?

42) 16; Minnesota trailed the host New York Giants 19-3 at halftime and 22-13 late in the fourth quarter before winning 23-22 on Dec. 27, 1997.

43) Amp Lee had 11 catches and a touchdown.

44) 34 points; Minnesota trounced host New Orleans 44-10 on Jan. 3, 1988.

45) Anthony Carter, who had 10 catches and also had 30 yards rushing. His yardage total set a league playoff record while all-world receiver Jerry Rice was held to three catches for 27 yards by an inspired Viking defense.

46) Carl Eller. The lethargic Minnesota team trailed 7-3 at the half but Eller's emotional outburst designed to exhort his team seemed to work as the host team went on to a 27-20 triumph. John Gilliam scored twice on throws from Fran Tarkenton in the second half on a day with 19-degree temps. Eller's rage included throwing the chalkboard against a wall, pounding his fists against metal doors, and emitting a few colorful phrases.

47) Cris Carter had nine playoff touchdowns; Randy Moss had eight.

48) Best: Randall Cunningham (85.9); five games, nine touchdowns, three interceptions. Worst: Fran Tarkenton: (58.6); 11 games, 11 touchdowns, 17 interceptions.

49) Roger Staubach and Drew Pearson. Trailing 14-10, Staubach faced a 4th and 16 from his own 25 yard-line and hit Pearson on the sideline for a 25-yard gain. Following a dropped pass by Preston Pearson, the former Heisman Trophy winner from Navy hurled a long pass down the middle of the field. Viking cornerback Nate Wright, covering Pearson, suddenly goes down to the ground as Pearson snags the ball on his hip at the five yard-line and trots into the end zone. Viking supporters yelled for offensive interference, claiming that Pearson had pushed Wright as he attempted to go for the ball. However, back judge Jerry Bergman never threw a flag and perhaps the best Viking team ever assembled was one and done.

50) Wally Hilgenberg

51) Brent McClanahan. The Arizona State runner ran 20 times for 101 yards while Chuck Foreman had 105 yards in the same number of carries. Both Foreman and Sammy White scored twice in the win.

52) Billy Martin, who caught a one-yard pass from Joe Kapp in the 24-14 loss to Baltimore on Dec. 22, 1968. He split tight-end duties with John Beasley and also shared the punting duties with King Hill. Martin punted 28 times for a 37.4-yard average in his only season with the team. He had 10 receptions for 101 yards and a touchdown in the regular season.

53) Leroy Hoard

54) It was Christmas Day in 1971 and many were concerned that the significant religious holiday was being usurped by pro football. Rev. Dick Smith of St. Patrick's Episcopal Church in Bloomington offered an 11:00 a.m. non-denominational service a few hundred yards away at the Met Center, where the North Stars played their NHL games. More than 3,000 people attended and most of the churchgoers were able to saunter their way over to make the noon start. The New York newspaper did a story on the 45-minute service. Heavenly help was given to Dallas that day, as the Cowboys edged the Vikings.

55) Tommy Kramer, Wade Wilson, and Rich Gannon.

56) Bobby Bryant. Nate Allen blocked Tom Dempsey's field goal attempt and the ball bounced perfectly to Bryant as he raced the length of the field untouched. The Rams refused to try to score a touchdown with fourth and goal from inside the Viking one-yard line. Bryant later made another interception to foil another Ram drive.

57) 27 times in 52 seasons.

58) Joe Webb. The Alabama-Birmingham product started against Green Bay in a wild-card game on Jan. 5, 2013 when year-long starter Christian Ponder (triceps injury) was unable to play. Webb was 11-30 for 180 yards with one touchdown and one interception in a 24-10 loss. Webb had only taken three snaps during the entire 2012 season and hadn't started a game since the last game of the 2010 season.

18 The Super Bowl

1) The Vikings have competed in four Super Bowls and, of course, lost each of them. In how many of those contests were the Vikings actually favored to win?

2) Since their last appearance in Super Bowl XI (Jan. 10, 1977), which NFL teams besides the Vikings have not played in the "big" game?

3) What is the only other NFL team other than the Vikings to chalk up a 0-4 Super Bowl record?

4) Fran Tarkenton started in three Super Bowls for the Vikings; who was the other quarterback to start a Super Bowl for Minnesota?

5) How many total touchdowns did the Vikings score in their four Super Bowls?

6) Who were the ten players who played on all four of Minnesota's Super Bowl teams?

7) What special teams player scored the Vikings only touchdown in Super Bowl IX, a 16-6 loss to Pittsburgh?

8) The largest crowd ever to watch the Vikings saw them play in which Super Bowl?

9) What Viking receiver had a collision with NFL Films cameraman and future president Steve Sabol during Super Bowl IX?

10) Who scored the first Super Bowl touchdown for the Vikings?

11) How many total points did the Viking score in their four Super Bowl losses?

12) In what stadium did Minnesota play two Super Bowls?

13) Who was the MVP of Super Bowl XI for Oakland, a wide receiver with a nifty moustache?

14) What future Viking kicked three first-half field goals in Kansas City's 23-7 Super Bowl victory on Jan. 11, 1970?

15) How many yards rushing did All-Pro Chuck Foreman have in three Super Bowl efforts?

16) What Viking linebacker blocked Raider standout Ray Guy's punt deep in Oakland territory early in Super Bowl XI and recovered it at the Raider three-yard line?

Mick Tingelhoff

17) What Miami battering ram set a then-record 145 yards rushing (33 carries) and ran for two touchdowns as the Dolphins won their second-straight Super Bowl with a 24-7 win over Minnesota on Jan. 13, 1974?

18) In Super Bowl IX in New Orleans, Pittsburgh led 2-0 after a listless first half. How did they score the safety?

19) What seven players started in all four of the Super Bowls the Vikings participated in—two on offense and five on defense?

20) In Super Bowl XI, what Viking receiver was leveled by hard-hitting Oakland Raider safety Jack Tatum, yet managed to miraculously hold onto the ball despite having his helmet knocked off?

21) In Super Bowl VIII, what Hall of Fame quarterback needed to throw just seven passes (completing six) in his team's victory over the Vikings on Jan. 13, 1974?

22) What former Viking draft pick and Outland Trophy award winner for the University of Minnesota starred at linebacker for Kansas City when the Chiefs beat Minnesota in Super Bowl IV?

23) What rugged running back from Penn State ran roughshod over the Vikings in Super Bowl IX, rushing for 158 yards and a touchdown in 33 carries?

24) While it was cool by California standards (52 degrees) at the Rose Bowl in Pasadena for Super Bowl XI, what was the temperature back in the Twin Cities during that game?

25) What Viking figure was fined $5,000 by the NFL, the maximum at the time, for complaining about the practice facilities provided by the league prior to Super Bowl VIII in Houston?

26) What AFC team held the Vikings offense to just 17 yards rushing and only 119 total yards in Super Bowl IX, and what was the nickname for their stout defense?

27) In perhaps an omen to come, how many turnovers did the Vikings have in their first Super Bowl played on Jan. 11, 1970, in New Orleans?

28) Who are the only four quarterbacks to play for the Vikings in the Super Bowl?

29) In all four Super Bowl efforts, the Viking offense was inept in the first half. How many points did they score total in the first halves of those four contests?

30) What was the face value for a ticket at Tulane Stadium in New Orleans when the Vikings faced the Chiefs in Super Bowl IV?

31) In one of the few "lighter" moments in Minnesota Super Bowl lore, what three Viking players were responsible for getting a rise out of broadcaster Howard Cosell prior to Super Bowl IV?

32) Who was the head coach of the Kansas City Chiefs in Super Bowl IV, who became famous (or infamous, depending on who you were pulling for) for his candid remarks regarding the Vikings failures as he was being recorded by microphone?

33) What opposing head coach in one of the four Viking Super Bowls hailed from Minnesota?

1) One. In Super Bowl IV, the Vikings were favored to beat the Kansas City Chiefs by 13 points and lost 23-7. Ouch! Really, a 29-point differential! It still hurts 43 years later!

2) Detroit Lions, New York Jets, and Kansas City Chiefs. Otherwise, every other team in the NFL has been to a Super Bowl since the Vikings lost to Oakland 35 years ago. Note, the Cleveland Browns franchise moved to Baltimore in 1996 and won Super Bowl XXXV by beating the New York Giants 34-7 on Jan. 28, 2001 and also Super Bowl XLVII by downing San Francisco 34-31 on Feb. 5, 2013.

3) Buffalo Bills (1991-94). Denver had been 0-4 before winning Super Bowl XXXII and XXXIII following the 1998 and 1999 seasons to stand 2-4. New England is the only other franchise to lose four games but they have also won three Super Bowls titles.

4) Joe Kapp (Jan. 11, 1970 in Super Bowl IV versus Kansas City)

5) Five (one vs. Kansas City, one vs. Miami, one vs. Pittsburgh, and two vs. Oakland)

6) Fred Cox, Carl Eller, Wally Hilgenberg, Paul Krause, Jim Marshall, Alan Page, Roy Winston, Mick Tingelhoff, Ed White, and Ron Yary.

7) Terry Brown. The defensive back recovered a blocked punt in the end zone after Matt Blair blocked Bobby Walden's punt. Unfortunately, Fred Cox then missed the conversion.

8) Super Bowl XI at the Rose Bowl in Pasadena, California when 103,438 saw the Vikings lose their third Super Bowl in four years on Jan. 9, 1977 to Oakland 32-14.

9) John Gilliam. Sabol was used to contact on a football field, being a running back at Colorado College in the early 1960's.

10) Dave Osborn scored on a 4-yard run in the third quarter of the Vikings 23-7 loss to Kansas City in Super Bowl IV.

11) 34; meanwhile, the winners scored 95!

12) Tulane Stadium in New Orleans, Louisiana. (Super Bowl IV and IX).

Dave Osborn

13) Fred Biletnikoff, who had four catches for 79 yards.

14) Jan Stenerud, a future Hall of Famer who kicked for the Vikings in 1984 and 1985.

15) 80 in 36 attempts, a paltry 2.2 average.

16) Fred McNeil. However, on the next play, Oakland's Phil Villapiano nailed Brent McClanahan and Willie Hall recovered the fumble to end the threat. Oakland scored on a field goal to set the tone for yet another Minnesota loss.

17) Larry Csonka.

18) Steeler defensive lineman Dwight Smith tackled Fran Tarkenton in the end zone in the second quarter.

19) Center Mick Tingelhoff and tackle Ron Yary on offense; on defense, ends Carl Eller and Jim Marshall, tackle Alan Page, linebacker Wally Hilgenberg, and safety Paul Krause.

20) Sammy White, who had one of Minnesota's two touchdowns with an eight-yard grab in the 32-14 loss.

21) Bob Griese. The former Purdue great handed off to Csonka, Jim Kiick and Mercury Morris all day as Miami won consecutive NFL titles.

22) Bobby Bell, the Gopher great who was their second round pick in 1963. He chose to sign with the AFL Chiefs and is now enshrined in the Pro Football Hall of Fame.

23) Franco Harris, who was the MVP. Meanwhile, Chuck Foreman had 18 yards in 12 carries for the NFC champs. It was the Steelers first appearance in the Super Bowl.

24) -17 degrees (Fahrenheit) as Oakland dumped the Vikings 32-14.

25) Bud Grant. The Vikings head coach wasn't pleased with the less than adequate set-up at James M. Delmar High School in Houston.

26) Pittsburgh and the "Steel Curtain" defense.

27) Five (two fumbles and three interceptions). It led to a 23-7 upset defeat to Kansas City. In fact, on their first five possessions, Minnesota fumbled twice and dropped a pass that would have led to a first down.

28) Joe Kapp, Gary Cuozzo, Fran Tarkenton, and Bob Lee.

29) 0 (yes, zero, zip, nothing).

30) $15

31) Wally Hilgenberg, Alan Page, and Bob Lurtsema, stationed a floor above, simultaneously dumped their own wastebasket of water on Cosell's head. The bombastic ABC reporter was interviewing Fran Tarkenton at the motel where the Vikings were staying. An irate Cosell, who had his hairpiece askew, began a spew of epithets and curse words that could be heard halfway to New York.

32) Hank Stram. One of the quotes was, "They're running around like a Chinese fire drill."

33) John Madden. The Oakland Raiders coach, a victor in Super Bowl XI, was born in Austin in 1936 but his family moved to California when he was a youngster. Madden was enshrined in the Hall of Fame in 2006 and became a cultural icon as a color analyst on network television from 1979 to 2008. Madden (.763) has the highest winning percentage for any head coach in NFL history for those coaches who have won at least 100 games (103-32-7).

Fans carry away a goalpost after the final game played at Met Stadium, a 10-6 loss to Kansas City on Dec. 20, 1981.

19 Potpourri

1) The Viking logo, depicting the fierce warrior from Scandinavia, has been utilized officially since what year?

2) For how many seasons did the Vikings conduct their summer training in northern Minnesota?

3) Who are the only two Vikings players ever to play for the club whose last name started with the letter....."U"?

4) What is the name of the team's training facilities and in what Twin Cities suburb is its headquarters located?

5) Only two running backs in NFL history have a higher rushing yards per game average (minimum 50 games) than Adrian Peterson (99.4). Who are they?

6) What is the Vikings Opening Day record over its 52 seasons (1961-2012)?

7) Four players in Viking history have first and last names that total just six letters. Who are they?

8) In August of 1959, Minneapolis businessmen Bill Boyer, H.P. Skoglund, and Max Winter were awarded a franchise in the new American Football League. Five months later, in January of 1960, the three afore-mentioned gentlemen and Bernie Ridder, reneged on their agreement with the AFL after being promised the 14th franchise in the National Football League. Where did the AFL franchise set for the Twin Cities eventually end up?

9) One of the two primary logos for the Minnesota Vikings is a white Viking horn (outlined in gold) adorned on a purple helmet. What is the other?

10) Among the 32 current NFL franchises, how do the Vikings rank in all-time winning percentage?

11) How many football players have played at least one game with the Minnesota Vikings over the past 52 seasons?

12) Who are the three players to have competed for the Vikings without first playing college football?

13) How many players that played in the Division III Minnesota Intercollegiate Athletic Conference have played for the Vikings?

14) What early Viking employee recommended that the term "Vikings" be used as the nickname for the fledgling new franchise as one of his first acts as the team's general manager?

15) How many Gopher football players have played for the NFL Vikings?

16) What former Viking quarterback is the son-in-law of former Viking hero Bill Brown?

17) After playing four years with the Vikings, what good-looking Ivy Leaguer became a fine actor, being best known for his role as a policeman in *Hill Street Blues*?

18) What term was given to the Vikings relentless front four from the late 1960's and 1970's, one of the top four or five defensive lines in league history?

19) How many total games have the Vikings played in their history, counting both regular season and post-season games?

20) What is the address of the Vikings headquarters/practice facility in Eden Prairie?

21) What Viking player once introduced himself by saying, "I play third string center for the Minnesota Vikings behind Mick Tingelhoff and Mick Tingelhoff hurt"?

22) What is the current limit for the active roster for the Vikings (and for all NFL teams)?

23) What former Viking running back competed in the 1992 Winter Olympics in Albertville, France?

24) What Minnesota cities have hosted an NFL training camp besides Bemidji and Mankato, which have both hosted the Vikings?

25) Though it is largely meaningless, what is the Vikings all-time record in pre-season games?

26) What position did the following Viking players play: Paul Edinger (1995), Teddy Garcia (1989), Chuck Nelson (1986-88), and Doug Brien (2002)?

27) What is the most common last name among players who have competed for the Minnesota Vikings?

28) What Viking players have started at quarterback for another franchise in the Super Bowl?

29) What stalwart Viking came up with the idea of the "nerf" football while he was playing for the club in 1970?

30) What is the name of the official mascot of the Minnesota Vikings?

31) How many quarterbacks have started a game for the Vikings?

32) Of the more than 1,000 Viking players to have played for the

club, which two come first and last, alphabetically?

33) What do the following former Viking players have in common: John Campbell (1963-64), Paul Faust (1967), Bruce Holmes (1993), and Craig Sauer (2000)?

34) What Viking Hall of Famer was drafted not only by the Vikings but by the Boston Patriots?

35) What opposing player has scored the most touchdowns against the Vikings?

36) Which of the following Viking heroes was the only one to finish his NFL career with Minnesota: Cris Carter, Chuck Foreman, Alan Page, Carl Eller, or Paul Krause?

37) There have been five pairs of Viking players who have shared the exact same first and last name. Who are they?

38) What was the name of the Viking mascot that became the official mascot of the Minnesota Vikings Children's Fund and took part in the 1995 Celebrity Mascot Olympics before being retired before the 2000 season?

39) What other professional sports franchise did Max Winter (one of the original Viking owners) own at one time?

40) What native Minnesotan and eleven-year Viking veteran was nominated for the NFL's Walter Payton Man of the Year six times?

41) Add up the uniform numbers of the following Viking greats (Fran Tarkenton, Joey Browner, Robert Smith, and Jeff Siemon) and then subtract the uniform numbers of Fred Cox, Chuck Foreman, Jim Marshall, and Gary Anderson and what Viking number would you match?

42) What former popular Viking is the only athlete to have competed in a Super Bowl, a Rose Bowl, and a NCAA Basketball Final Four?

43) Who are the lightest and heaviest players ever to play for the Vikings?

44) Before Brett Favre wore #4 for the Vikings in 2009 and 2010,

who was the only other quarterback in Viking history to wear that number?

45) What Viking tight end once held the NCAA basketball record for best career field-goal percentage?

46) Who is the only non-kicker to wear jersey #1 for the Vikings?

47) What do the following players have in common: Ron Yary, Joey Browner, Kenechi Udeze, and Matt Kalil?

48) What do Hugh McElhenny, Warren Moon, and Chuck Nelson have in common?

49) Who are the tallest and shortest players ever to play for the Vikings?

50) A Viking mascot since 1994, what is the name for the wild-eyed, motorcycle-driving fellow who usually goes by the name of Joseph Juranitch?

51) Believe it or not, the Vikings have had five quarterbacks who have had two different stints as a signal-caller for the team. Who are they?

52) What Viking running back from the 1980's witnessed his son win the Most Outstanding Player award in the 2011 NCAA Hockey Frozen Four at Xcel Center in St. Paul?

53) Which four non-players have been honored in the Minnesota Vikings Ring of Honor?

54) What is the Vikings all-time record against their divisional rivals Green Bay, Chicago, and Detroit?

55) How have the Vikings fared playing on days of the week other than Sundays and Mondays (regular season only)?

56) In what year was a Viking home game "blacked out" most recently?

57) What is the Vikings record in Monday night games?

58) Who are the only players to lead the Vikings in both rushing and receiving in the same season?

59) What three quarterbacks have had the most Opening Day starts for the Vikings?

60) The Vikings have played six times on Thanksgiving Day—three times at Detroit and three times at Dallas. What is their record in those Turkey Day contests?

61) When was the last time the Vikings recorded a shutout win?

Gary Zimmerman

62) When was the last time the Vikings participated in a tie game?

63) For NFL teams that have been playing continuously since at least 1961, how do the Vikings rank in regard to the shortest stretch for consecutive losing seasons?

64) Wearing #45 in the Vikings defensive backfield for over a decade, what was the nickname of cornerback Ed Sharockman (1961-72)?

65) What entertaining Viking offensive lineman, a center on Notre Dame's national champion club in 1977, wore red-colored elbow pads so his mother could see him in the pile-ups?

66) What Viking quarterback went two seasons in a row with more interceptions than touchdown passes but was still the starter the third season?

67) What Viking player was known as Super Freak for his great speed and jumping ability?

68) When Twin Cities Federal was looking for a backup player who was a complete unknown with a funny name for commercials prior to the 1973 season, who were the two other candidates for the job that Bob Lurtsema eventually landed?

69) Who is the oldest player ever to compete for the Vikings?

70) What Viking player was leading the NFL in receptions midway through the 2012 season before being sidelined by a serious ankle injury?

71) Who holds the Viking record for most career receptions by a running back?

72) What kicker missed not one but two extra points (consecutive, too) in a 45-39 loss to Buffalo on Sept. 15, 2002?

73) Who was the first former Viking player to sound the gjallar-horn when it was introduced in 2007?

74) How many Viking runners have gained 1,000 yards in a season?

75) What two Viking quarterbacks rank 12th and 13th in career yards per carry in the NFL?

76) Starting with the 2011 season, what is the starting kickoff yard-line for NFL games?

77) Who is the lowest-drafted player in Viking history ever to earn a Pro Bowl berth—or even a starting berth, for that matter?

78) What five men have played in at least 200 games for the Vikings?

79) What two Heisman Trophy winners have played for Minnesota?

80) Which teams have more division titles since the 1970 AFL/NFL merger than the Vikings (16)?

81) Who are the only Viking players to earn the prestigious Walter Payton Man of the Year award?

82) What current Viking pro scout and Richmond, Minnesota, native played wide receiver for the winningest coach in college football history?

83) What receiver was 4 for 8 passing during his tenure with Minnesota for 106 yards, two touchdowns, and an interception?

84) Has a non-lineman ever led the Vikings in sacks in a season?

85) What two running backs, perhaps the two best running and receiving duos in Viking lore, ended their careers with exactly the same number of rushing and receiving touchdowns?

86) Has the team's leading receiver in a season ever gone without scoring a receiving touchdown?

87) Which players started every game their rookie season?

88) What kickoff man holds the Vikings record for most touchbacks in a season?

89) How do the Vikings rank in playoff appearances and division titles since their first game in 1961, compared to division rivals Green Bay, Detroit, and Chicago?

90) In what college stadium did the Vikings open up the 2002 season playing the Chicago Bears?

91) Which teams do the Vikings have a losing record against?

92) Have the Vikings ever played a regular season game in a foreign country?

93) In what four overseas cities have the Vikings played a pre-season game?

94) What three teams have a winning record playing the Vikings in Minnesota?

95) What two players have worn four different numbers during their tenure with Minnesota?

96) Who are the only NFL teams the Vikings have never defeated on the road?

97) What is the Vikings overall record in overtime games?

98) Who are the only teams with a better record since the 1970 AFL/NFL merger than the Vikings (374-288-2)?

99) Five of the top 16 all-time scoring leaders in NFL history kicked for the Vikings at some point in their lengthy careers. Who are they?

100) In his first game as a Viking on Sept. 11, 2005, what defensive back returned an interception 88 yards for a touchdown against visiting Tampa Bay?

101) Which Viking running backs have thrown touchdown passes?

102) Among Minnesota natives, what player has played in and started the most games for the Vikings?

103) Of all the Vikings who have played in at least 100 games (regular season), which players have started every game they ever played with the Vikings?

104) Which former Viking is the president of the local chapter of the NFL Alumni Association?

105) Which legendary football program did the following Viking stars compete for collegiately—Cris Carter, Jim Marshall, Robert Smith, Korey Stringer, and Antoine Winfield?

106) What Viking quarterback once passed for five touchdowns in back-to-back games on the road?

1) 1966. The logo is of a stern-faced warrior with a gold skull cap, white horns, and gold-beaded hair. An alternate logo, a fanciful purple "V" with gold trim, was added in 1998.

2) Six (1961-66) at Bemidji State University.

3) Kenechi Udeze (2004-08), a defensive end from USC who was their top pick in 2004 and Artie Ulmer (1997), a linebacker and special teams star from Valdosta State in Georgia.

4) Winter Park (named after former owner Max Winter) in Eden Prairie. After first being located in a small office in Edina, the Vikings moved into the new facility, which housed the team's offices, locker-room, and practice fields. When the Twins moved out of the Metrodome to Target Field, the Vikings then moved their ticket operation to downtown Minneapolis.

5) Jim Brown (104.3) and Barry Sanders (99.8). Terrell Davis (97.5) is fourth. Peterson has 8,849 yards in 89 career games (51 yards short of averaging 100 per game through six seasons).

6) 29-22-1; Minnesota is 18-6 at home and 11-16-1 on the road. Their most common opponent on "Opening Day" has been San Francisco and Green Bay, six times each.

7) Amp Lee (RB - 1994-96); Bob Lee (QB/P - 1969-72; 75-78); Jim Leo (DE, 1961-62), and Al Noga (DE, 1988-92). Tied for the longest name are Adimchinobe Echemnandu, a Cal player from Nigeria who played two games as a running back in 2005, and McLeod Bethel-Thompson, a QB from Sacramento State (2012).

8) Oakland, California.

9) A profile of a blond Norseman.

10) Sixth (54.5%). The Chicago Bears (57.8%) are tops followed by Dallas (57.3%), Miami (56.8%), Green Bay (56.5%), and San Francisco (55.5%).

11) 1,016 (including 18 new players on the roster in 2012).

12) Darren Bennett (punter, 2004-05); Willie Spencer (running back, 1976); and Tom Wilson (running back, 1963).

13) Nine (9); they include three from Concordia-Moorhead, two each from St. Thomas and Gustavus Adolphus, and one each from St. John's and Macalester.

14) Bert Rose, who felt that "Vikings" represented both an aggressive person with the will to win and also that it fit the Nordic tradition of the Midwest, and Minnesotans, in particular.

15) 29 Gophers have played for the Vikings.

16) Rich Gannon, who married Brown's daughter Shelley, an All-American gymnast at Minnesota.

17) Ed Marinaro, who rushed for 1,007 yards and had 1,008 receiving yards.

18) Purple People Eaters (Carl Eller, Alan Page, Jim Marshall, and Gary Larsen). In the mid-1970's, Larsen was replaced by Doug Sutherland. Purple People Eaters was in reference to a popular hit song by Sheb Wooley from 1958.

19) 836. In addition, they have played 236 pre-season games.

20) 9520 Viking Drive

21) Godfrey Zaunbrecher, who played 16 games from 1971-73.

22) 45; additionally, up to eight players may be placed on the practice roster for a total of 53 on the active roster.

23) Herschel Walker. He finished seventh in the two-man bobsled. He also tried out for the four-man bobsled team but was cut.

24) Northfield at St. Olaf College (Dallas Cowboys, 1961); St. Peter at Gustavus Adolphus (New York Giants, 1952-53); Hibbing (Philadelphia Eagles, 1950-51; and Duluth (Chicago Cardinals, 1939)

25) 141-91-3

26) Kicker

27) Johnson (isn't it only fitting for Minnesota!). There have been 19 Johnson's over the years with 17 Smith's, 12 Williams', and 10 Browns'.

28) Jim McMahon (Chicago), Brad Johnson (Tampa Bay), and Rich Gannon (Oakland).

29) Fred Cox. The Viking kicker came up with the idea working with a fellow named John Mattox and they brought their idea to Parker Brothers, who started producing the cushy foam balls in 1972.

30) Viktor the Viking

31) 30; of that total, no less than 12 of them started less than 10 games in their Viking career.

32) Husain Abdullah (2008-12), a safety from Washington State is first and Gary Zimmerman (1986-92), a tackle from Oregon, is last.

33) All were former Gopher stalwarts who later played linebacker for the Vikings. Campbell, from Wadena, was a wide receiver with the Gophers. Sauer hailed from Sartell.

34) Fran Tarkenton. Besides being the Vikings third-round pick in the 1961 draft, the Georgia quarterback was also drafted by the upstart AFL club in the fifth round.

35) Walter Payton. The Chicago Bears Hall of Famer scored 18 of his 110 career touchdowns versus the Vikings.

36) Paul Krause. Meanwhile, Carter finished with Miami, Foreman with New England, Page with Chicago, and Eller with Seattle.

37) Derrick Alexander, Barry Bennett, Charlie Johnson, Mike Jones, and Robert Smith. A first-round draft pick in 1995 out of Florida State, defensive end Derrick Laborn Alexander played four seasons with the Vikings and recorded 17.5 sacks. Derrick Scott Alexander, a wide receiver out of Michigan, played for the Vikings in 2002, when he caught 14 passes for 134 yards and one touchdown. Barry Martin Bennett, a St. Paul native who played at Concordia-Moorhead, played one game at defensive end in 1988 after playing previously for New Orleans and the New York Jets. Barry S. Bennett was a punter on the 1974 team from Quachita Baptist. Colorado nose tackle Charlie Johnson played from 1982-84 with four sacks while Oklahoma State grad Charlie Johnson has played both left tackle (2011) and left guard (2012) for the current team. Mike Anthony Jones (sixth-round choice in 1983) was a wide receiver from Tennessee State from 1983-85 and totaled 90 catches for 1,327 yards and five touchdowns while Mike Lenere Jones (third-round pick in 1990) was a tight end from Texas A &M from 1990-91 who caught two balls for two

touchdowns. Robert Scott Smith (first-round pick in 1993) from Ohio State is the second-leading rusher in Viking history after a stellar career from 1993-2000. Robert Benjamin Smith was a defensive end from Grambling and played in 1985.

38) Vikadontis Rex

39) Minneapolis Lakers. Winter became part owner of the basketball franchise in 1947 along with Sid Hartman, Ben Berger, and Morris Chalfin.

40) Matt Birk. As a Baltimore Raven, he finally won the award and was recognized at the Super Bowl in February of 2012. The following season, he was the starting center for the Super Bowl champions Ravens.

41) Four (4). Ever heard of a fellow named Brett Favre!

42) Joe Kapp. The fun-loving quarterback brought his California Golden Bears to the 1959 Rose Bowl, he was the Vikings starting quarterback in Super Bowl IV, and he was a guard on the California team that was in the 1959 Final Four.

43) Offensive tackle Bryant McKinnie (2002-10) weighed 365 in his final season with the Vikings in 2010 and reportedly weighed nearly 400 pounds in the summer of 2011, when he was put on the inactive list and later released during training camp. On the other end of the scale, wide receiver Eric Guliford (1993-94) weighed in at just 165 pounds on his 5'8" frame.

44) Archie Manning (1983-84)

45) Joe Senser, who made 66.2% of his shots playing for West Chester State (1975-79). Six others have now surpassed his record, however.

46) Quarterback Warren Moon (1994-96).

47) All were first-round draft picks from Southern California: Yary (1968), Browner (1983), Udeze (2004), and Kalil (2012).

48) Each were stars at the University of Washington and are in the Husky Hall of Fame.

49) Bryant McKinnie, the beast from Miami, was 6'8" as the starting offensive tackle from 2002-10. Meanwhile, the shortest player in team history is kick returner/punt returner Eddie Payton (1980-

82), who was just 5'6".

50) Ragnar

51) Fran Tarkenton (1961-66, 1972-78); Bob Berry (1965-67, 1973-75); Bob Lee (1969-72, 1975-78); Brad Johnson (1994-98, 2005-06); and Gus Frerotte (2003-04,2008).

52) Ted Brown. His son, J.T., was a vital cog when the UMD Bulldogs took their first-ever national crown.

53) Bud Grant (head coach), Jerry Burns (assistant and head coach), Jim Finks (general manager), and Fred Zamberletti (trainer).

54) The Vikings are 49-55-1 against Green Bay, 53-49-2 against Chicago, and 68-33-2 against Detroit. In addition, they were 31-17 against Tampa Bay when the Bucs were in the NFC Central Division from 1978-2001 and 31-22 overall.

55) Tuesdays (0-1); Thursdays (10-8), Fridays (1-2), Saturdays (4-1).

56) 1997

57) 26-29

58) Tommy Mason (1962), Bill Brown (1964), Dave Osborn (1967), Chuck Foreman (1974, 1975, 1976), Ted Brown (1981, 1982), and Darrin Nelson (1983).

59) Fran Tarkenton (9), Tommy Kramer (6), and Daunte Culpepper (6).

60) 5-1 (tied with Miami for best all-time)

61) On Dec. 5, 1993, the Vikings blanked host Detroit 13-0 at the Pontiac Silverdome. The Vikings had five interceptions, three by linebacker Jack Del Rio.

62) On Nov. 26, 1978, the Vikings tied the Packers 10-10. Their only other tie since overtime was created came on Sept. 19, 1976 when Minnesota tied the Los Angeles Rams by the same score.

63) First. The Vikings have never gone more than three years in a row without a winning season. The Jets and the Ravens/original Cleveland franchise each have had stretches of four losing seasons in a row.

64) "Bozo"

65) David Huffman, who was a fun-loving backup at both center and guard for 11 years (1979-83, 85-90). He was just 41 when he died in an auto accident on Nov. 21, 1998, not far from his alma mater.

66) Joe Kapp. In 1967, he had eight touchdown passes and 17 interceptions with a 48.2 quarterback rating. In 1968, Joe had 10 TD passes and 17 interceptions with a 58.8 rating. However, in 1969, he led the Vikings to a 12-2 record and their first Super Bowl.

67) Randy Moss

68) Center Godfrey Zaunbrecher and linebacker Carl Gersbach.

69) Morten Anderson was 44 when he was the team's kicker in 2004. Gary Anderson was 43 in his final season kicking in 2002.

Vikings mascot Hub Meeds on the sideline at Met Stadium.

70) Percy Harvin. The flanker had 62 catches for 677 yards after nine games and was certain to be a Pro Bowler and was even in the discussion for MVP before getting hurt in Seattle. Traded to Seattle prior to the 2013 season for draft picks, Harvin piled up 7,168 all-purpose yards in just four seasons, scored 29 touchdowns and totaled 280 receptions.

71) Ted Brown (339). Chuck Foreman (336) and Rickey Young (292) follow. Young has the seasonal record with 88 catches in 1978.

72) Doug Brien

73) Chuck Foreman. Since then, the following players have also performed the ceremonial task: Carl Eller, Heath Farwell, Robert Griffith, John Randle, Paul Krause, Robert Smith, Rufus Bess, Jim Marshall, Randall McDaniel, Scott Studwell,

Mick Tingelhoff, Joe Kapp, Stu Voigt, Greg Coleman, Gene Washington, Mike Morris, Sidney Rice, Jeff Siemon, Fred Cox, Chris Doleman, Matt Blair, and Ted Brown. Others to perform the ceremonial duty include Hub Meeds, Bud Grant, Jerry Burns, and Fred Zamberletti.

74) Seven. Adrian Peterson (2007-2010, 2012), Robert Smith (1997-2000), Chuck Foreman (1975-1977), Terry Allen (1992, 1994), Ted Brown (1981), Chester Taylor (2006), and Michael Bennett (2002).

75) Fran Tarkenton (5.45) and Daunte Culpepper (5.2).

76) 35-yard line. From 1994-2010, it was set at the 30-yard line; from 1974-93, it was also at the 35. Prior to that, it was set at the 40-yard line.

77) Milt Sunde (20th round pick in 1964 and 1966 Pro Bowler).

78) Jim Marshall (270), Mick Tingelhoff (240), Fred Cox (210), Carl Eller (209), and Scott Studwell (202).

79) Herschel Walker (1982-Georgia) and Gino Torretta (1992-Miami). Adrian Peterson (2004) and Toby Gerhart (2009) both finished second.

80) Pittsburgh (20), San Francisco (19), and Dallas (17).

81) Cris Carter (1999) and Madieu Williams (2010).

82) Ryan Monnens. He played for St. John's head coach John Gagliardi, who had a record of 489-138-11 in 64 collegiate seasons (60 with the Johnnies). Gagliardi retired following the 2012 season after coaching his last college game at the age of 86.

83) Randy Moss. In addition, running back Alfred Anderson was 4-9 for 112 yards and two touchdowns and an interception, almost identical to Moss' numbers.

84) Yes. Linebacker Matt Blair had six in 1981 and linebacker Ben Leber had five in 2007. In both instances, however, they tied two defensive linemen.

85) Bill Brown and Chuck Foreman; each had 52 rushing and 23 receiving.

86) Yes. Darrin Nelson (51 in 1983) and Steve Jordan (68 in 1985).

87) Gary Zimmerman (1986), Todd Steussie (1994), Dewayne Washington (1994), Kevin Williams (2003), Matt Kalil (2012), and Harrison Smith (2012) started all 16 games. Plus, kicker Blair Walsh participated in all 16 games in 2012. Prior to the expanded schedule, Mick Tingelhoff (1962), Paul Flately (1963), Carl Eller (1964), and Sammy White (1976) started all 14 games.

88) Blair Walsh had 53 in his rookie year in 2012. He booted 61.6% of his kickoffs into the end zone in earning his way into the Pro Bowl, which set an NFL rookie record.

89) Minnesota (27) is first in playoff appearances. Green Bay (22) is second with Chicago (15), and Detroit (10) following. Minnesota (18) is also first in division titles with Chicago (10), Green Bay (10), and Detroit (3) following.

90) Memorial Stadium in Champaign, Illinois, the home field of the University of Illinois. The Bears moved their home games there while Solider Stadium was being refurbished. The Vikings squandered a 23-13 fourth quarter lead and lost 27-23.

91) Green Bay (49-55-1); Indianapolis/Baltimore Colts (8-15); Kansas City (4-7); Miami (4-7); New England (4-7); New York Jets (1-8); Oakland (4-10); San Diego (5-6); Seattle (5-7), and Washington (10-12).

92) No. However, the Vikings are slated to play the Pittsburgh Steelers at Wembley Stadium in London on Sept. 29, 2013. It will be the fourth week of the season and will be followed by a bye for Minnesota. It will also count as one of the eight home games for the Vikings. The NFL has played one game a year in London since 2007 but the Jaguars and 49ers will also play in London in 2013.

93) London, England (28-10 win over St. Louis Cardinals on Aug. 6, 1983); Goteborg, Sweden (28-21 win over Chicago Bears on Aug. 15, 1988); Berlin, Germany (20-6 win over Buffalo on Aug. 7, 1993), and Tokyo, Japan (17-9 win over Kansas City on Aug. 6, 1994)

94) New York Jets (3-1), Oakland Raiders (4-3), and Washington Redskins (6-4). Green Bay, incidentally, is 25-26 playing in Minnesota.

95) Chris Martin, a linebacker from Auburn, wore numbers 56, 94, 98, and 57 from 1984-88. Andrew Jordan, a tight from Western

Carolina, wore numbers 85, 43, 83, and 89 from 1994-97 and from 1999-2001.

96) Indianapolis (0-11; 0-8 while in Baltimore, 0-3 in Indianapolis) and the New York Jets (0-5).

97) 19 wins, 20 losses, and two ties.

98) Pittsburgh (404-258-2), Miami (392-270-2), Dallas (389-275-0), Denver (380-278-6), and San Francisco (375-285-4).

99) Morten Anderson (2004), Gary Anderson (1998-2002), Jan Stenerud (1984-85), Ryan Longwell (2006-11), and Eddie Murray (1997). Morten Anderson is first with 2,544 points with Gary Anderson second with 2,434. Stenerud is 12th with 1,699 while Longwell is 13th with 1,687 and Murray 16th with 1,594.

100) Darren Sharper

101) Alfred Anderson (2), Darrin Nelson, Mewelde Moore, Chester Taylor, Keith Henderson, D.J. Dozier, and Tommy Mason. Anderson threw both of his during the 1984 season.

102) Matt Birk (St. Paul) played in 146 games from 1998-08 and started 123 in a row.

103) Jim Marshall (240), Mick Tingelhoff (240), Kevin Williams (156), Todd Steussie (111), and Gary Zimmerman (108).

104) Kurt Knoff, a safety from 1979-82. It has 100 members (most of whom have played for the Vikings) and has been in existence for over 30 years.

105) Ohio State University.

106) Daunte Culpepper (2004). The former Central Florida standout threw five at Houston on Oct. 10 and five at New Orleans on Oct. 17. He also threw five scoring tosses earlier in the season at Dallas on Sept. 12.

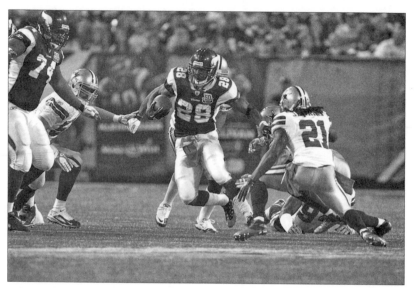

Adrian Peterson (28) eyes yardage against Dallas with the help of Bryant McKinnie (74).

20 Individual Records

1) What Viking rookie running back set the NFL single-game rushing record with 296 yards in just his eighth professional contest?

2) A Pro Football Hall of Famer, what Viking safety still holds the NFL mark for most interceptions in a career with 81?

3) Which Viking defensive standout is tied for first all-time in NFL history with four career safeties?

4) Which Viking linebacker holds the franchise record for most career tackles, most tackles in a season, and most tackles in a game?

5) What Viking defensive player holds the franchise mark with 130 sacks?

6) What Viking player has the longest kickoff return in NFL history without scoring a touchdown?

7) Who is the only player in club annals to score a touchdown four different ways?

8) What backup receiver holds the team record for most "special teams" tackles?

9) What Viking rusher holds the NFL record for most yards gained in one month?

10) What Viking runner holds the NFL record for most yards in one half?

11) What diminutive kicker set the Viking mark for most points in a single season with 164 points in 1998, which led the NFL?

12) What Viking defensive end holds the Viking and NFL record for most fumbles recovered in a season?

13) Who leads the Vikings in career interceptions?

14) Who is the Vikings all-time single-season leader in touchdowns scored?

15) On Oct. 22, 2006, what running back set the Viking record for longest run from scrimmage with a 95-yard touchdown scamper at Seattle?

16) Who holds the franchise record for most career rushing yards?

17) Who was the Vikings kicking specialist in 1989 who booted barefoot?

18) What non-quarterback has thrown the most passes in Viking history?

19) Who holds the Viking record for the longest punt with an 84-yarder?

20) What Viking running back holds the team record for most fumbles in a season with 14?

21) What Viking receiver and quarterback are tied with 12 other tandems as they hooked up on a 99-yard touchdown pass play against the Chicago Bears at the Metrodome on Nov. 30, 2008?

22) Who was the first Viking to rush for 1,000 yards in a season?

23) Who was the first Viking receiver to reach 1,000 receiving yards in a season?

24) What fellow holds the Viking record for best win-loss percentage as a starting quarterback? (Minimum 10 games)

25) What two stalwart defensive linemen for the Vikings share the team record with two safeties in one season?

26) What Viking receiver holds the team record for all-purpose yards?

27) What defensive back established the Minnesota mark for longest interception return?

28) What straight-on kicker holds the franchise record with 282 field goals?

29) What Viking linebacker set the record for longest fumble return?

30) Which Viking quarterback holds the team mark for single-game passing yards?

31) Which athletic linebacker for the Vikings has the all-time high with 20 career blocked kicks?

32) Although he didn't lead the league that year, what Viking holds the franchise record with 10 interceptions in 1975?

33) What Viking defensive end holds the team single-season mark for sacks?

34) What Viking runner holds the single-season rushing record?

35) Who holds the Minnesota mark for most fumble recoveries in a game?

36) What Viking receiver holds the single-season record for most receptions?

37) What Viking player holds the team record for highest career kickoff return average?

38) What Viking quarterback holds the Minnesota record for most touchdowns passes in a single season?

39) What player holds the single-season mark for the highest punting average?

40) What player holds the career mark for highest punt return average?

41) What Viking player holds the record for most career receptions?

42) Who holds the Minnesota record for most passing yards in one season?

43) Who is Minnesota's all-time leading scorer?

44) With 33,098 yards, who is the Viking leader in career passing yards?

45) What player is the only Viking in history to record five kickoff return touchdowns?

46) Who holds the single-season mark for highest punt return average?

47) What cornerback set a season mark and tied a career Viking mark with three interception returns for touchdowns in 1998?

48) What quarterback holds the career mark (minimum 100 pass attempts) for the lowest interception percentage at 2.23%?

49) What legendary Viking player holds the franchise record for most seasons played with the team?

50) What Viking defensive back holds the record for longest punt return?

51) What swift Vikings running back holds the all-time NFL career record for the longest average on his touchdown runs?

52) What popular figure in Vikings history holds the career mark for rushing attempts?

53) What two Viking safeties are tied with the most consecutive games with an interception with six?

54) What noted Viking kicker went six years without missing an extra point?

55) What non-running back holds the Minnesota career mark for rushing yards per carry (minimum 250 carries)?

56) What two former Viking teammates share the single-season record for most touchdown receptions?

57) Who holds the franchise record for most rushing touchdowns in a career?

58) What quarterback holds the Viking mark for most consecutive games with a touchdown pass?

59) What man holds the Minnesota record for wins as a starting quarterback?

60) What fellow has the Viking record for most career receiving yards?

61) What crafty Viking safety holds the one-season record for most interception return yards?

62) What two teammates hold the Minnesota mark for most seasons leading the team in sacks?

63) What South African-born kicker from Syracuse holds the NFL record for most consecutive field goals made (regular and post-season) with 46?

64) What Viking defender has the all-time NFL record for most consecutive games with a sack with 11?

65) What Minnesota receiver holds the NFL record for most consecutive seasons with 120 or more catches?

66) What two place-kickers share the Vikings record for longest field goal?

67) Who holds the NFL record for most consecutive games started?

68) What Viking runner has the most 100-yard rushing games?

69) What Viking kicker has the most field goals of at least 50 yards in a season?

70) Who has the most rushing touchdowns in one season?

71) Who became the first receiver in NFL history to average more than 100 yards per game and at least one touchdown per game over the course of a season spanning at least 12 games?

72) What quarterback holds the mark for most consecutive passes completed?

73) Who kicked field goals in 31 straight games?

74) What defender has 300 more solo tackles than any other Viking?

75) What Viking has the single-game record for sacks with five?

76) Who holds the franchise mark for scoring in consecutive games?

77) The Viking record for most completions in a single game is 38. What quarterback did it twice?

78) Who holds the franchise mark for most games played?

79) Which two Vikings have returned two punts for touchdowns?

Scott Studwell (55) and Keith Millard (75).

80) With 110, which Viking holds the career record for most touchdowns?

81) Who has the best yards-per-punt average in Vikings history?

82) Who has the highest yards per reception average for the Vikings?

83) What quarterback holds both the career and season mark for most interceptions?

84) With a minimum of four catches, who holds the single-game record for most yards per reception?

85) With 852 yards, who holds the career record for most interception return yards?

86) Who became the first Viking to lead the NFL in scoring with

121 points in 1969 and followed it with a league-leading total of 125 in 1970?

87) What Viking quarterback tied an NFL record by throwing for seven touchdowns in a 52-12 whipping of the Baltimore Colts at Met Stadium on Sept. 28, 1969?

88) Who is the only Viking kicker to boot a field goal of fifty yards or more in three consecutive games?

89) Which Viking quarterback leads the club with 239 career touchdown passes?

90) What player holds the single-season mark for highest kickoff return average?

91) What Viking punter also performed as the team's kickoff man for several seasons?

92) Who holds the rookie record for most touchdown receptions?

93) Who holds the team mark for most reception yards in a season?

94) Who is the Vikings all-time leader in pass completions with 2,635?

95) Who has the team record for most field goals in a game?

96) What Viking kicker led the NFL three times in field goals made?

97) What receiver holds the team record with the most 1,000-yard receiving seasons?

98) Who are the only players to score touchdowns in a season at least three different ways?

99) What Viking rookies have led the team in scoring?

100) Which quarterback holds the career mark for completion percentage?

101) Who holds the team record for consecutive passes without an interception?

102) Who recorded the longest scoring play in Viking history?

103) Who was the first Viking to rush for 100 yards or more in a single game?

104) What Viking runner has the most runs of at least 50 yards?

105) Who holds the mark for most 100-yard rushing games in a season?

106) What longtime cornerback averaged 20.1 yards for each of his interceptions?

107) What defender holds the franchise mark for most solo tackles in a season?

108) Which two quarterbacks are tied with the most 300-yard passing games with 19?

109) Which two teammates have the most 100-yard receiving games?

110) Who has the team record for scoring touchdowns in consecutive games?

111) What runner has the franchise mark for most consecutive games with at least 100 yards?

112) What punter booted 565 punts without a block?

113) What receiver led the team in catches in 10 straight seasons?

114) What player led the team in scoring in 11 consecutive years?

115) Which non-kickers have led the Vikings in scoring?

116) Which three defensive backs led the team in interceptions four times?

117) Who holds the single game mark for most receptions with 15?

118) Which Viking rookies were selected NFL Player of the Week more than once?

119) Who has scored the most career touchdowns among Viking defenders?

120) Who is the Viking career leader in takeaways (interceptions and fumble recoveries)?

121) Who holds the record for most touches (rushes, receptions, or returns) without a fumble in his career with the Vikings?

122) What top draft choice played 26 major-league games for the New York Mets?

123) What player once led the team in receiving yards with a paltry 282 yards?

124) Which five players have led the team in tackles and interceptions in the same year?

125) Who holds the rookie scoring record with 141 points?

126) What Viking player was third in the NFL in tackles in consecutive seasons?

127) Which two Viking running backs surpassed 5,000 rushing yards and 3,000 receiving yards?

128) Who holds the team mark for most tackles by a defensive back?

129) Who are the only two Vikings to score four touchdowns in a game?

130) Which two Viking kickers share the single-season mark for field goals with 35?

131) What Viking holds the team record for consecutive rushes (478) without a lost fumble?

1) Adrian Peterson. The Palestine, Texas, native and former Oklahoma star broke the previous record of 295 yards by Jamaal Lewis (2003) with his fantastic effort on Nov. 4, 2007, at the Metrodome against the San Diego Chargers. Peterson had 43 first-half yards but then rushed for 253 more in the second half.

2) Paul Krause. Blessed with great hands, Krause played center field in the Vikings powerful defense and he picked off 53 of his 81 thefts in eight seasons with the Vikings (1968-75). An eight-time Pro-Bowler, Krause had 1,185 return yards on those interceptions for an average of nearly 15 yards per return. Krause graduated from Iowa and played the first four years of his career with the Redskins and has been a long-time Dakota County Commissioner.

3) Jared Allen. Since joining the Vikings in 2008, the feisty pass-rusher has tied Ted Hendricks and Doug English with four safeties (two in 2008, and one each in 2009, and 2011). Alan Page is tied with several others with three.

4) Scott Studwell. A ninth-round draft pick out of Illinois, the intense middle linebacker had a total of 1,981 tackles over his 14-year career from 1977-90 and started 161 games. In 1981, he had a season-record 230 tackles and in a 1985 game versus Dallas, he collected 24 tackles. He was in the Pro Bowl in 1987 and 1988.

5) Carl Eller. Jim Marshall had 127.

6) Percy Harvin. On Nov. 27, 2011, the Florida speedster ran a kickoff back 104 yards before being caught from behind by Atlanta's Chris Owens at the Falcon three-yard line. To add insult to injury, the Vikings turned the ball over on downs and ended up losing 24-14.

7) David Palmer (two punt returns, one rushing, one receiving, one kickoff return).

8) Chris Walsh had 147 tackles from 1994-02.

9) Adrian Peterson rushed for 861 yards in five games in December of 2012; Dec. 2 (210 at Green Bay); Dec. 9 (154 against Chicago); Dec. 16 (212 at St. Louis); Dec. 23 (86 at Houston), and Dec. 30 (199 against Green Bay). Adrian averaged 172.2 yards per game.

10) Adrian Peterson had 253 second-half yards on Nov. 4, 2007 at the Metrodome when he ran for 296 yards against San Diego. His

second-half total alone would be tied for ninth-best for one game. Peterson had 146 yards in the fourth quarter, too, another Viking record.

11) Gary Anderson, who was 39 years old at the time. Anderson's number stands as the fifth-highest scoring year in league history.

12) Don Hultz with nine in 1963. He also had 10.5 sacks in his only season with Minnesota.

13) Paul Krause had 53 interceptions from 1968-79. Bobby Bryant is a close second with 51 thefts from 1968-80.

14) Chuck Foreman scored 22 touchdowns (13 rushing, nine receiving) in 1975.

15) Chester Taylor

16) Adrian Peterson (8,849); he has averaged 5.0 yards per carry in 89 career games. It took him only 74 games to set the Viking record. Robert Smith (6,818) is second after averaging 4.8 per carry in his eight seasons (98 games) with the club (1993-2000).

17) Rich Karlis

18) Alfred Anderson, a running back. He threw nine passes, completing four for 112 yards and two touchdowns.

19) Harry Newsome, who booted nearly the length of the field in a game on Dec. 20, 1992 at Three Rivers Stadium in Pittsburgh. He was aided by a 16 mile-per-hour wind. Newsome was second in the league in punting average in 1991 and 1992.

20) Tommy Mason (1963)

21) Bernard Berrian (WR) and Gus Frerotte (QB). Berrian ran the final 54 yards after catching Frerotte's pass at the Viking 46.

22) Chuck Foreman, who rushed for 1,070 yards and 13 touchdowns in 1975.

23) John Gilliam (1,035 yards in 1972). Gilliam led the NFL that year with 22 yards per reception.

24) Gus Frerotte (76.9% ; 10-3 in 13 starts). Gary Cuozzo is next at 76.2% . Cuozzo was 16-5 as a starter but benefitted from great Viking defenses from 1968-1971. Randall Cunningham is next at 69.6% while Daunte Culpepper is worst at 47.5% (38-42).

25) Jared Allen (2008) and Alan Page (1971).

26) Cris Carter (12,410; all but 24 receiving). Darrin Nelson had 10,365.

27) Reggie Rutland (nee Najee Mustafaa), who picked off Los Angeles Rams quarterback Jim Everett and sprinted 97 yards for a touchdown on Dec. 15, 1991.

28) Fred Cox

29) Dwayne Ruud, who raced 94 yards with a fumble on Dec. 6, 1998 against Chicago.

30) Tommy Kramer, who had 490 yards on Nov. 2, 1986 in a 44-38 overtime win on the road over Washington.

31) Matt Blair. The Iowa State alum, who had a penchant for being able to jump high and time his leaps perfectly, was a key member of Bud Grant's specialty teams.

32) Paul Krause

33) Jared Allen (22 in 2011), eclipsing Chris

Cris Carter.

Doleman's total of 21 in 1989. Allen had 3.5 sacks in the final game against Chicago Bear quarterback Josh McCown but couldn't get another, which would have exceeded the NFL record of 22.5 by Michael Strahan of the New York Giants.

34) Adrian Peterson, who totaled 2,097 yards in 2012, besting his 2008 mark of 1,760. Peterson came within nine yards of breaking Eric Dickerson's NFL mark of 2,105 set in 1984. He won the rushing title by a whopping 484 yards. Adrian averaged 131.1 yards per game and 6.026 per rush—fourth-best in NFL history for one season behind Jim Brown (6.4 in 1963), Barry Sanders (6.1 in 1997), and O.J. Simpson (6.033 in 1973).

35) Joey Browner, who recovered three fumbles on Sept. 8, 1985, versus San Francisco. The 49ers fumbled seven times in the game and lost five of them.

36) Cris Carter, who not only caught 122 balls in 1994 but repeated it in 1995.

37) Percy Harvin (27.9 per return). The former Florida flash returned 114 kicks for 3,183 yards in just four seasons with five touchdowns.

38) Daunte Culpepper (39 in 2004).

39) Chris Kluwe, whose average gross punt in 2008 was 47.6.

40) Mewelde Moore (10.4) returned 74 punts for 768 yards from 2004-07. Tommy Mason had a higher average (10.5 per return) but doesn't meet the minimum required 50 returns. He returned 46 punts for 483 yards in his six seasons (1961-66).

41) Cris Carter (1,004). Enshrined in the Pro Football Hall of Fame in 2013, Carter also holds the franchise mark for most consecutive games with a reception (111). No one in the NFL had more receptions (779) or touchdowns (90) between 1993 and 2000 than Carter, and only Tim Brown had more receiving yards than Carter's 9,456 during that period. He caught 70-plus passes in a season 10 times.

42) Daunte Culpepper (4,717 in 2004).

43) Fred Cox (1,365).

44) Fran Tarkenton

45) Percy Harvin had five kick return touchdowns in just four seasons (two in 2009 and one each in 2010, 2011, and 2012.

46) Troy Walters averaged 14.46 yards on 15 returns (minimum) in 2000.

47) Jimmy Hitchcock. Others with three career interception return touchdowns include Rip Hawkins, Bobby Bryant, Ed Sharockman, Joey Browner, Audray McMillian, Dewayne Washington, and Darren Sharper.

48) Sean Salisbury (1992-94) with just nine interceptions in 404 pass attempts.

49) Jim Marshall (1961-79) played 19 seasons for the Vikings. Center Mick Tingelhoff (1962-78), who played 17 years, is the only other player to play more than 15 years for the club. Carl Eller, Ron Yary, Roy Winston, and Fred Cox all played 15 years.

50) Charlie West returned a punt 98 yards for a touchdown against Washington in 1968.

51) Robert Smith, who averaged 27.2 yards on his 32 rushing touchdowns. Meanwhile, Adrian Peterson has averaged 16.3 yards on his 76 rushing scores.

52) Adrian Peterson (1,754).

53) Paul Krause (1968) and Brian Russell (2003).

54) Fred Cox. Freddie the Foot booted 199 straight conversions from Sept. 14, 1968 through Sept. 15, 1974.

55) Quarterback Fran Tarkenton averaged 5.49 yards per rush in his two stints with the team (1961-66, 1972-78) as he accumulated 2,548 yards on 464 rushes. Another quarterback, Daunte Culpepper, is second on the list with 5.45 yards per rush from 1999 to 2005 (2,476 yards on 454 rushes).

56) Cris Carter (1995) and Randy Moss (1998 and 2003) are tied with 17 scoring grabs. Moss also had 15 in 2000 and Carter had 13 in 1997 and 1999, as did Moss in 2004.

57) Adrian Peterson has 76 rushing scores after six seasons (2007-12) while Bill Brown and Chuck Foreman are tied for second with 52.

58) Daunte Culpepper threw a TD pass in 24 straight games between the 2000 and 2001 seasons.

59) Fran Tarkenton won 91 games in his 13 seasons with Minnesota.

60) Cris Carter had 12,383 yards in his 12 seasons with the Vikes, including eight-straight years when he totaled at least 1,000 yards.

61) Darren Sharper, who totaled 276 yards in 2005 after swiping nine passes. He also holds the one-game record with 123 yards (against Washington, when he pilfered three passes, which also ties him with 10 others who have done so).

62) Alan Page and Jim Marshall (each had six).

63) Gary Anderson (Dec. 15, 1997 - Jan. 17, 1999).

64) Jared Allen (2010 and 2011).

65) Cris Carter (2; 1994 and 1995). Carter caught 122 balls in each season.

66) Paul Edinger kicked a 56-yarder against Green Bay on Oct. 23, 2005. Blair Walsh kicked a 56-yarder at Houston on Dec. 23, 2012.

67) Brett Favre started 321 consecutive games at quarterback from Sept. 27, 1992 to Dec. 5, 2010 (total includes regular season and playoffs). Of course, Favre only played the last 31 of those games with the Vikings in 2009 and 2010 after playing at Green Bay from 1992-2007 and with the New York Jets in 2008.

68) Adrian Peterson has 37, including 10 each in both 2008 and 2012.

69) Blair Walsh, a rookie, was 10 for 10 from 50 yards out and further in 2012. No one else has ever had more than eight in a season.

70) Adrian Peterson had 18 rushing touchdowns in 2009.

71) Randy Moss. In 2003, the Marshall product caught 111 passes for 1,632 yards and 17 touchdowns.

72) Tommy Kramer. He completed 16 in a row in a 19-7 loss at Green Bay Nov. 11, 1979 and finished 27-38 for 262 yards.

73) Fred Cox (1968-70), the second-best mark in NFL history to Matt Stover (38).

74) Scott Studwell (1,308). Jeff Siemon is second with 1,008.

75) Randy Holloway got a fistful against Atlanta on Sept. 16, 1984.

76) Fred Cox. The kicker scored in 151 straight games from 1963-73.

77) Tommy Kramer (once versus Cleveland in 1980 and once versus Green Bay in 1981).

78) Jim Marshall (289). Mick Tingelhoff (259) is second. Both totals include 19 playoff games.

79) David Palmer and Mewelde Moore.

80) Cris Carter

81) Chris Kluwe (44.4). Kluwe punted 623 times for 27,683 yards.

82) Gordy Smith, with an outstanding average of 22.4 from 1961-65.

83) Fran Tarkenton (194 career, 32 in 1978).

84) Randy Moss (38.0 at Green Bay, Oct. 5, 1998)

85) Paul Krause

86) Fred Cox, who was a Pro-Bowler both seasons.

87) Joe Kapp, whose threw for 449 yards (28-43) that sunny day. Kapp joined Adrian Burk, Sid Luckman, Y.A. Title, and George Blanda to tie the all-time mark.

88) Blair Walsh. The rookie did so in his first three games of his career in 2012.

89) Fran Tarkenton

90) Percy Harvin averaged 35.9 yards in 2012 after averaging 32.5 in 2011, the second-best mark in team history.

91) Mitch Berger

92) Randy Moss (17 in 1998)

93) Randy Moss (1,632 in 2003)

94) Fran Tarkenton

95) Rich Karlis booted seven field goals in a 23-21 overtime win over the Los Angeles Rams on Nov. 5, 1989. Karlis had kicks of 20, 24, 22, 25, 29, 36, and 40 yards without a miss. The Vikings were stopped four times inside the Rams 10-yard line.

96) Fred Cox (1965, 1969, and 1970).

97) Cris Carter went eight straight years with at least 1,000 yards (1993-2000).

98) Percy Harvin (2010, 2011, 2012), Mewelde Moore (2005), Herschel Walker (1989), Bill Brown (1963), and Hugh McElhenny (1961).

99) Kickers Jim Christopherson (61 points -1962), Fred Cox (75 points - 1963), and Blair Walsh (141 points - 2012).

100) Daunte Culpepper (64.4). He also owns the single-season mark with 69.2% in 2004.

101) Warren Moon (193).

102) Percy Harvin. The Florida flash took the opening kick for a 105-yard touchdown in a 20-13 win at Detroit on Sept. 30, 2012.

103) Raymond Hayes (123 yards versus L.A. Rams on Dec. 3, 1961).

104) Adrian Peterson has 18 through his first six seasons. Robert Smith had 12. Peterson had seven alone in 2012, tied with Barry Sanders for the most in one season.

105) Adrian Peterson, who had 10 each in both 2008 and 2012.

106) Ed Sharockman, who had three touchdowns among his 40 picks.

107) Jeff Siemon (170 in 1978). That same season, he also amassed 229 total tackles, second all-time for a single season in team history.

108) Tommy Kramer and Daunte Culpepper. Warren Moon (10) is the only other passer in double digits.

109) Randy Moss (41) and Cris Carter (40).

110) Randy Moss (10 between 2003 and 2004).

111) Adrian Peterson had eight straight in 2012, a stretch where he ran for 1,313 yards or an average of 164 yards per game.

112) Greg Coleman (1979-87).

113) Cris Carter (1991-2000).

114) Fred Cox (1963-1973). He also led the team in scoring in 1976 and holds the team mark for most seasons leading the team in scoring with 12.

115) Jerry Reichow (1961), Chuck Foreman (1974, 1985, tie 1977), Sammy White (tie 1977), Cris Carter (1997), and Randy Moss (tie 2003).

116) Ed Sharockman, Bobby Bryant, and Joey Browner.

117) Rickey Young (at New England on Dec. 16, 1979). However, those short little swing passes from Tommy Kramer netted just 80 yards and no touchdowns.

118) Adrian Peterson (2007) and Blair Walsh (2012).

119) Ed Sharockman (6). He scored three on interception returns, two on returns of blocked punts, and one on a fumble recovery return.

120) Paul Krause - 64 (53 interceptions and 11 fumble recoveries). Bobby Bryant is second with 58 (51 interceptions and seven fumble recoveries).

121) Scottie Graham (368).

122) D.J. Dozier (14th overall pick in 1987).

123) Dave Osborn (1967 - 14 games).

124) Rip Hawkins (1961), Tommy Hannon (1979), Joey Browner (1987), Kailee Wong (2000), and Greg Biekert (2002).

125) Blair Walsh (2012). The Georgia standout broke Randy Moss' mark of 106 set in 1998. Walsh was just a field goal away from tying the NFL record of 144 established by Kevin Butler of Chicago in 1985. Walsh was fourth in the league in scoring.

126) Chad Greenway (2011 and 2012). Greenway has led the Vikings in tackles five straight seasons (2008-12).

127) Bill Brown (5,757 rush, 3,177 receive) and Chuck Foreman (5,879 rush, 3,057 receive).

128) Joey Browner (1,098).

129) Chuck Foreman (Dec. 20, 1975 at Buffalo) and Ahmad Rashad (Sept. 2, 1979 vs. San Francisco).

130) Gary Anderson (1998) and Blair Walsh (2012).

131) Robert Smith (1996-98).

Matt Blair (59), Fred McNeill (54), Alan Page (88), and Jim Marshall (70) watch the offense from the sideline at Met Stadium in 1975.

21 Team Records

1) What is the team record for consecutive wins?

2) What is the team record for most wins in a season?

3) What dubious NFL record did the Vikings set during the 2011 season in regard to pass defense?

4) What is Minnesota's record for most consecutive division championships?

5) In which season did the Vikings win all eight of their home games?

6) Against which NFL team did the Viking once have a 13-game winning streak?

7) What is the Vikings record in the 790 regular season games they have played through 2012?

8) How many opponent fumbles did the Vikings recover in 1963, still an NFL record today?

9) Only four teams in NFL history have scored at least 50 points in three games in a season; which year did the Vikings do it?

10) In what two seasons did the Vikings finish with a 3-13 record, ten games under .500?

11) In what season did the Vikings average an impressive 34.8 points a game?

12) What is the Viking mark for most consecutive wins to begin a season?

13) From 1969 to 1978, the Vikings had an incredible record playing at home. What was their record playing at Met Stadium during that 10-year stretch?

14) What is the Viking record for most consecutive winning seasons?

15) Incredibly, what year or years did the Vikings defense give up an average of less than 10 points per game?

16) How many ties have the Vikings played to since the NFL created overtime play?

17) The 1981 Vikings own the NFL record for the most pass attempts in a season. How many?

18) The only team to allow four kickoff return touchdowns in a season is the 1998 Viking squad; how many?

19) The 1991 Dolphins and the 1997 Vikings share the league record for most two-point conversions in a season; how many?

20) What is the Viking record for most consecutive losing seasons?

21) In what season did the Vikings total a franchise record 36 interceptions?

22) Based on percentages, what is the worst season in Viking history?

23) In what year did the Vikings score a franchise record 64 touchdowns, an average of four per game?

24) In what year did the Viking lose just three fumbles the entire season?

25) Of all NFL teams that have been playing continuously since 1961, the Vikings are tied with Dallas with the least losing seasons over the past 52 years. How many?

26) In 1989, the Vikings set a team record with how many sacks?

27) The Vikings hold the NFL record for scoring touchdowns on both a punt return and a kick return the most times in a game with how many?

28) What is the franchise mark for most interceptions in a game?

29) What is the most lopsided win in Viking history?

30) In what season did the Vikings allow a franchise low of 25 sacks?

31) What is the Viking record for consecutive losses?

32) What is the franchise mark for consecutive home games won?

33) What are the most points scored in a game by the Vikings?

34) What is the record for fewest yards gained by an opponent in a game?

35) What is the record for the most blocked kicks in a game?

36) What is the team mark for most points scored in a quarter and a half, respectively?

37) What is the largest deficit the Vikings have overcome to win a game?

38) What is the team record for most yards gained in a single game?

39) What is the team record for most wins in a season, including post-season?

40) What is the record for consecutive losses on the road?

41) What is the team mark for consecutive games without a fumble?

42) Amazingly, in what season did the Vikings total just 36 penalties?

43) What is the least amount of first downs earned by the Vikings in a game?

44) Have the Viking ever recorded two safeties in a game?

45) Establishing an NFL record, in how many straight games did the Vikings score a touchdown from 1995-2001?

46) What is the largest margin of defeat in Minnesota Vikings history?

47) In what season did the Vikings total a franchise low of 16 sacks?

48) While the Vikings have had the top-rated defense in six seasons, what was the only year they had the NFL's top offense?

49) What is the least number of passes completed by the Vikings in a game?

50) Incredibly, what year did the Vikings defense hold opponents to just 195 yards per game?

51) In their 760 regular season games over 52 seasons, have the Vikings outscored its opponents or have they been outscored overall?

52) Through its 52 seasons, how many seasons did the Vikings outscore its opponents and how many times were they outscored?

53) What is the greatest fourth-quarter deficit ever overcome by the Vikings?

54) What is the greatest one-season improvement in regard to wins in team history?

55) Of all NFL teams that have been playing continuously since 1961, the Vikings have the shortest stretch of consecutive losing seasons. How many?

1) 12 (1969). In that 14-game season, the Vikings actually lost their first game to the New York Giants and their final game to Atlanta but won every game in between. The 12-game streak was the longest in the NFL in 35 years.

2) 15 (15-1 record in 1998)

3) They went nine consecutive games without an interception, a gap that saw opposing quarterbacks complete an astounding 72.1% of their passes (212 of 294) for 2,647 yards and 27 touchdowns. The streak went from Oct. 9 (Jamarca Sanford -2, Asher Allen) until the second half at Washington on Dec. 24 when Mistral Raymond finally pilfered a pass.

4) Six (NFC Central Division 1973-78)

5) 1998. However, in the 14-game schedule in effect from 1961-1978, the Vikings were also perfect at home in 1969, 1970, 1973 and 1975. Each of the aforementioned years, they went 7-0 at home. In 1976, they were 6-0-1, with their only blemish a 10-10 tie with the Los Angeles Rams in their first home tilt.

6) Detroit Lions (1968-74).

7) 426-355-9. Add in their 19-27 playoff mark and they are 445-382-9 overall.

8) 31; they also hold the NFL record for forcing the most fumbles with 50 that season.

9) 1969; the Vikings beat Baltimore 52-14, Cleveland 51-3, and Pittsburgh 52-14.

10) 1984 and 2011

11) 1998, a year when they shattered the NFL record for points in a season with 556. Their highest output was 50 against Jacksonville and their lowest was 24 each against Tampa Bay and Cincinnati. New England holds the mark with 589 points in 2007.

12) 10 in 1975; their first loss 31-30 was to host Washington on Nov. 30. In 1973, they were 9-0 before losing to Atlanta 20-14 on Nov. 19.

13) 56-14 (80%)

Fred Cox boots an extra point with Paul Krause holding.

14) Six (1973-78)

15) 1969 and 1971. In '69, the Vikings allowed a league-low of 133
points in the 14-game regular season, an average of 9.5 points a
game. Two years later, they gave up 139. Amazingly, in 1970, they
almost did it, allowing just 143.

16) Two (Green Bay, 10-10 tie on Nov. 26, 1978 and Los Angeles
Rams, a 10-10 tie on Sept. 19, 1976).

17) 709 (Tommy Kramer- 593; Steve Dils - 102; Wade Wilson -13;
Ted Brown- 1)

18) Four

19) 13

20) Three (1961-63).

21) 1998

22) 1961 (2-11-1) for 15.3%. Both 1984 (3-13) and 2011 (3-13) are next, tied at 18.7%.

23) 1998

24) 1980

25) 15. Pittsburgh has 16 while Green Bay and Oakland are next with 17 losing seasons over the past 52 years.

26) 71

27) Three. 1999 (Robert Tate- kick; Randy Moss - punt); 2005 (Koren Robinson - kick; Mewelde Moore - punt); and 2012 (Percy Harvin - kick; Marcus Sherels - punt).

28) Six. (At Tampa Bay, Oct. 23, 1988 and at Pittsburgh, Sept. 24, 1995)

29) A 51-3 whipping of Cleveland on Nov. 9, 1969 at Met Stadium.

30) 1998

31) Eight (2001-02)

32) 15 (1974-76)

33) 54 in a victory over Dallas in 1970.

34) 60 by Atlanta on Nov. 11, 1975. The Falcons had 43 yards rushing and just 17 passing as Kim McQuilken was 5-26 with five interceptions.

35) Four. In a game at Tampa Bay on Nov. 25, 1979, the Vikings blocked two extra-point attempts, a field goal, and a punt in a 23-22 triumph.

36) 28 (seven occasions) and 38 (second half versus Jacksonville Dec. 20, 1998).

37) 24 versus San Francisco on Dec. 4, 1977. The Vikings trailed 24-0 in the third quarter before backup quarterback Tommy Kramer tossed three fourth-quarter touchdowns, including the game-winner of 69 yards to Sammy White.

38) 622 (versus Baltimore on Sept. 28, 1969)

39) 16 (1998)

40) 16 (2000-02)

41) 10 (1998-99)

42) 1961 (14 games)

43) Three. Tarvaris Jackson was 10-20 for 50 yards passing and the Vikings rushed for 77 yards as host Green Bay won 9-7 on Dec. 21, 2006

44) Yes, twice. (At Atlanta on Oct, 5, 2003 and vs. Green Bay on Nov. 9, 2008).

45) 97

46) 44 points. Host San Francisco hammered Minnesota 51-7 on Dec. 8, 1984.

47) 1961; in contrast, they allowed 61.

48) 2003 (fourth-ranked in both rushing and passing)

49) Two (Yes, one more than one!) Joe Kapp was a woeful 2-11 for 25 yards with two interceptions. Amazingly, the Vikings won 10-7 at Green Bay on Oct. 15, 1967. Bad weather was not a factor, either, as the game was played in 56-degree temperatures with a slight wind. Minnesota rushed for 158 yards to offset the putrid passing game. Zeke Bratkowski was 15-25 for 240 yards passing for the Packers.

50) 1969 (2,720 yards in 14 games)

51) The Vikings have scored 16,982 points and allowed 16,082 in 790 games for an average score of: Minnesota: 21.4   Opponents: 20.3.

52) In 29 seasons, the Vikings have outscored their opponents and in 23 seasons they have been outscored by the opponents.

53) 23 points. On Dec. 1, 1985, visiting Minnesota trailed Philadelphia 23-0 with just 8:30 remaining. Wade Wilson hit Allen Rice for a seven-yard TD and then Willie Teal returned a fumble 65 yards for a score. Wilson then connected with Anthony Carter on a 36-yard touchdown pass before hitting A.C. with another 42-yard toss to win 28-23 before the startled fans at Veterans Stadium.

54) Seven. In 2011, the Vikings were 3-13 in 2011 but improved to 10-6 in 2012.

55) Three (1961-63). The Baltimore Ravens (Cleveland Browns prior to 1996) are second with just four straight losing seasons with Dallas, Green Bay, and Washington all with five-straight losing seasons.

Ron Yary (73) in action against the Lions.

22 Statistical Records

(Regular season only)

Most Seasons

1 Jim Marshall - 19 (1961-79)
2 Mick Tingelhoff - 17 (1962-78)
3 Fred Cox - 15 (1963-77)
  Roy Winston - 15 (1962-76)
  Carl Eller - 15 (1964-78)
  Ron Yary - 15 (1968-82)

Games Started

1 Jim Marshall - 270 (1961-79)
2 Mick Tingelhoff - 240 (1962-78)
3 Carl Eller - 201 (1964-78)
4 Randall McDaniel - 188 (1988-99)
5 Tim Irwin - 181 (1981-93)

Points Scored (Career)

1 Fred Cox - 1,365 (1963-77)
2 Cris Carter - 670 (1990-01)
3 Ryan Longwell - 633 (2006-11)
4 Fuad Reveiz - 598 (1990-95)
5 Randy Moss - 552 (1998-04, 10)

Touchdowns (Career)

1 Cris Carter - 110 (1990-2001)
2 Randy Moss - 92 (1998-04, 10)
3 Adrian Peterson - 80 (2007-12)
4 Bill Brown - 76 (1962-74)
5 Chuck Foreman - 75 (1973-79)

Games Played

1 Jim Marshall - 270 (1961-79)
2 Mick Tingelhoff - 240 (1962-78)
3 Fred Cox - 210 (1963-77)
4 Carl Eller - 209 (1964-78)
5 Scott Studwell - 202 (1977-90)
  Randall McDaniel - 202 (1988-99)

Consecutive Games Played

1 Jim Marshall - 270 (1961-79)
2 Mick Tingelhoff - 240 (1962-78)
3 Fred Cox - 210 (1963-77)
4 Randall McDaniel - 202 (1988-99)
5 Carl Eller - 201 (1964-78)

Points Scored (Season)

1 Gary Anderson - 164 (1998)
2 Blair Walsh - 141 (2012)
3 Chuck Foreman - 132 (1975)
  Fuad Reveiz - 132 (1995)
  Ryan Longwell - 132 (2009)

Touchdowns (Season)

1) Chuck Foreman - 22 (1975)
2) Adrian Peterson - 18 (2009)
3) Cris Carter - 17 (1995)
  Randy Moss - 17 (1998)
  Randy Moss - 17 (2003)

Rushing Touchdowns (Career)
1 Adrian Peterson - 76 (2007-12)
2 Bill Brown - 52 (1962-74)
  Chuck Foreman - 52 (1973-79)
4 Ted Brown - 40 (1979-86)
5 Robert Smith - 32 (1993-00)

Rushing Touchdowns (Season)
1 Adrian Peterson - 18 (2009)
2 Chuck Foreman - 13 (1975)
  Chuck Foreman - 13 (1976)
  Terry Allen - 13 (1992)
5 Adrian Peterson - 12 (2007)
  Adrian Peterson - 12 (2010)
  Adrian Peterson - 12 (2011)
  Adrian Peterson - 12 (2012)

Receiving Touchdowns (Career)
1 Cris Carter - 110 (1990-2001)
2 Randy Moss - 92 (1998-04, 10)
3 Anthony Carter - 52 (1985-93)
4 Sammy White - 50 (1976-86)
5 Ahmad Rashad - 34 (1976-82)

Receiving Touchdowns (Season)
1 Cris Carter - 17 (1995)
  Randy Moss - 17 (1998)
  Randy Moss - 17 (2000)
  Randy Moss - 17 (2003)
5 Cris Carter - 13 (1997)
  Cris Carter - 13 (1999)
  Randy Moss - 13 (2004)

Touchdown Passes (Career)
1 Fran Tarkenton - 239
2 Tommy Kramer - 159
3 Daunte Culpepper - 135
4 Wade Wilson - 66
5 Brad Johnson - 65

Touchdown Passes (Season)
1 Daunte Culpepper - 39 (2004)
2 Randall Cunningham - 34 (1998)
3 Warren Moon - 33 (1995)
  Daunte Culpepper - 33 (2000)
  Brett Favre - 33 (2009)

Touchdown Passes (Game)
1 Joe Kapp - 7 (9/28/69 vs. Balt.)
2 Tommy Kramer - 6 (9/28/86 vs. G.B.)
3 Tommy Kramer - 5 (11/28/82 vs. Chi.)
  Daunte Culpepper - 5 (9/12/04 vs. Dal.)
  Daunte Culpepper - 5 (10/10/04 vs. Hou.)
  Daunte Culpepper - 5 (10/17/04 vs. N.O.)

Rushing Yards (Career)

1 Adrian Peterson - 8,849 (2007-12)
2 Robert Smith - 6,818 (1993-2000)
3 Chuck Foreman - 5,879 (1973-79)
4 Bill Brown - 5,757 (1962-74)
5 Ted Brown - 4,546 (1979-86)

Rushing Yards (Season)

1 Adrian Peterson - 2,097 (2012)
2 Adrian Peterson - 1,760 (2008)
3 Robert Smith - 1,521 (2000)
4 Adrian Peterson - 1,383 (2009)
5 Adrian Peterson - 1,341 (2007)

Rushing Attempts (Career)

1 Adrian Peterson - 1,754 (2007-12)
2 Bill Brown - 1,627 (1962-74)
3 Chuck Foreman - 1,529 (1973-79)
4 Robert Smith - 1,411 (1993-2000)
5 Dave Osborn - 1,173 (1965-75)

Rushing Yards Per Carry (Career)
(minimum 250 carries)

1 Fran Tarkenton - 5.49 (1961-66; 72-78)
2 Daunte Culpepper - 5.45 (1999-05)
3 Adrian Peterson - 5.05 (2007-12)
4 Mewelde Moore - 4.87 (2004-07)
5 Robert Smith - 4.83 (1993-2000)

Most Rushing Yards (Game)

1 Adrian Peterson - 296 (11/4/07 vs. San Diego)
2 Adrian Peterson - 224 (10/14/07 vs. Chicago)
3 Adrian Peterson - 212 (12/16/12 vs. St.Louis)
4 Adrian Peterson - 210 (12/2/12 vs. Green Bay)
5 Chuck Foreman - 200 (10/24/76 vs. Philadelphia)

Most Receptions (Season)

1 Cris Carter - 122 (1994)
  Cris Carter - 122 (1995)
3 Randy Moss - 111 (2003)
4 Randy Moss - 106 (2002)
5 Cris Carter - 96 (1996)
  Cris Carter - 96 (2000)

Reception Yards (Career)

1 Cris Carter - 12,383 (1990-01)
2 Randy Moss - 9,316 (1998-04, 10)
3 Anthony Carter - 7,636 (1985-93)
4 Jake Reed - 6,433 (1992-01)
5 Sammy White - 6,400 (1976-85)

Receiving Yards (Season)

1 Randy Moss - 1,632 (2003)
2 Randy Moss - 1,437 (2000)
3 Randy Moss - 1,413 (1999)
4 Cris Carter - 1,371 (1995)
5 Randy Moss - 1,347 (2002)

Most Receptions (Career)

1 Cris Carter - 1,004 (1990-01)
2 Randy Moss - 587 (1998-04, 10)
3 Steve Jordan - 498 (1982-94)
4 Anthony Carter - 478 (1985-93)
5 Jake Reed - 413 (1992-01)

Receiving Yards/Catch (Career)
(minimum 50 catches)
1) Gordie Smith - 22.4 (1961-65)
2) John Gilliam - 22.0 (1972-75)
3) Kelly Campbell - 18.6 (2002-04)
4) Gene Washington - 17.9 (1967-72)
5) Hassan Jones - 16.8 (1986-92)

Most Receptions (Game)
1 Rickey Young (15) 12/16/79 vs. N.E.
2 Cris Carter (14) 10/2/94 vs. Arizona
3 Cris Carter (12), on five occasions;
Bob Grim, Ted Brown, Rickey Young,
Darrin Nelson, Jake Reed, and
Mewelde Moore - (12) once each.

Receiving Yards (Game)
1 Sammy White - 210 (11/7/76 vs. Detroit)
2 Randy Moss - 204 (11/14/99 vs. Chicago)
3 Paul Flately - 202 (10/24/65 vs. Chicago)
4 Sidney Rice - 201 (11/5/09 vs. Detroit)
5 Randy Moss - 190 (10/5/98 vs. Green Bay)

Quarterback Wins (Career)
1 Fran Tarkenton - 91 (1961-66; 72-78)
2 Tommy Kramer - 54 (1977-89)
3 Daunte Culpepper - 38 (1999-05)
4 Brad Johnson - 28 (1994-98; 05-06)
5 Wade Wilson - 27 (1981-91)

Passing Yards (Career)
1 Fran Tarkenton - 33,098 (1961-66; 72-78)
2 Tommy Kramer - 24,775 (1977-89)
3 Daunte Culpepper - 20,162 (1999-05)
4 Wade Wilson - 12,135 (1981-91)
5 Brad Johnson - 11,098 (1994-98; 05-06)

Pass Completions (Career)
1 Fran Tarkenton - 2,635 (1961-66; 72-78)
2 Tommy Kramer - 2,011 (1977-89)
3 Daunte Culpepper - 1,678 (1999-05)
4 Brad Johnson - 1,036 (1994-98; 05-06)
5 Wade Wilson - 929 (1981-91)

Passing Yards (Season)

1 Daunte Culpepper - 4,717 (2004)

2 Warren Moon - 4,264 (1994)

3 Warren Moon - 4,228 (1995)

4 Brett Favre - 4,202 (2009)

5 Daunte Culpepper - 3,937 (2000)

Pass Completions (Season)

1 Daunte Culpepper - 379 (2004)

2 Warren Moon - 377 (1995)

3 Warren Moon - 371 (1994)

4 Brett Favre - 363 (2009)

5 Fran Tarkenton - 345 (1978)

Passing Yards (Game)

1) Tommy Kramer - 490 (11/2/86)

2) Tommy Kramer - 456 (12/14/80)

3) Joe Kapp - 449 (9/28/69)

4) Brett Favre - 446 (11/7/09)

5) Tommy Kramer - 444 (1/11/81)

Pass Completions (Game)

1 Tommy Kramer - 38 (12/14/80)

Tommy Kramer - 38 (11/29/81)

3 Steve Dils - 37 (9/5/81)

Daunte Culpepper - 37 (9/20/04)

5 Brett Favre - 36 (11/7/10)

Quarterback Rating (Career)

1 Randall Cunningham - 94.2 (1997-99)

Jeff George - 94.2 (1999)

3 Brett Favre - 92.2 (2009-10)

4 Daunte Culpepper - 91.5 (1999-05)

5 Warren Moon - 82.8 (1994-96)

Longest Pass Completion

1 Gus Frerotte/Bernard Berrian - 99 (2008)

2 F. Tarkenton/Charley Ferguson - 89 (1962)

3 Gus Frerotte/Bernard Berrian - 86 (2008)

4 Joe Kapp/Gene Washington - 85 (1967)

Warren Moon/Qadry Ismail - 85 (1995)

Completion Percentage (Career)

1 Brett Favre - 65.2%

2 Daunte Culpepper - 64.4%

3 Brad Johnson - 62.0%

4 Warren Moon - 60.7%

5 Jim McMahon - 60.4%

Interceptions Thrown (Career)

1 Fran Tarkenton - 194

2 Tommy Kramer - 157

3 Daunte Culpepper - 86

4 Wade Wilson - 75

5 Brad Johnson - 48

Kick Return Average (Career)

(minimum 50 returns)

1 Percy Harvin - 27.9
2 Charlie West - 25.5
3 Buster Rhymes - 25.1
4 Clinton Jones - 24.8
5 Darrin Nelson - 22.8

Kick Return Yardage (Career)

1 Darrin Nelson - 3,619
2 David Palmer - 3,274
3 Qadry Ismail - 3,273
4 Percy Harvin - 3,183
5 Eddie Payton - 2,353

Punt Return Average (Career)

(minimum 50 returns)

1 Mewelde Moore - 10.4
2 David Palmer - 9.94
3 Bill Butler - 9.91
4 Leo Lewis - 9.3
5 Marcus Sherels - 8.7

Punt Return Yardage (Career)

1 Leo Lewis - 1,812
2 David Palmer - 1,610
3 Charlie West - 820
4 Mewelde Moore - 768
5 Eddie Payton - 733

Field Goals (Career)

1 Fred Cox - 282 (1963-77)
2 Ryan Longwell - 135 (2006-11)
3 Fuad Reveiz - 133 (1990-95)
4 Gary Anderson - 109 (1998-02)
5 Rick Danmeier - 70 (1977-83)

Field Goals (Season)

1 Gary Anderson - 35 (1998)
  Blair Walsh - 35 (2012)
3 Fuad Reveiz - 34 (1994)
4 Rich Karlis - 31 (1989)
5 Fred Cox - 30 (1970)

Field Goals (Game)

1 Rich Karlis - 7 (11/5/89 vs. LA. Rams)
2 Gary Anderson - 6 (12/13/98 vs. Baltimore Ravens)
3 Fred Cox - 5 (9/23/73 vs. Chicago Bears)
  Rich Karlis - 5 (12/10/89 vs. Atlanta Falcons)
  Rich Karlis - 5 (12/25/89 vs. Cinncinati Bengals)
  Gary Anderson - 5 (9/20/98 vs. Detroit Lions)
  Gary Anderson - 5 (10/10/99 vs. Chicago Bears)
  Ryan Longwell - 5 (9/14/08 vs. Indianapolis Colts)

Field Goal Percentage (Career)

(minimum 35 attempts)

1 Blair Walsh - 92.1% (2012)

2 Ryan Longwell - 86.0% (2006-11)

3 Gary Anderson - 84.5% (1998-02)

4 Rich Karlis - 79.5% (1989)

5 Fuad Reveiz - 77.8% (1990-95)

Punting Average (Career)

1 Chris Kluwe - 44.4 (2005-12)

2 Harry Newsome - 43.8 (1990-93)

3 Mitch Berger - 43.5 (1996-01)

4 Bobby Walden - 42.9 (1964-67)

5 Mike Saxon - 41.9 (1994-95)

Interceptions (Career)

1 Paul Krause - 53 (1968-79)

2 Bobby Bryant - 51 (1967-80)

3 Ed Sharockman - 40 (1962-72)

4 Joey Browner - 37 (1983-91)

5 Nate Wright - 31 (1971-80) 5)

Interceptions (Season)

1 Paul Krause - 10 (1975)

2 Orlando Thomas - 9 (1995)

  Brian Russell - 9 (2003)

  Darren Sharper - 9 (2005)

5 Bobby Bryant - 8 (1969)

  Isaac Holt - 8 (1986)

  Carl Lee - 8 (1988)

  Audray McMillian - 8 (1992)

Tackles (Career)

1 Scott Studwell - 1,928 (1977-90)

2 Matt Blair - 1,452 (1974-85)

3 Jeff Siemon - 1,382 (1972-82)

4 Alan Page - 1,120 (1967-78)

5 Joey Browner - 1,098 (1983-91)

Tackles (Season)

1 Scott Studwell - 230 (1981)

2 Jeff Siemon - 229 (1978)

3 Matt Blair - 220 (1981)

4 Scott Studwell - 215 (1983)

5 Scott Studwell - 213 (1984)

Tackles (Game)

1) Scott Studwell - 24 (11/17/85 vs. Detroit Lions)

2) Chad Greenway - 22 (11/20/11 vs. Oakland Raiders)

3) Scott Studwell - 21 (9/24/89 vs. Pittsburgh Steelers)

  Ed McDaniel - 21 (9/4/94 vs. Green Bay Packers)

Sacks (Career)

1 Carl Eller - 130 (1964-78)
2 Jim Marshall - 127 (1961-79)
3 John Randle - 114 (1990-00)
4 Alan Page - 108 (1967-78)
5 Chris Doleman - 96.5 (1985-93;99)

Sacks (Season)

1 Jared Allen - 22 (2011)
2 Chris Doleman - 21 (1989)
3 Keith Millard - 18 (1989)
  Alan Page - 18 (1976)
5 John Randle - 15.5 (1997)

Sacks (Game)

1 Randy Holloway - 5 (9/16/84 vs. Atl)
2 Jared Allen - 4.5 (10/5/09 vs. G.B)
3 Accomplished by many, most recently
    Kevin Williams - 4 (10/12/08 vs. Detroit)

Blocked Kicks (Career)

1 Matt Blair - 20 (1974-85)
2 Alan Page - 16 (1967-78)
3 Tim Irwin - 10 (1981-93)
4 Carl Eller - 9 (1964-78)

Fumbles Recovered (Career)

1 Jim Marshall - 29 (1961-79)
2 Carl Eller - 23 (1964-78)
3 Matt Blair - 20 (1974-85)
4 Alan Page - 19 (1967-78)
5 Fred McNeill - 16 (1974-85)
  Scott Studwell - 16 (1977-90)

23 Year-by-Year Record

Year	Rcrd	PF	PA	Coach	Finish	Playoff Result
Western Division (1961-1966)						
1961	3-11	285	407	Van Brocklin	7th	
1962	2-11-1	254	410	Van Brocklin	6th	
1963	5-8-1	309	390	Van Brocklin	T-4th	
1964	8-5-1	355	296	Van Brocklin	T-2nd	
1965	7-7	383	403	Van Brocklin	T-5th	
1966	4-9-1	212	304	Van Brocklin	T-6th	
Central Division (1967-2001)						
1967	3-8-3	233	294	Grant	4th	
1968	8-6	282	242	Grant	1st	Loss at Baltimore
1969	12-2	379	133	Grant	1st	Super Bowl loss to Kansas City
1970	12-2	335	143	Grant	1st	Loss to S.F. at home
1971	11-3	245	139	Grant	1st	Loss to Dallas at home
1972	7-7	301	252	Grant	3rd	
1973	12-2	296	198	Grant	1st	Super Bowl loss to Miami
1974	10-4	310	195	Grant	1st	Super Bowl loss to Pitt.
1975	12-2	377	180	Grant	1st	Loss to Dallas at home
1976	11-2-1	305	176	Grant	1st	Super Bowl loss to Oakland
1977	9-5	231	227	Grant	1st	1-1; loss at Dallas
1978	8-7-1	294	306	Grant	1st	Loss at L.A. Rams
1979	7-9	259	337	Grant	3rd	
1980	9-7	318	308	Grant	1st	Loss at Philadelphia
1981	7-9	325	369	Grant	4th	
1982	5-4	187	198	Grant	(strike)	1-1; Loss at Washington
1983	8-8	316	348	Grant	4th	

Year	Rcrd	PF	PA	Coach	Finish	Playoff Result
1984	3-13	276	484	Steckel	5th	
1985	7-9	346	259	Grant	3rd	
1986	9-7	398	273	Burns	2nd	
1987	8-7	336	335	Burns	2nd	2-1; Loss to Washington
1988	11-5	406	233	Burns	2nd	1-1; Loss at S.F.
1989	10-6	351	275	Burns	1st	Loss at S.F.
1990	6-10	351	326	Burns	5th	
1991	8-8	301	306	Burns	3rd	
1992	11-5	374	249	Green	1st	Loss to Washington
1993	9-7	277	290	Green	2nd	Loss at NY Giants
1994	10-6	356	314	Green	1st	Loss at home to Chicago
1995	8-8	412	385	Green	4th	
1996	9-7	298	315	Green	2nd	Loss at Dallas
1997	9-7	354	359	Green	4th	1-1; Loss at San Francisco
1998	15-1	556	296	Green	1st	1-1; Loss to Atlanta
1999	10-6	399	335	Green	2nd	1-1; Loss to St. Louis
2000	11-5	397	371	Green	1st	1-1; Loss to N.Y. Giants
2001	5-11	290	390	Green (5-10)		
				Tice (0-1)	4th	

NFC North Division (2002–2012)

Year	Rcrd	PF	PA	Coach	Finish	Playoff Result
2002	6-10	390	442	Tice	2nd	
2003	9-7	416	353	Tice	2nd	
2004	8-8	405	395	Tice	2nd	1-1; Loss at Philly
2005	9-7	306	344	Tice	2nd	
2006	6-10	282	327	Childress	3rd	
2007	8-8	365	311	Childress	2nd	
2008	10-6	379	333	Childress	1st	Loss to Philly at home
2009	12-4	470	312	Childress	1st	1-1; Loss at N.O.
2010	6-10	281	348	Childress (3-7)		
				Frazier (3-3)	3rd	
2011	3-13	340	449	Frazier	4th	
2012	10-6	379	348	Frazier	2nd	Loss at Green Bay

Regular Season Record ♦ 426-355-9

Playoff Record ♦ 19-27

Overall Record ♦ 445-382-9

24 Minnesota Vikings All-Time Roster (1961-2012)

(Players on active roster for one game to qualify)

Name	Position	College	Number	Years Played
Abdullah, Husain	S	Wash. State	39	2008-11
Abrams, Bobby	LB	Michigan	50	1993-94
Arche, Steve	LB	SW Missouri	53	1987
Adams, Scott	G	Georgia	72	1991-93
Adams, Tom	WR	Minn.-Duluth	85	1962
Adams, Tony	QB	Utah State	7	1987
Addickes, John	C	Baylor	68	1989
Adibi, Xavier	LB	Virginia Tech	57	2011
Alderman, Grady	T	Detroit	67	1961-74
Alex, Keith	G	Texas A & M	63	1995
Alexander, Derrick L.	DE	Florida State	90	1995-98
Alexander, Derrick S.	WR	Michigan	82	2002
Alexander, Rufus	LB	Oklahoma	57	2008
Alipate, Tuineau	LB	Wash. State	53	1995
Allen, Asher	CB	Georgia	21	2009-11
Allen, Jared	DE	Idaho State	69	2008-12
Allen, Nate	CB	Texas Southern	25	1976-79
Allen, Terry	RB	Clemson	21	1991-94
Allison, Aundrae	WR	East Carolina	84	2007-08
Anderson, Morten	K	Michigan State	7	2004
Anderson, Alfred	RB	Baylor	46	1984-91
Anderson, Gary	K	Syracuse	1	1998-2002
Anderson, Scott	C	Missouri	56	1974, 1976
Angulo, Richard	TE	Western N.M.	86	2003-05
Anno, Sam	LB	USC	53	1987-88
Araguz, Leo	P	Stephen F. Austin	2	2003
Arbubakrr, Hasson	DE	Texas Tech	69	1984
Arceneaux, Emmanuel	WR	Alcorn State	16	2011
Archer, R. J.	QB	William & Mary	16	2010
Aromashodu, Devin	WR	Auburn	19	2011-12

Name	Position	College	Number	Years Played
Arrobio, Chuck	T	USC	79	1966
Ashley, Walker Lee	LB	Penn State	58	1983-88, 90
Asiata, Matt	FB	Utah	48	2012
Asper, Mark	G	Oregon	79	2012
Athas, Pete	CB	Tennessee	45	1975
Avery, John	RB	Mississippi	33	2003
Awasom, Adrian	DE	North Texas	67	2011
Ayanbadejo, Obafemi	FB	San Diego State	49	1998-99
Ayodele, Remi	DT	Oklahoma	92	2011
Badger, Brad	G	Stanford	74	2000-01
Baker, Al	DE	Colorado State	77,60	1988
Baker, Rashad	S	Tennessee	28	2006
Baker, Robert	WR	Auburn	86	2003
Baldwin, Randy	RB	Mississippi	37	1991
Ball, Jerry	DT	SMU	96	1997-99
Ballard, Christian	DT/DE	Iowa	99	2011-12
Ballman, Gary	TE	Michigan State	85	1973
Banks, Antonio	S	Virginia Tech	30	1998-00
Barker, Roy	DT	North Carolina	92	1992-95,00
Barnes, Bill	RB	Wake Forest	33	1965-66
Barnes, Tomur	CB	North Texas	23	1996
Barnett, Harlon	S	Michigan State	42	1995-96
Baskett, Hank	WR	New Mexico	19	2010
Bass, Anthony	DB	Bethune-Cookman	32/38	1998-99
Bates, D'Wayne	WR	Northwestern	85	2002-03
Battle, Jim	G	Southern Illinois	63	1963
Bavaro, David	LB	Syracuse	52	1992
Rick Bayless	RB	Iowa	32	1989
Baylor, Tim	S	Morgan State	47	1979-80
Beamon, Autry	S	East Texas State	27	1975-76
Beasley, John	TE	California	87	1967-73
Bebout, Nick	T	Wyoming	63	1980
Bedsole, Hal	TE	USC	86	1964-66
Bell, Rick	RB	St. John's (MN)	33	1983
Bennett, Barry M.	DE	Concordia (MN)	78	1988

Name	Position	College	Number	Years Played
Bennett, Barry S.	P	Quachita Baptist	12	1974
Bennett, Darren	P	None	2	2004-05
Bennett, Michael	RB	Wisconsin	23	2001-05
Bercich, Pete	LB	Notre Dame	56/50	1995-00
Berger, Joe	G/C	Michigan Tech	61	2011-12
Berger, Mitch	P	Colorado	17	1996-01
Berrian, Bernard	WR	Fresno State	87	2008-11
Berry, Bob	QB	Oregon	17	1965-67,73-76
Berry, Ray	LB	Baylor	50	1987-92
Berton, Sean	TE	North Carolina St.	45/87/44	2003-04
Bess, Rufus	CB	South Carolina St.	21	1982-87
Bethea, Ryan	WR	South Carolina	85	1988
Bethel-Thompson, McLeod	QB	Sacramento State	4	2012
Biekert, Greg	LB	Colorado	55/54	2002-03
Birk, Matt	C	Harvard	75/78	1998-08
Bishop, Bill	DT	North Texas State	73	1961
Bishop, Keith	QB	Wheaton	12	1987
Blahak, Joe	CB	Nebraska	21	1974-75,77
Blair, Matt	LB	Iowa State	59	1974-85
Blair, Paul	T	Oklahoma State	68	1990
Bland, Tony	WR	Florida A & M	18/84	1996-98
Blanton, Robert	S	Notre Dame	36	2012
Blue, Greg	S	Georgia	20	2006
Bobo, Orlando	G	N.E. Louisiana	74	1997-98
Boireau, Michael	DE	Miami (Florida)	92/96	2000
Bolin, Bookie	G	Mississippi	66	1968-69
Bollinger, Brooks	QB	Wisconsin	9	2006-07
Bolston, Conrad	DT	Maryland	60	2007
Bomar, Rhett	QB	Sam Houston State	3	2010
Bono, Steve	QB	UCLA	13	1985-86
Booker, Lorenzo	RB	Florida State	27	2010-11
Boone, David	DE	Eastern Michigan	71	1974
Booty, John David	QB	USC	4	2008
Bouman, Todd	QB	St. Cloud State	8	1997-02
Bowie, Larry	G	Purdue	61	1962-68

Name	Position	College	Number	Years Played
Boyd, Brent	G	UCLA	62	1980-86
Boyd, Malik	CB	Southern	36	1994
Boylan, Jim	WR	Washington State	80	1963
Bradford, Ronnie	S	Colorado	26	2002
Brady, Jeff	LB	Kentucky	50	1995-97
Bramlett, Don	DT	Carson-Newman	61	1987
Braxton, David	LB	Wake Forest	53	1989-90
Breitenstein, Bob	T	Tulsa	75	1967
Brewer, Jack	S	Minnesota	42	2002-03
Brien, Doug	K	California	4	2002
Briggs, Greg	S	Texas Southern	43/54	1997-98
Brim, James	WR	Wake Forest	84	1987
Brim, Michael	CB	Virginia Union	44	1989-90
Brinkley, Jasper	LB	South Carolina	54	2009-12
Brister, Bubby	QB	N.E. Louisiana	6	2000
Britt, Charlie	S	Georgia	28	1964
Bromell, Lorenzo	DE	Clemson	91	2002
Brown, Bill	RB	Illinois	30	1962-74
Brown, Ivory Lee	RB	Ark. - Pine Bluff	22	1993
Brown, Larry	WR	Mankato State	80	1987
Brown, Norris	TE	Georgia	86	1983
Brown, Pat	T	Central Florida	79	2010-11
Brown, Ralph	CB	Nebraska	33	1994-95
Brown, Richard	LB	San Diego State	52	1994-96
Brown, Robert	TE	Alcorn A & M	89	1971
Brown, Ted	RB	N. C. State	23	1979-86
Brown, Terry	S	Oklahoma State	24	1972-75
Browner, Joey	S	USC	47	1983-91
Bruer, Bob	TE	Mankato State	82	1980-84
Brune, Larry	S	Rice	24	1980
Bruno, Dave	P	Moraine Valley	13	1987
Bryant, Bobby	CB	South Carolina	20	1967-80
Bryant, Tim	LB	S. Mississippi	94	1987
Buetow, Bart	T	Minnesota	74	1976-77
Bundra, Mike	DT	USC	75	1964

Name	Position	College	Number	Years Played
Burrough, John	DE	Wyoming	91	1999-00
Burton, Brandon	CB	Utah	36	2011-12
Burton, Derek	T	Oklahoma State	71	1987
Burton, Stephen	WR	W. Texas A & M	11	2011-12
Burleson, Nate	WR	Nevada	81	2003-05
Butler, Billy	S/RB	Tenn-Chattanooga	22	1962-64
Butler, Duane	S	Illinois State	31	1997-98
Byers, Ken	G	Cincinnati	66	1964-66
Caesar, Ivan	LB	Boston College	53	1991
Caleb, Jamie	RB	Grambling	23	1961
Calland, Lee	CB	Louisville	23	1963-65
Camarillo, Greg	WR	Stanford	85	2010-11
Campbell, John	LB	Minnesota	55	1963-64
Campbell, Kelly	WR	Georgia Tech	16	2002-04
Cappelman, Bill	QB	Florida State	17	1970
Carlson, John	TE	Notre Dame	89	2012
Carman, John	T	Georgia Tech	65	2002
Carpenter, Preston	TE	Arkansas	40	1966
Carpenter, Ron	S	Miami (Ohio)	36	1993
Carroll, Jay	TE	Minnesota	84	1985
Carter, Anthony	WR	Michigan	81	1985-93
Carter, Cris	WR	Ohio State	80	1990-01
Carter, Dale	CB	Tennessee	21	2001
Carter, Jason	WR	Texas A & M	11	2006
Carter, Tyrone	CB	Minnesota	22/37	2000-01
Carson, Malcolm	G	Tenn-Chattanooga	56	1984
Casper, Dave	TE	Notre Dame	44	1983
Cercone, Matt	TE	Arizona State	44/89	2000-02
Chamberlain, Byron	TE	Wayne State	87	2001-02
Chapman, Doug	RB	Marshall	23/34	2000-03
Charles, John	S	Purdue	25	1970
Chavous, Corey	S/CB	Vanderbilt	21	2002-05
Chealander, Hal	QB	Mississippi State	16	1974
Christopherson, Jim	K/LB	Concordia-Moorhead	36	1962
Christy, Jeff	C	Pittsburgh	62	1993-99

Name	Position	College	Number	Years Played
Chukwurah, Patrick	LB/DE	Wyoming	50	2001-02
Ciurciu, Vinny	LB	Boston College	50/54	2007-08
Clabo, Neil	P	Tennessee	12	1975-77
Clairborne, Chris	LB	USC	55	2003-04
Clark, Jesse	RB	Arkansas	33	1989-90
Clark, Kenny	WR	Central Florida	89	2003-04
Clarke, Ken	DT	Syracuse	71	1989-91
Clarke, Leon	WR	USC	81	1963
Clemons, Duane	DE	California	92	1996-99
Cobb, Marvin	S	USC 2	6	1980
Cobb, Robert	DE	Texas	63	1984
Coffman, Paul	TE	Kansas State	89	1988
Cole, Audie	LB	North Carolina State	57	2012
Cole, Colin	DT	Iowa	92	2003
Coleman, Al	CB	Tennessee State	37	1967
Coleman, Dan	DE	Murray State	9	1987
Coleman, Greg	P	Florida A & M	8	1978-87
Colinet, Stalin	DE	Boston College	99/93	1997-99,01
Collins, Calvin	G	Texas A & M	65	2001
Collins, Dwight	WR	Pittsburgh	84	1984
Collins, Fabray	LB	Southern Illinois	59	1987
Colter, Jeff	CB	Kansas	43	1984
Conaty, Billy	C	Virginia Tech	63	2004
Cook, Chris	CB	Virginia	31	2010-12
Cook, Ryan	T	New Mexico	62	2006-10
Cooks, Kerry	S	Iowa	20	1998
Cooper, Adrian	TE	Oklahoma	87	1994-95
Cooper, Jon	C	Oklahoma	68	2009-10
Cooper, Marquis	LB	Washington	50	2006
Cornish, Frank	C	UCLA	63	1994
Cortez, Jose	K	Oregon State	1	2003-04
Council, Keith	DE	Hampton	95	1999
Cowart, Sam	LB	Florida State	55	2005
Cox, Fred	K	Pittsburgh	14	1963-77
Craig, Roger	RB	Nebraska	33	1992-93

Name	Position	College	Number	Years Played
Craig, Steve	TE	Northwestern	84	1974-78
Crawford, Brian	T	Western Oregon	73	2001
Crockett, Henri	LB	Florida State	52	2002-03
Crumpler, Carlester	TE	East Carolina	87	1999
Culpepper, Brad	DT	Florida	77	1992-93
Culpepper, Daunte	QB	Central Florida	12/11	1999-05
Culpepper, Ed	DT	Alabama	71	1961
Cunningham, Doug	WR	Rice	89	1979
Cunningham, Randall	QB	UNLV	7	1997-99
Cunningham, Rick	T	Texas A & M	67	1995
Cuozzo, Gary	QB	Virginia	15	1968-71
Curtis, Travis	S	West Virginia	49	1989
Daffney, Bernard	G	Tennessee	71/75	1992-94
Dale, Carroll	WR	Virginia Tech	84	1973
Dalton, Antico	LB	Hampton	50	1999
Daniels, Brian	G	Colorado	63	2007
Daniels, LeShun	G	Ohio State	69	1997
Danmeier, Rick	K	Sioux Falls	7	1977-83
Darden, Tony	CB	Texas Tech	32/25	1998
Daugherty, Ron	WR	Northwestern	82	1987
Davis, Brian	CB	Nebraska	34	1994
Davis, Doug	T	Kentucky	71	1966-72
Davis, Greg	K	Citadel	5	1997
Davis, Isaac	G	Arkansas	63	1998
Davis, John	TE	Emporia State	86	2000
Davis, Nick	WR	Wisconsin	17/86	2002-03
Davis, Rod	LB	So. Mississippi	58/50	2004-06
Dawson, Dale	K	Eastern Kentucky	4	1987
Dawson, Rhett	WR	Florida State	86	1973
Dean, Larry	LB	Valdosta State	51	2011-12
Dean, Ted	S	Wichita State	24	1964
DeGeare, Chris	G	Wake Forest	72	2010
Del Rio, Jack	LB	USC	55	1992-95
Delaney, Jarrod	WR	TCU	89	1989
DeLong, Greg	TE	North Carolina	85	1995-98

Name	Position	College	Number	Years Played
Demery, Calvin	WR	Arizona State	27	1972
Denny, Earl	RB	Missouri	28	1967-68
Denson, Al	WR	Florida A & M	86	1971
Denton, Bob	DE	Pacific	62	1961-64
Derby, Dean	DB	Washington	25	1961-62
Devine, Kevin	CB	California	27	1999
Dick, Jim	LB	North Dakota State	52	1987
Dickson, Paul	DT	Baylor	76	1961-70
Dill, Scott	T	Memphis State	76	1996-97
Dillon, Terry	CB	Montana	25	1963
Dils, Steve	QB	Stanford	12	1979-84
D'Imperio, Ryan	RB	Rutgers	44	2011
Dishman, Cris	CB	Purdue	25	2000
Dixon, David	G	Arizona State	71	1994-04
Doleman, Chris	DE/LB	Pittsburgh	56	1985-93,99
Donahue, Oscar	WR	San Jose State	84	1962
Dorsey, Nat	T	Georgia Tech	65	2004
Doss, Mike	S	Ohio State	21	2007
Dozier, D.J.	RB	Penn State	42	1987-91
Dozier, Ukee	CB	Minnesota	48	2005
Dugan, Bill	G	Penn State	56	1984
Dugan, Jeff	TE	Maryland	83	2004-10
Dumler, Doug	C	Nebraska	57	1976-77
Dusbabek, Mark	LB	Minnesota	59	1989-92
Early, Michael	G	Norfolk State	64	2002
Echemandu, A.	RB	California	39	2005
Edinger, Paul	K	Michigan State	1	2005
Edwards, Brad	S	South Carolina	27	1988-89
Edwards, Dixon	LB	Michigan State	5	1996-98
Edwards, Davonte	CB	North Carolina State	36	2005-06
Edwards, Jimmy	RB	NE Louisiana	32	1979
Edwards, Ray	DE	Purdue	91	2006-10
Eilers, Pat	S	Notre Dame	24	1990-91
Eischied, Mike	P	Upper Iowa	11	1972-74
Eley, Clifton	TE	Mississippi State	86	1987

Name	Position	College	Number	Years Played
Eller, Carl	DE	Minnesota	81	1964-78
Elling, Aaron	K	Wyoming	8	2003-04
Ellison, Rhett	TE	USC	40	2012
Elshire, Neil	DE	Oregon	65/73	1981-86
Emmanuel, Charles	S	West Virginia	47	1997
Epstein, Hayden	K	Michigan State	6	2002
Evans, Charles	RB	Clark	29	1993-98
Evans, David	CB	Central Arkansas	26	1986-87
Evans, Fred	DT	Texas St. San Marcos	90	2007-12
Everett, Eric	CB	Texas Tech	31	1992
Farber, Hap	LB	Mississippi	51	1970
Farwell, Heath	LB	San Diego State	59	2005-10
Fason, Ciatrick	RB	Florida	35	2005-06
Faust, Paul	LB	Minnesota	54	1967
Favre, Brett	QB	So. Mississippi	4	2009-10
Fears, Willie	DT	Northwestern St.	91	1990
Feasel, Grant	T	Abilene Christian	64	1984-86
Felton, Jerome	FB	Furman	42	2012
Fenney, Rick	RB	Washington	31	1987-91
Ferguson, Bob	RB	Ohio State	35	1963
Ferguson, Charley	WR	Tennessee State	84	1962
Ferguson, Robert	WR	Texas A & M	89	2007-08
Fielder, Jay	QB	Dartmouth	11	1998
Finch, Steve	WR	Elmhurst	85	1987
Fisk, Jason	DT	Stanford	72	1995-98
Fitzgerald, Jamie	CB	Idaho State	29	1987
Fitzgerald, Mike	CB	Iowa State	37	1966-67
Flately, Paul	WR	Northwestern	85	1963-67
Fonoti, Toniu	G	Nebraska	79	2005
Foote, Chris	C	USC	62	1987-91
Foreman, Chuck	RB	Miami (Florida)	44	1973-79
Fowler, Melvin	C	Maryland	67	2005
Fowlkes, Dennis	LB	West Virginia	50	1983-85
Frampton, Eric	S	Washington State	37	2007-11
Frankhauser, Tom	S	Purdue	40	1962-63

Name	Position	College	Number	Years Played
Frank, Donald	CB	Winston-Salem	37	1995
Freeman, Steve	S	Mississippi	22	1987
Frerotte, Gus	QB	Tulsa	12	2003-04,08
Frisch, David	TE	Colorado State	83	1996
Frye, Phil	RB	California Lutheran	37	1987
Fuller, Corey	CB	Florida State	27	1995-98
Fullington, Darrell	S	Miami (Florida)	29	1988-90
Fusco, Brandon	C/G	Slippery Rock	63	2011-12
Galbreath, Tony	RB	Missouri	32	1981-83
Gallagher, Frank	G	North Carolina	66	1973
Gallery, Jim	K	Minnesota	6	1990
Gallishaw, Laroni	CB	Murray State	28	2005
Galvin, John	LB	Boston College	90	1989
Gannon, Rich	QB	Delaware	16	1987-92
Garcia, Teddy	K	NE Louisiana	2	1989
Garnett, David	LB	Stanford	54	1993-94,96
Garnett, Winfield	DT	Ohio State	92	2001
Gault, Billy	CB	Texas Christian	44	1961
Gay, William	DE	USC	78	1988
George, Jeff	QB	Illinois	3	1999
George, Ron	LB	Stanford	55	1997
Gerak, John	TE/G	Penn State	46/66	1993-96
Gerhart, Toby	RB	Stanford	32	2010-12
Gersbach, Carl	LB	West Chester	56	1971-72
Gillespie, Willie	WR	Tenn-Chattanooga	86	1987
Gilliam, John	WR	South Carolina State	42	1972-75
Glenn, Jason	LB	Texas A & M	55	2006
Glenn, Vencie	S	Indiana State	25	1992-94
Glover, Andrew	TE	Grambling	82	1997-99
Goff, Robert	DT	Auburn	94	1996
Goldberg, Adam	G	Wyoming	73	2004-05
Goodridge, Bob	WR	Vanderbilt	82	1968
Goodrum, Charles	G	Florida A & M	68	1972-78
Goodwin, Hunter	TE	Texas A & M	87/83	1996-98,02-03
Gordon, Charles	CB	Kansas	41	2006-08

Name	Position	College	Number	Years Played
Graham, Scottie	RB	Ohio State	31	1993-96
Graves, Rory	T	Ohio State	73	1993
Gray, Torrian	S	Virginia Tech	23	1997-98
Grecni, Dick	LB	Ohio	50	1961
Green, Robert	RB	William and Mary	32	1997
Greene, Marcellus	CB	Arizona	25	1984
Greenway, Chad	LB	Iowa	52	2006-12
Griffen, Everson	DE	USC	97	2010-12
Griffin, Cedric	CB	Texas	23	2006-11
Griffith, Robert	S	San Diego State	24	1994-01
Grigsby, Otis	DE	Kentucky	73	2007-08
Grim, Bob	WR	Oregon State	27/26	1967-71,76-77
Groce, Ron	RB	Macalester	47	1976
Guggemos, Neal	DB	St. Thomas	41	1986-87
Guion, Letroy	DT	Florida State	98	2008-12
Guliford, Eric	WR	Arizona State	84	1993-94
Gustafson, Jim	WR	St. Thomas	80	1985-90
Haayer, Adam	T	Minnesota	72	2002, 04
Habib, Brian	G	Washington	91/74	1988-92
Hackbart, Dale	S	Wisconsin	49	1966-70
Haines, John	DT	Texas	90	1984
Haley, Dick	WR	Pittsburgh	28	1961
Hall, Lemanski	LB	Alabama	55	2000-02
Hall, Steven	S	Kentucky	23	1996
Hall, Tom	WR	Minnesota	86/28	1964-66,68-69
Hall, Windlan	S	Arizona State	40	1976-77
Hamilton, Wes	G	Tulsa	61	1976-85
Hammonds, Shelly	CB	Penn State	23	1995
Hampton, Alonzo	CB	Pittsburgh	25	1990
Hanks, Ben	LB	Florida	51	1996
Hannon, Tom	S	Michigan State	45	1977-84
Hansen, Don	LB	Illinois	55	1966-67
Hanson, Mark	G	Mankato State	63	1987
Hargrove, Jim	LB	Howard Payne	50	1967-70
Harrell, Sam	RB	East Carolina	36	1980-82,87

Name	Position	College	Number	Years Played
Harris, Bill	RB	Colorado	35	1969-70
Harris, Darryl	RB	Arizona	32	1988
Harris, James	DE	Temple	99	1993-95
Harris, Joe	LB	Georgia Tech	52	1979
Harris, John	S	Arizona State	44	1985-86
Harris, Napoleon	LB	Northwestern	58/99	2005-06,08
Harris, Paul	LB	USC	57	1978
Harris, Robert	DE	Southern	90	1992-94
Harris, Steve	RB	Northern Iowa	32	1987
Harrison, Martin	DE	Washington State	95/91	1994-96,99
Harrison, Todd	TE	North Carolina State	48	1993
Hartenstine, Mike	DT	Penn State	78	1987
Hartwig, Keith	WR	Arizona	86	1977
Harvin, Percy	WR	Florida	12	2009-12
Haslerig, Clint	WR	Michigan	87	1975
Hasselback, Don	TE	Colorado	88	1984
Hatchette, Matthew	WR	Langston	89/19	1997-00
Hawkins, Mike	CB	Oklahoma	37	2006
Hawkins, Rip	LB	North Carolina	58	1961-65
Hayden, Leo	RB	Ohio State	44	1971
Hayes, Ray	RB	Central Oklahoma	32	1961
Hazuga, Jeff	DE	Wisconsin-Stout	90	2001
Henderson, E. J.	LB	Maryland	56	2003-11
Henderson, Erin	LB	Maryland	50	2008-12
Henderson, John	WR	Michigan	80	1968-72
Henderson, Keith	RB	Georgia	30	1992
Henderson, Wymon	CB	UNLV	34	1987-88
Hernandez, Matt	T	Purdue	60	1984
Herrera, Anthony	G	Tennessee	67/64	2004-11
Herron, David	LB	Michigan State	58	2007-08
Hicks, Artis	G	Memphis State	79	2006-09
Hicks, Maurice	RB	North Carolina A & T	43	2008
Hilgenberg, Wally	LB	Iowa	58	1968-79
Hill, Gary	S	USC	43	1965
Hill, King	P, QB	Rice	10	1968

Name	Position	College	Number	Years Played
Hill, Shaun	QB	Maryland	12/13	2002-05
Hillary, Ira	WR	South Carolina	89	1990
Hilton, Carl	TE	Houston	82	1986-89
Hilton, John	TE	Richmond	85	1970
Hinkle, George	DT	Arizona	98	1992
Hinton, Chris	T	Northwestern	75/78	1994-95
Hitchcock, Jimmy	CB	North Carolina	37	1998-99
Hoag, Ryan	WR	Gustavus Adolphus	18	2004
Hoard, Leroy	RB	Michigan	44	1996-99
Holcomb, Kelly	QB	Middle Tennessee St.	13	2007
Holland, Darius	DT	Colorado	93	2002
Holland, John	WR	Tennessee State	85	1974
Holloway, Randy	DE	Pittsburgh	75	1978-84
Holmberg, Rob	LB	Penn State	51	1999
Holmes, Bruce	LB	Minnesota	54	1993
Holt, Isaac	CB	Alcorn State	30	1985-89
Horan, Mike	P	Long Beach State	2	1986
Hough, Jim	G	Utah State	51	1978-86
Houston, Bobby	LB	North Carolina State	55	1998
Hovan, Chris	DT	Boston College	99	2000-04
Howard, Bryan	S	Tennessee State	24	1982
Howard, David	LB	Long Beach State	51/99	1985-89
Howard, Willie	DL	Stanford	91	2001-02
Howell, Leroy	DT	Appalachian State	92	1986
Howry, Keenan	WR	Oregon	82	2003-05
Huffman, David	G/T	Notre Dame	56/72	1979-83,85-90
Hultz, Don	DE	Southern Mississippi	83	1963
Hunter, Will	S	Syracuse	25/31	2005-06
Humphrey, Jay	T	Texas	67	1999
Hutchinson, Steve	G	Michigan	76	2006-11
Huth, Gary	G	Wake Forest	65	1961-63
Iglesias, Juaquin	WR	Oklahoma	84	2010
Igwebuike, Donald	K	Clemson	4	1990
Ingram, Darryl	TE	California	86	1989
Irvin, Ken	CB/S	Memphis State	22	2003-05

Name	Position	College	Number	Years Played
Irwin, Tim	T	Tennessee	76	1981-93
Ismail, Qadry	WR	Syracuse	82	1993-96
Israel, Ron	DB	Notre Dame	37	2003
Jackson, Alfred	CB	San Diego State	25	1995-96
Jackson, Harold	WR	Colorado	89	1982
Jackson, Joe	DT	New Mexico State	76	1977
Jackson, Tarvaris	QB	Alabama State	7	2006-10
Jacquet, Nate	WR	San Diego State	83	2000-01
James, Cedric	WR	TCU	89/13	2002
James, Dick	RB	Oregon	47	1965
James, Erasmus	DE	Wisconsin	99	2005-07
Jefferson, A.J.	CB	Fresno State	24	2012
Jenke, Noel	LB	Minnesota	52	1971
Jenkins, Carlos	LB	Michigan State	51	1991-94
Jenkins, Izel	CB	North Carolina State	28	1993
Jenkins, Michael	WR	Ohio State	84	2011-12
Jobko, Bill	LB	Ohio State	57	1963-65
Johnson, Bethel	WR	Texas A & M	81	2006
Johnson, Brad	QB	Florida State	14	1992-98, 2005-06
Johnson, Charlie	NT	Colorado	65	1982-84
Johnson, Charlie E.	T/G	Oklahoma State	74	2011-12
Johnson, Chase	T	Wyoming	75	2007
Johnson, Chris	S	San Diego State	35	1996
Johnson, Dennis	LB	USC	52	1980-85
Johnson, Eddie	P	Idaho State	4	2003
Johnson, Gene	S	Cincinnati	41	1961
Johnson, Henry	LB	Georgia Tech	53	1980-83
Johnson, Jaymar	WR	Jackson State	11	2009-10
Johnson, Joe	WR	Notre Dame	89	1992
Johnson, Ken	S	Florida A & M	22	1989-90
Johnson, Lee	P	BYU	12	2001
Johnson, Marcus	T	Mississippi	72	2005-08
Johnson, Olrick	LB	Florida A & M	55	1999
Johnson, Sammy	RB	North Carolina	48	1976-78
Johnson, Spencer	DT	Auburn	97	2004-07

Name	Position	College	Number	Years Played
Johnson, Tyrell	S	Arkansas State	25	2008-11
Johnstone, Lance	DE	Temple	51	2001-05
Jones, Chris	WR	Jackson State	15	2005
Jones, Clinton	RB	Michigan State	26	1967-72
Jones, Hassan	WR	Florida State	84	1986-92
Jones, Henry	S	Illinois	21	2001
Jones, Mike A.	WR	Tennessee State	82	1983-85
Jones, Mike L.	TE	Texas A & M	89	1990-91
Jones, Rushen	CB	Vanderbilt	31	2003-04
Jones, Shawn	S	Georgia Tech	32	1993
Jordan, Andrew	TE	W. Carolina	85/43/83/89	1994-97,99-01
Jordan, Jeff	S	Tulsa	22	1966-67
Jordan, Steve	TE	Brown	83	1982-94
Joyce, Don	DE	Tulane	83	1961
Kalil, Matt	T	USC	75	2012
Kalis, Todd	G	Arizona State	69	1988-93
Kapp, Joe	QB	California	11	1967-69
Karlis, Rich	K	Cincinnati	3	1989
Kassulke, Karl	DB	Drake	29	1963-72
Katula, Matt	LS	Wisconsin	48	2011
Kellar, Mark	RB	Northern Illinois	39	1976-78
Kelly, Eric	CB	Kentucky	25	2001-03
Kelly, Lewis	T/G	South Carolina St.	61	2001-03
Kennedy, Jimmy	DT	Penn State	73	2008-10
Kent, Joey	WR	Tennessee	83	2000
Keys, Brady	CB	Colorado State	43	1967
Kidd, Keith	WR	Arkansas	80	1987
Killings, Cedric	DT	Carson-Newman	95	2002-03
King, Caleb	RB	Georgia	38	2011
King, Phil	RB	Vanderbilt	24	1965-66
Kingsriter, Doug	TE	Minnesota	89	1973-75
Kirby, John	LB	Nebraska	36	1964-68
Kirksey, William	LB	Southern Mississippi	52	1990
Kleinsasser, Jim	TE/FB	North Dakota	40/85	1999-11
Kluwe, Chris	K	UCLA	4/5	2005-12

Name	Position	College	Number	Years Played
Knoff, Kurt	S	Kansas	25	1979-82
Koch, Greg	G	Arkansas	68	1987
Kolodziej, Ross	DE	Wisconsin	96	2006
Kosens, Terry	S	Hofstra	26	1963
Kramer, Kent	TE	Minnesota	89	1969-70
Kramer, Tommy	QB	Rice	9	1977-89
Krause, Paul	S	Iowa	22	1968-79
Kropog, Troy	T	Tulane	78	2012
Krueger, Todd	QB	Northern Michigan	5	1987
Lacey, Bob	C	North Carolina	59	1964
Lacina, Corbin	G	Augustana	63	1999-02
Lamson, Chuck	S	Wyoming	21	1962-63
Langer, Jim	C	South Dakota St.	58	1980-81
Lapham, Bill	C	Iowa	51	1961
Larsen, Gary	DT	Concordia-Moorhead	77	1965-74
Lash, Jim	WR	Northwestern	82	1973-76
Lawson, Steve	G	Kansas	65	1973-75
Leber, Ben	LB	Kansas State	51	2006-10
LeCount, Terry	WR	Florida	80	1979-83,87
Lee, Amp	RB	Florida State	32	1994-96
Lee, Bob	QB, P	Pacific	19	1969-72,75-78
Lee, Carl	CB	Marshall	39	1983-93
Leman, J.	LB	Illinois	57	2009
Leo, Jim	DE	Cincinnati	59	1961-62
Lester, Darrell	RB	McNeese State	31	1964
Lewis, Dave	RB	Northern Iowa	49	1987
Lewis, Greg	WR	Illinois	17	2009-10
Lewis, Leo	WR	Missouri	87	1981-91
Liddiard, Brody	TE/LS	Colorado	43	2001-03
Linden, Errol	T	Houston	73	1962-65
Lindsay, Everett	T/G	Mississippi	61/62	1993-98,2001-03
Lindsey, Jim	RB	Arkansas	21	1966-72
Lingenfelter, Bob	T	Nebraska	76	1978
Livingston, Cliff	LB	UCLA	55	1962
Livingston, Mike	QB	SMU	13	1980

Name	Position	College	Number	Years Played
Liwienski, Chris	T/G	Indiana	76	1998-05
Loadholt, Phil	T	Oklahoma	71	2009-12
Loeffler, Cullen	LS	Texas	46	2004-12
Louallen, Fletcher	S	Livingston	38	1987
Longwell, Ryan	K	California	8	2006-11
Love, Demarcus	T	Arkansas	75	2011
Love, Terry	S	Murray State	23	1987
Lowdermilk, Kirk	C	Ohio State	63	1985-92
Lowe, Omare	S	Washington	25	2004
Luce, Derrel	LB	Baylor	57	1979-80
Lurtsema, Bob	DE	Western Michigan	75	1971-76
Lush, Mike	S	East Stroudsburg	27	1986
Lynch, James	FB	Maryland	35	2003
Lyon, Billy	DL	Marshall	96	2003
MacDonald, Mark	G	Boston College	71	1985-88
Mackbee, Earsell	CB	Utah State	46	1965-69
Malano, Mike	G	San Diego State	69	2002
Manley, James	DT	Vanderbilt	75	1996-97
Mann, Maurice	WR	Washington	17	2006
Manning, Archie	QB	Mississippi	4	1983-84
Manusky, Greg	LB	Colgate	91	1991-93
Marinaro, Ed	RB	Cornell	49	1972-75
Marshall, Jim	DE	Ohio State	70	1961-79
Marshall, Larry	S	Maryland	48	1974
Martin, Amos	LB	Louisville	55	1972-76
Martin, Billy	TE	Georgia Tech	89	1968
Martin, Chris	LB	Auburn	56/94/98/57	1984-88
Martin, Doug	DE	Washington	79	1980-89
Martin, Steve	DT	Missouri	90	2004
Mason, Tommy	RB	Tulane	20	1961-66
Maurer, Andy	G	Oregon	66	1974-75
May, Chad	QB	Kansas State	5	1995
Mayberry, Doug	RB	Utah State	35	1961-62
Mayes, Mike	CB	LSU	23	1991
Mays, Kivuusama	LB	North Carolina	53	1998-99

Name	Position	College	Number	Years Played
Mays, Stafford	DT	Washington	73	1987-88
McCauley, Marcus	CB	Fresno State	31/21	2007-08
McClanahan, Brent	RB	Arizona State	33	1973-80
McClendon, Skip	DE	Arizona State	96	1992
McCormick, John	QB/P	Massachusetts	15	1962
McCullum, Sam	WR	Montana State	84/80	1974-75,82-83
McCurry, Mike	G	Indiana	74	1987
McDaniel, Ed	LB	Clemson	58	1992-2001
McDaniel, Randall	T	Arizona State	64	1988-99
McDole, Mardye	WR	Mississippi State	88	1981-83
McDonald, Ramos	CB	New Mexico	34	1998-99
McElhenny, Hugh	RB	Washington	39	1961-62
McElroy, Reggie	T	West Texas State	60	1994
McGill, Mike	LB	Notre Dame	55	1968-70
McGriggs, Lamar	S	Western Illinois	37	1993-94
McKeever, Marlin	TE	USC	86	1967
McKenzie, Tyrone	LB	South Florida	58	2012
McKinnie, Bryant	T	Miami (Florida)	74	2002-10
McMahon, Jim	QB	BYU	9	1993
McMillian, Audray	CB	Houston	26	1989-93
McMullen, Billy	WR	Virginia	12	2006
McNabb, Donovan	QB	Syracuse	5	2011
McNeil, Tom	P	Stephen F. Austin	12	1970
McNeill, Fred	LB	UCLA	54	1974-85
McQuaid, Dan	T	UNLV	60	1988
McWatters, Bill	RB	North Texas	32	1964
McWilliams, Johnny	TE	USC	87	2000
Meamber, Tim	LB	Washington	53	1985
Mercer, Mike	K	Arizona State	18	1961-62
Merriweather, Mike	LB	Pacific	57	1989-92
Meylan, Wayne	LB	Nebraska	56	1970
Micech, Phil	DE	Wisconsin-Platteville	98	1987
Michel, Tom	RB	East Carolina	21	1964
Middleton, Dave	WR	Auburn	84	1961
Millard, Keith	DT	Washington State	75	1985-91

Name	Position	College	Number	Years Played
Miller, Corey	LB	South Carolina	55/59	1999
Miller, Kevin	WR	Louisville	87	1978-80
Miller, Larry	QB	Northern Iowa	5	1987
Miller, Robert	RB	Kansas	35	1975-80
Miller, Romaro	QB	Mississippi	14	2001
Million, Ted	G	Duke	64	1987
Mills, Garrett	TE	Tulsa	45	2007-09
Mills, John Henry	FB	Wake Forest	45	1999
Mincy, Charles	S	Washington	21	1995
Mitchell, Jayme	DE	Mississippi	92	2006-10
Mitchell, Marvin	LB	Tennessee	55	2012
Mitchell, Mel	G	Tennessee State	68	1980
Mitrione, Matt	DT	Purdue	71	2005
Mixon, Kenny	DE	LSU	79	2002-04
Molden, Fred	DT	Jackson State	90	1987
Monty, Pete	LB	Wisconsin	94	2001
Moon, Warren	QB	Washington	1	1994-96
Moore, Leonard	RB	Jackson State	45	1987
Moore, Manfred	RB	USC	36	1977
Moore, Mewelde	RB	Tulane	30	2004-07
Morgan, Dan	S	Nevada-Reno	31	1999-01
Morrell, Kyle	S	BYU	35	1985-86
Morris, Jack	CB	Oregon	40	1961
Morris, Mike	C	NE Missouri State	68	1991-99
Morrow, Harold	RB	Auburn	33	1996-02
Mosley, C.J.	DT	Missouri	96	2005
Moss, Eric	OL	Ohio State	79	1997
Moss, Randy	WR	Marshall	84	1998-04, 10
Mostardi, Rich	S	Kent State	24	1961
Mularkey, Mike	TE	Florida	86	1983-88
Mullaney, Mark	DE	Colorado State	77	1975-87
Munsey, Nelson	CB	Wyoming	31	1978
Murphy, Fred	TE	Georgia Tech	88	1961
Murphy, Yo	WR	Idaho	19	1999
Murray, Eddie	K	Tulane	3	1997

Name	Position	College	Number	Years Played
Myers, Frank	T	Texas A & M	74	1978-80
Najarian, Peter	LB	Minnesota	51/59	1987
Nance, Martin	WR	Miami (Florida)	15	2006
Nattiel, Mike	LB	Florida	59	2003-04
Ned, Larry	RB	San Diego State	28	2004-04
Nelson, Ben	WR	St. Cloud State	17	2004
Nelson, Chuck	K	Washington	1	1986-88
Nelson, Darrin	RB	Stanford	20	1982-89,91-92
Nelson, David	RB	Heidelberg	32	1984
Nelson, Jim	LB	Penn State	56	2000-02
Nelson, Rhett	CB	Colorado State	38	2003-04
Newbill, Richard	LB	Miami (Florida)	53	1990
Newman, Keith	LB	North Carolina	52	2004-05
Newman, Pat	WR	Utah State	86	1990
Newsome, Harry	P	Wake Forest	18	1990-93
Newton, Tim	DT	Florida	96	1985-89
Niehaus, Steve	DT	Notre Dame	71	1979
Nix, Roosevelt	DT	Central State	79	1994
Noga, Al	DE	Hawaii	99	1988-92
Nord, Keith	S	St. Cloud State	49	1979-85
Norman, Tony	DE	Iowa State	97	1987
Northern, Gabe	DE/LB	LSU	90	2000
Novoselsky, Brent	TE	Pennsylvania	85	1989-94
Obee, Terry	WR	Oregon	89	1991
O'Brien, Dave	G	Boston College	74	1963-64
O'Neal, Andre	LB	Marshall	96	2001
O'Sullivan, J.T.	QB	California-Davis	7	2005
Offord, Willie	S	South Carolina	24	2002-05
Onatolu, Kenny	LB	Nebraska-Omaha	55	2009-11
Ori, Frank	G	Northern Iowa	69	1987
Osborne, Clancy	LB	Arizona State	31	1961-62
Osborn, Dave	RB	North Dakota	41	1965-75
Owens, Richard	TE	Louisville	89/49/45	2004-06
Page, Alan	DT	Notre Dame	88	1967-78
Page, Jarrad	S	UCLA	24	2011

Name	Position	College	Number	Years Played
Palmer, David	WR/RB	Alabama	22	1994-00
Palmer, Mitch	LS	Colorado State	51	2000
Parker, Anthony	CB	Arizona State	27	1992-94
Parks, Rickey	WR	Arkansas-Pine Bluff	81	1987
Pascal, Doug	RB	North Carolina	40	1980-81
Patton, Jerry	DT	Nebraska	79	1971
Paup, Bryce	DE	Northern Iowa	95	2000
Paymah, Karl	CB	Washington State	41	2009
Payton, Eddie	RB, KR	Jackson State	31	1980-82
Pearson, Jayice	S	Washington	24	1993
Pentecost, John	G	UCLA	66	1967
Perreault, Pete	G	Long Beach State	68	1971
Perry, Jason	S	North Carolina State	31	2002
Pesonen, Dick	CB	Minnesota-Duluth	22	1961
Peterson, Adrian	RB	Oklahoma	28	2007-12
Peterson, Ken	C	Utah	66	1961
Phillips, Anthony	CB	Texas A & M, Kingsville	28	1998
Phillips, Bobby	RB	Virginia Union	30	1995
Phillips, Jim	WR	Auburn	82	1965-67
Phillips, Joe	DT	SMU	75/79/91	1986,99
Pinner, Artose	RB	Kentucky	22	2006
Ploeger, Kurt	DT	Gustavus Adolphus	63	1987
Poage, Ray	TE	Texas	86	1963
Poltl, Randy	S	Stanford	29	1974
Ponder, Christian	QB	Florida State	7	2011-12
Porter, Ron	LB	Idaho	52	1973
Powell, Art	WR	San Jose State	24	1968
Powers, John	TE	Notre Dame	83	1966
Prentice, Travis	RB	Miami (Ohio)	30	2001
Prestel, Jim	DT	Idaho	79	1961-65
Prior, Anthony	CB	Washington State	40	1996-97
Provost, Ted	CB	Ohio State	28	1970
Pyle, Palmer	G	Michigan State	66	1964
Quinn, Kelly	LB	Michigan State	92	1987
Rabold, Mike	G	Indiana	64	1961-62

Name	Position	College	Number	Years Played
Radovich, Drew	T	USC	60	2008
Ramsey, Patrick	QB	Tulane	9	2010
Randle, John	DT	Texas A & I	93	1990-2000
Randolph, Al	CB	Iowa	34	1973
Rashad, Ahmad	WR	Oregon	28	1976-82
Rasmussen, Randy	G	Minnesota	52	1987-89
Raymond, Mistral	S	South Florida	41	2011-12
Reaves, John	QB	Florida	11	1979
Redwine, Jarvis	RB	Nebraska	22	1981-83
Reed, Bob	RB	Pacific	27	1962-63
Reed, D'Aundre	DE	Arizona	91	2011-12
Reed, Jake	WR	Grambling	86	1991-99,01
Reed, Oscar	RB	Colorado State	32	1968-74
Rehder, Tom	G	Notre Dame	73	1992
Reichow, Jerry	WR	Iowa	89	1961-64
Reisner, Allen	TE	Iowa	89	2011-12
Reilly, Mike	LB	Iowa	56	1969
Renfroe, Gilbert	QB	Tennessee St.	14	1990
Rentzel, Lance	WR	Oklahoma	19	1965-66
Reveiz, Fuad	K	Tennessee	7	1990-95
Reynaud, Darius	WR	West Virginia	82	2008-09
Rhymes, Buster	WR	Oklahoma	88	1985-87
Ricardo, Benny	K	San Diego St.	1	1983
Rice, Allen	RB	Baylor	36	1984-90
Rice, Sidney	WR	South Carolina	18	2007-10
Richardson, Greg	WR	Alabama	89	1987-88
Richardson, Kyle	P	Arkansas St.	5	2002
Richardson, Tony	FB	Auburn	49	2006-07
Riley, Steve	T	USC	78	1974-84
Robbins, Fred	DT	Wake Forest	98	2000-03
Robinson, Gerald	DE	Auburn	95	1986-87
Robinson, Josh	CB	Central Florida	21	2012
Robinson, Marcus	WR	South Carolina	87	2004-06
Robison, Brian	DE	Texas	96	2007-12
Rodenhauser, Mark	C	Illinois	60	1989

Name	Position	College	Number	Years Played
Rogers, Chris	CB	Howard	29	1999
Rogers, Nick	LB	Georgia Tech	58	2002-03
Roller, Dave	DT	Kentucky	76	1979-80
Rose, George	CB	Auburn	47	1964-66
Rosenfels, Sage	QB	Iowa State	2/18	2009, 11
Rosenthal, Mike	T	Notre Dame	75	2003-06
Rosnagle, Ted	S	Portland State	28	1985,87
Ross, Derek	CB	Ohio State	37	2004
Rouse, Curtis	G	Tennessee-Chattanooga	68	1982-86
Rowe, Ray	TE	San Diego State	89	1994
Rowland, Justin	CB	Texas Christian	47	1961
Rubke, Karl	LB	USC	54	1961
Rudd, Dwayne	LB	Alabama	57	1997-00
Rudolph, Kyle	TE	Notre Dame	82	2011-12
Ruether, Mike	C	Texas	65	1994
Russ, Pat	DT	Purdue	75	1963
Russell, Brian	S	San Diego State	27	2002-04
Rutland, Reggie	CB	Georgia Tech	48	1987-92
Salisbury, Sean	QB	USC	12	1990-94
Sams, Ron	C	Pittsburgh	72	1984
Sanders, Ken	DE	Howard Payne	89	1980-81
Sanford, Jamarca	S	Mississippi	33	2009-12
Sapp, Benny	CB	Northern Iowa	22	2008-09,11
Sapp, Bob	G	Washington	78	1997-98
Sauer, Craig	LB	Minnesota	59	1997-98
Sawyer, Talance	DE	UNLV	97	1999-03
Saxon, Mike	P	San Diego State	4	1994-95
Scardina, John	T	Lincoln	78	1987
Schenk, Ed	TE	Central Florida	89	1987
Schmidt, Roy	G	Long Beach State	68	1971
Schmitz, Bob	LB	Montana	54	1966
Schnelker, Bob	TE	Bowling Green	85	1961
Schreiber, Adam	C	Texas	60	1990-93
Schuh, Jeff	LB	Minnesota	53	1986
Schwartz, Geoff	G	Oregon	76	2012

Name	Position	College	Number	Years Played
Scott, Carey	CB	Kentucky State	41	2002
Scott, Darion	DE	Ohio State	98	2004-07
Scott, Randy	LB	Alabama	50	1987
Scott, Todd	S	SW Louisiana	38	1991-94
Scribner, Bucky	P	Kansas	13	1987-89
Selesky, Ron	C	North Central	60	1987
Sendejo, Andrew	S	Rice	34	2011-12
Sendlein, Robin	LB	Texas	57	1981-84
Senser, Joe	TE	West Chester State	81	1979-84
Serwanga, Wasswa	CB	UCLA	29	2000-01
Sharockman, Ed	CB	Pittsburgh	45	1962-72
Sharper, Darren	S	William and Mary	42	2005-08
Shaw, George	QB	Oregon	14	1961
Shaw, Terrance	CB	Sam Houston State	25	2004
Shay, Jerry	DT	Purdue	73	1966-67
Sheppard, Ashley	LB	Clemson	59	1993-95
Sheppard, Lito	CB	Florida	29	2010
Sherels, Marcus	CB	Minnesota	35	2010-12
Sherman, Will	WR	St. Mary's (California)	43	1961
Shiancoe, Visanthe	TE	Morgan State	81	2007-11
Shields, Lebron	DE	Tennessee	77	1961
Shuler, Mickey	TE	Penn State	82/86	2010-11
Siemon, Jeff	LB	Stanford	50	1972-82
Simkus, Arnold	DT	Michigan	69	1967
Simpson, Howard	T	Auburn	75	1964
Simpson, Jerome	WR	Coastal Carolina	81	2012
Sims, William	LB	SW Louisiana	57	1994
Sisson, Scott	K	Georgia Tech	9	1996
Slaton, Mark	S	South Dakota	35	1987
Smiley, Larry	DE	Texas Southern	74	1973
Smith, Cedric	RB	Florida	30	1990
Smith, Daryl	CB	North Alabama	25	1989
Smith, Dwight	S	Akron	24	2006-07
Smith, Fernando	DE	Jackson State	95/92	1994-97,2000
Smith, Gordon	TE	Missouri	87	1961-65

Name	Position	College	Number	Years Played
Smith, Greg	DT	Kansas	91	1984
Smith, Harrison	S	Notre Dame	22	2012
Smith, Jim	RB	Elon	43	1987
Smith, Khreem	DE	Oklahoma State	90	2006
Smith, Lyman	DT	Duke	79	1978
Smith, Onterrio	RB	Oregon	32	2003-04
Smith, Raonall	LB	Washington State	57	2002-05
Smith, Robert B.	DE	Grambling	74	1985
Smith, Robert S.	RB	Ohio State	26/20	1993-00
Smith, Rod	CB	Notre Dame	47	1996
Smith, Steve	DE	Michigan	74	1968-70
Smith, Wayne	CB	Purdue	40	1987
Smoot, Fred	CB	Mississippi State	27/21	2005-06
Snead, Norm	QB	Wake Forest	16	1971
Snider, Matt	FB	Richmond	44	2001
Solomon, Ariel	G	Colorado	69	1996
Solomon, Jesse	LB	Florida State	54	1986-89
Spencer, Willie	RB	None	31	1976
Stackhouse, Charles	RB	Mississippi	44/45	2003
Starks, Tim	CB	Kent State	34	1987
Steele, Robert	WR	North Alabama	82	1979
Stein, Bob	LB	Minnesota	52	1975
Stenerud, Jan	K	Montana State	3	1984-85
Stensrud, Mike	DT	Iowa State	74	1986
Stepanek, Joe	DT	Minnesota	73	1987
Stephens, Mac	LB	Minnesota	95	1991
Steussie, Todd	T	California	73	1994-00
Stewart, James	RB	Miami (Florida)	28	1995
Stewart, Mark	LB	Washington	95	1983-84
Stills, Ken	S	Wisconsin	2	1990
Stonebreaker, Steve	LB/TE	Detroit	82	1962-63
Strauthers, Thomas	DE	Jackson State	94	1989-91
Strickland, Fred	LB	Purdue	53	1993
Stringer, Korey	T	Ohio State	77	1995-00
Studwell, Scott	LB	Illinois	55	1977-90

Name	Position	College	Number	Years Played
Sullivan, John	C	Notre Dame	65	2008-12
Sumner, Charlie	CB	William and Mary	26	1961-62
Sunde, Milt	G	Minnesota	64	1964-74
Sutherland, Doug	DT	Superior State	69	1971-81
Sutton, Archie	T	Illinois	72	1965-67
Sverchek, Paul	DT	Cal-Poly (SLO)	94	1984
Swain, Bill	LB	Oregon	52	1964
Swain, John	CB	Miami (Florida)	29	1981-84
Swilley, Dennis	C	Texas A & M	67	1977-83,85-87
Tahi, Naufahu	FB	BYU	38	2006-10
Talley, Darryl	LB	West Virginia	55	1996
Tapeh, Thomas	RB	Minnesota	44	2008
Tarkenton, Fran	QB	Georgia	10	1961-66, 72-78
Tate, Robert	CB/WR	Cincinnati	28/83	1997-01
Tatman, Pete	RB	Nebraska	33	1967
Tausch, Terry	G	Texas	66	1982-88
Taylor, Chester	RB	Toledo	29	2006-09
Taylor, Eric	DE	Memphis State	90	2005
Taylor, Travis	WR	Florida	89	2005-06
Teal, Willie	CB	LSU	37	1980-86
Teeter, Mike	DT	Michigan	67	1991
Tennell, Derek	TE	UCLA	46	1992-93
Thibodeaux, Keith	CB	Northwestern St.	27	1999-2001
Thomas, Andre	RB	Mississippi	35	1987
Thomas, Broderick	LB	Nebraska	51	1995
Thomas, Dontarrious	LB	Auburn	54/55	2004-08
Thomas, Henry	DT	LSU	97	1987-94
Thomas, Orlando	S	Southwest Louisiana	42/43	1995-01
Thornton, John	DT	Cincinnati	94	1993
Tice, Mike	TE	Maryland	87/83	1992-93,95
Tilleman, Mike	DT	Montana	74	1966
Tingelhoff, Mick	C	Nebraska	53	1962-78
Tobey, Dave	LB	Oregon	51	1966-67
Todman, Jordan	RB	Connecticut	29	2011
Torretta, Gino	QB	Miami (Florida)	13	1993
Triplett, Mel	RB	Toledo	33	1961-62

Name	Position	College	Number	Years Played
Truelove, Tony	RB	Livingston	32	1987
Truitt, Orlando	WR	Mississippi State	89	1993
Tuaolo, Esera	DT	Oregon State	98/95	1992-96
Tucker, Bob	TE	Bloomsburg State	38	1977-80
Turner, John	S	Miami (Florida)	27	1978-83,85-87
Turner, Maurice	RB	Utah State	24	1984-85
Turner, Mike	T	Louisiana State	61	1987
Udeze, Kenechi	DE	USC	95	2004-08
Ulmer, Artie	LB	Valdosta State	53	1997
VanderKelen, Ron	QB	Wisconsin	15	1963-67
Vanhorse, Sean	CB	Howard	37	1996
Vargo, Larry	S	Detroit	25	1964-65
Vaughan, Ruben	DT	Colorado	69	1984
Vella, John	T	USC	71	1980
Vellone, Jim	G	USC	63	1966-70
Voigt, Stu	TE	Wisconsin	83	1970-80
Waddy, Bill	WR	Colorado	88	1984
Wade, Bobby	WR	Arizona	19	2007-08
Wagoner, Dan	S	Kansas	31	1984
Waiters, Van	LB	Indiana	54	1992
Walden, Bobby	P	Georgia	39	1964-67
Walker, Adam	RB	Carthage	49	1987
Walker, Denard	CB	LSU	26	2003
Walker, Frank	CB	Tuskegee	41	2010
Walker, Herschel	RB	Georgia	34	1989-91
Walker, Jay	QB	Howard	6	1996-97
Walker, Jimmy	DT	Arkansas	93	1987
Wallace, Jackie	CB	Arizona	25	1973-74
Walsh, Blair	K	Georgia	3	2012
Walsh, Chris	WR	Stanford	81	1994-02
Walters, Troy	WR	Stanford	82	2000-01
Ward, John	G/DT	Oklahoma State	72	1970-75
Warwick, Lonnie	LB	Tennessee Tech	59	1965-72
Washington, Dewayne	CB	North Carolina State	20	1994-97
Washington, Gene	WR	Michigan State	84	1967-72
Washington, Harry	WR	Colorado State	80	1978

Name	Position	College	Number	Years Played
Washington, Keith	DE	UNLV	96	1995
Webb, Joe	QB	Alabama-Birmingham	14	2010-12
Webster, Kevin	C	Northern Iowa	68	1997
Welborne, Tripp	S	Michigan	32	1992
Welch, Thomas	T	Vanderbilt	66	2010
Wells, Mike	QB	Illinois	15	1973-74
West, Charlie	S	UTEP	40	1968-73
West, Ronnie	WR	Pittsburgh State	35	1992
Westbrooks, David	DE	Howard	92	1990
Wheeler, Leonard	CB	Troy State	37	1997
Whitaker, Danta	TE	Mississippi Valley St.	82	1992
Whitaker, Ronyell	CB	Virginia Tech	27	2006-07
White, Brad	DT	Tennessee	62	1987
White, Ed	G	California	62	1969-77
White, James	DT	Oklahoma State	72	1976-83
White, Jose	DT	Howard	97	1995
White, Sammy	WR	Grambling	85	1976-86
Whittle, Jason	C	SW Missouri State	65	2006
Wiggins, Jermaine	TE	Georgia	85	2004-06
Wilcots, Solomon	S	Colorado	41	1991
Wiley, Chuck	DE	LSU	94	2002-04
Williams, A.D.	WR	Pacific	82	1961
Williams, Ben	DE	Minnesota	98	1998
Williams, Brian	CB	North Carolina State	29	2002-05
Williams, Jeff	RB	Oklahoma State	23	1966
Williams, Jimmy	LB	Nebraska	58	1990-91
Williams, Kevin	DT	Oklahoma State	93	2003-12
Williams, Madieu	S	Maryland	20	2008-10
Williams, Moe	RB	Kentucky	21/20	1996-00, 2002-05
Williams, Pat	DT	Texas A & M	94	2005-10
Williams, Tank	S	Stanford	25	2006-07
Williams, Tony	DT	Memphis State	94	1997-00
Williams, Walt	CB	New Mexico State	44	1981-82
Williamson, Troy	WR	South Carolina	19/82	2005-07
Willis, Leonard	WR	Ohio State	80	1976
Wilson, Antonio	LB	Texas A & M-Comm.	59/54	2000-02

Name	Position	College	Number	Years Played
Wilson, Brett	RB	Illinois	27	1987
Wilson, David	S	California	24	1992
Wilson, Tom	RB	None	24	1963
Wilson, Wade	QB	East Texas State	11	1981-91
Wilson, Wayne	RB	Shepard	45	1986
Winfield, Antoine	CB	Ohio State	26	2004-12
Winfrey, Carl	LB	Wisconsin	36	1971
Winston, Roy	LB	LSU	60	1962-76
Wise, Phil	S	Nebraska-Omaha	29	1977-79
Wisne, Jerry	T	Notre Dame	79	2001
Winthrow, Cory	C	Washington State	60	1990-05
Wofford, James	RB	UNLV	44	2002
Wolfley, Craig	G	Syracuse	73	1990-91
Womack, Jeff	RB	Memphis State	33	1987
Wong, Kailee	LB	Stanford	52	1998-01
Wood, Mike	P	Missouri State	5	1978
Word, Barry	RB	Virginia	23	1993
Worthen, Shawn	DT	TCU	95	2001
Wright, Fearon	LB	Rhode Island	59	2001
Wright, Felix	S	Drake	22	1991-92
Wright, Jarius	WR	Arkansas	17	2012
Wright, Jeff	S	Minnesota	23	1971-78
Wright, Kenny	CB	Northwestern State	20	1999-01
Wright, Nate	CB	San Diego State	43	1971-80
Wyms, Ellis	DT	Mississippi State	97	2008
Wynn, Spergon	QB	SW Texas State	3	2001
Yakavonis, Ray	DT	E. Stroudsburg St.	91	1980-83
Yary, Ron	T	USC	73	1968-81
Yates, Max	LB	Marshall	50	2003-04
Young, Albert	RB	Iowa	34	2009-10
Young, Jim	RB	Queens (Ontario)	34	1965-66
Young, Rickey	RB	Jackson State	34	1978-83
Youso, Frank	T	Minnesota	72	1961-62
Zaunbrecher, Godfrey	C	LSU	51	1971-73
Zimmerman, Gary	T	Oregon	65	1986-92

The author at the Metrodome on December 30, 2012, a 37-34 win over Green Bay in the regular season finale.

Jim Hoey was born and raised in Taconite, Minnesota, and graduated from Greenway High School in Coleraine and St. Mary's University in Winona. He spent 34 years as a secondary social studies teacher and was a hockey and softball coach at both Shakopee and Farmington High Schools. His passion for Vikings football began in 1961, when, as a nine-year old, he watched the fledgling new franchise on a grainy black and white Setchell-Carlson television.

Over the years, he has missed very few of the team's 836 games (counting playoffs) and has fond memories of most of the 1,016 players who have played for the team over its 52-year history. Hoey's zeal for the Vikings shines through in this book's vast array of remarkable feats and curious, little-known facts, statistics, records and awards.

Hoey's first book, *Minnesota Twins Trivia*, was published in 2010 and his second book, *Puck Heaven*, a book on the Minnesota State Boys Hockey Tournament, appeared in 2011. Hoey is presently the Athletic Director at Trinity School at River Ridge in Eagan, where he lives with his wife Ann and son Eddie. Like most Viking die-hards, he is determined to live long enough to witness the team win that elusive Super Bowl title.